"*Accounting for Sustainability* is an excellent a wide-ranging textbook reflecting the m... the current sustainability agenda from an accounting perspective. This is a very useful book for students as well as practitioners."

—*Charles H. Cho, Professor of Accounting, Schulich School of Business, York University, Toronto, Canada; CSEAR Executive Council & Chair of the CSEAR International Associates Committee*

"As the world faces growing challenges around climate change, deforestation, habitat loss and a whole range of anthropogenic threats to people and planet, *Accounting for Sustainability* becomes ever more relevant and important. This book is a welcome addition to the sustainability literature, neatly summarising theory and practice from internal, management accounting for sustainability, to external sustainability reporting and integrated reporting, and their relationship with financial markets. An excellent read for students at all levels and practitioners."

—*Jill Atkins, Chair in Financial Management, Sheffield University Management School, University of Sheffield, UK; Chair BAFA SIG Corporate Governance*

"At a time when stakeholder reporting and non-financial disclosures are a must for corporate reporting, this book is a much-needed support not only for academics who are teaching sustainability reporting modules, but also for practitioners who would like to get a clear overview of the sustainability reporting landscape. It conveniently connects theory and practice, without losing rigour. The four parts into which the book is divided provide an interesting perspective from inside companies to external reporting to stakeholders."

—*Begoña Giner, Facultad d'Economia, Universitat de Valencia, Spain; Chair EAA Stakeholder Reporting Committee*

"This book provides a holistic overview on the ever-evolving ESG and a Green Finance landscape. It captures key developments in the space and offers extremely useful insights. Industry practitioners will benefit from the broad range of extra-financial perspectives, concepts, frameworks and tools, presented in a comprehensive manner and style."

—*Martina Macpherson, Senior Vice President, Strategic Partnerships & Engagement, MISA (ESG) at Moody's Investors Service; President of the Network for Sustainable Financial Partners (NSFM), UK*

"Over the past 30 years sustainability has become increasingly important to accounting, both to business practice and in academia. *Accounting for Sustainability* is a textbook that has been long needed for teaching sustainability in accounting modules at undergraduate as well as graduate level. This book explores a variety of challenges for companies and interested stakeholders providing a comprehensive review of core concepts and frameworks that are prominent reshaping the current world of accounting."

—Diogenis Baboukardos, Lecturer in Accounting at the University of Essex, Essex Business School, UK; Board Member of the British Accounting & Finance Association's Financial Accounting and Reporting Special Interest Group

Accounting for Sustainability

This book provides a broad overview of how sustainability reporting has grown, how it is used now and where it is heading.

Daily, we read and hear in various media about concepts such as corporate social responsibility (CSR), sustainability reporting, sustainability accounting, environmental reports, corporate citizenship or environmental management systems. *Accounting for Sustainability* decodes this terminology by providing an accessible introduction to the topic that explores sustainability reporting from an internal and external perspective. It begins with an overview of how sustainability reporting has emerged and why it is important, before moving on to cover definitions of key terms and specific theories and frameworks. Subsequent chapters explore the role of financial management, sustainability standards, accounting communication and capital markets.

With learning outcomes and study questions embedded in each chapter, this book will be of great interest to students of sustainability reporting and accounting, as well as practitioners taking related professional accreditations.

Gunnar Rimmel is Chair in Accounting and Corporate Reporting and Director of the Henley Centre for Accounting Research and Practice (HARP) at Henley Business School, University of Reading, UK. He is also a member of the Centre for Social and Environmental Research (CSEAR) Executive Council, European Accounting Association (EAA) Stakeholder Reporting Committee, and of the British Accounting and Finance Association – Financial Accounting and Reporting Special Interest Group (FARSIG) Council as well as member of the EFRAG European Lab Project Task Force on reporting of non-financial risks and opportunities and linkage to the business model (PTF-RNFRO).

Accounting for Sustainability

Edited by Gunnar Rimmel

Routledge
Taylor & Francis Group
LONDON AND NEW YORK

earthscan
from Routledge

First published 2021
by Routledge
2 Park Square, Milton Park, Abingdon, Oxon OX14 4RN

and by Routledge
52 Vanderbilt Avenue, New York, NY 10017

Routledge is an imprint of the Taylor & Francis Group, an informa business

Translation from the Swedish language edition:

Redovisning för hållbarhet by Gunnar Rimmel © Sanoma Utbildning AB 2018

ISBN: 9789152343883

British Library Cataloguing-in-Publication Data
A catalogue record for this book is available from the British Library

Library of Congress Cataloging-in-Publication Data
Names: Rimmel, Gunnar, editor.
Title: Accounting for sustainability / edited by Gunnar Rimmel.
Description: 1 Edition. | New York: Routledge, 2020. | Includes bibliographical references and index.
Identifiers: LCCN 2020014173 (print) | LCCN 2020014174 (ebook) | ISBN 9780367478926 (hardback) | ISBN 9780367478957 (paperback) | ISBN 9781003037200 (ebook)
Subjects: LCSH: Sustainable development reporting. | Social responsibility of business. | Environmental responsibility. | Environmental reporting.
Classification: LCC HD60.3 .A253 2020 (print) | LCC HD60.3 (ebook) | DDC 657/.32—dc23
LC record available at https://lccn.loc.gov/2020014173
LC ebook record available at https://lccn.loc.gov/2020014174

ISBN: 978-0-367-47892-6 (hbk)
ISBN: 978-0-367-47895-7 (pbk)
ISBN: 978-1-003-03720-0 (ebk)

Typeset in Bembo
by codeMantra

Contents

Figures

Tables

Contributors

Susanne Arvidsson, Ph.D., is associate professor in finance and accounting at Lund University School of Economics and Management. She graduated in 2003 with the dissertation "Demand and Supply of Information of Intangibles: The Case of Knowledge-Intense Companies". For the dissertation, she was awarded a three-year Wallander Scholarship by Jan Wallander and Tom Hedelius Foundation and Tore Browaldh's Foundation. Susanne has extensive research experience in the field of sustainability and heads several successful interdisciplinary research projects. She also has long experience from executive education directed to e.g. management teams and board of directors, Swedish judges as well as to participants from low- and mid-income countries in capacity building programmes related to Agenda 2030. Furthermore, Susanne is chairman of Swedish Corporate Sustainability Ranking (in partnership with the largest Swedish business paper Dagens Industri) and is initiator of the conference SUBREA and its network with close to 200 members form companies, governments, authorities, NGOs and senior researchers at both national and international levels.

Peter Beusch, Ph.D., is active and employed as an assistant professor at the Department of Business Administration at the School of Business, Economics and Law at Gothenburg University. He received his Ph.D. in 2007 at the School of Business, Economics and Law at the University of Gothenburg with the thesis "Contradicting Management Control Ideologies – A study of integration processes following cross-border acquisitions of large multinationals". He was part of the research program "Accounting for sustainability – communication through integrated reporting" and his current research is mainly about financial management and sustainability, but also the link between external and internal accounting. A research approach that permeates much of his work is pragmatic constructivism that helps to see the whole in decision making and all governance.

Berit Hartmann, Ph.D., is employed as a senior lecturer at the Department of Business Administration at the School of Business, Economics and Law at the University of Gothenburg. She graduated in 2014 at Jönköping International Business School. Her research focuses on international accounting and its connection to and influence on organisations and management.

Kristina Jonäll, Ph.D., is employed as an associate professor at the Department of Business Administration at the School of Business, Economics and Law at Gothenburg University. She graduated in 2009 at the School of Business, Economics and Law at the University of Gothenburg with the thesis "The image of the Good Company – text and figures in the CEO's letter. She is part of the research program "Accounting for sustainability – communication through integrated reporting".

Gunnar Rimmel, Ph.D., is Chair in Accounting & Corporate Reporting and director of the Henley Centre for Accounting Research & Practice (HARP) at Henley Business School, University of Reading, UK. He previously worked in Sweden as a professor of accounting at Jönköping International Business School. He received his doctorate in 2003 for the thesis "Human Resource Disclosures" from the School of Business at the School of Business, Economics and Law at the University of Gothenburg, Sweden. He published his articles in international academic journals such as Accounting, Auditing and Accountability Journal, Journal of Accounting and Public Policy and Accounting Forum. Furthermore, he has contributed more than twenty book chapters in international books. Since many years, he is an executive board member of the Center for Social and Environmental Accounting Research (CSEAR), board member of the British Accounting and Finance Association – Financial Accounting and Reporting Special Interest Group (FARSIG) and member of the European Accounting Association's – Stakeholder Reporting Committee (EAA SRC). He is also an editorial board member of the Accounting Forum, Social and Environmental Accountability Journal and the Journal of Business Models.

Svetlana Sabelfeld, Ph.D., is researcher and lecturer at the School of Business, Economics and Law at the University of Gothenburg. Her current research areas are accounting communication, sustainability and integrated reporting, and regulation of non-financial information. Her research received Oscar Sillén Prize in Sweden in 2014, and Emerald Literati Award for highly commended article in 2019.

Matti Skoog, Ph.D., is full professor in accounting and active as a researcher and teacher at the Åbo Akademi University and Stockholm University. He specializes in control systems and control processes and transformations in how both private and public organizations perceive, measure and manage performance. He has also authored a number of books and published in academic journals such as Accounting, Organization and Society, Accounting, Auditing and Accountability as well as Critical Perspectives of Accounting.

Preface

Why a book called Accountability for Sustainability?

Every day, we read and hear in various media about concepts such as sustainability, sustainability, corporate social responsibility (CSR), sustainability reporting, sustainability accounting, environmental reports, corporate citizenship or environmental management systems. Climate issues and their pressures for major changes that will affect society have also led to changes in the view of the subject of accounting by expanding reporting from only financial transactions and efficiency measurements to sustainability reporting.

Therefore, there is a book that provides a broad overview of how sustainability reporting has grown, how it is used now and where it is heading. Here we already want to point out that we consider the field broader than focusing on reporting. Therefore, we chose the title of the book *Accounting for Sustainability* consciously, as we want to give the reader the opportunity to get a basic overview of sustainability issues in accounting. The fact that we chose *for sustainability* in the title indicates that we believe that accounting, through its unique ability to identify, measure and communicate information, provides evidence that economic decisions can be taken for sustainability.

This book tries to take a different orientation compared to the few accounting books that concern the area of sustainability. Instead of sticking to an ideological position against entrepreneurship, growth economy or the financial market, as a number of accounting books in this field do, we would rather give a broad overview of the complexity and diversity of accounting for sustainability from internal processes to external reporting.

Therefore, the structure of the book is divided into four parts: Part 1 Background & Theoretical perspective; Part 2 Accounting for sustainability in Practice (internal perspective); Part 3 Reporting Sustainability (from internal to external perspective); Part 4 Capital market and Audit (external perspective).

Part 1 contains two chapters. *Chapter 1 Accounting for Sustainability – historical development of the field* provides an overview of accounting for sustainability. Accounting for sustainability reporting has been recognized as an important part of companies' information provision and the financial market has also begun to change its approach and attitude towards accounting for sustainability. The chapter gives a broad overview of how sustainability reporting has emerged and discusses why sustainability accounting is important. Many different definitions of sustainability are highlighted to show that there is a holistic view of sustainability both internally and externally. Chapter 1 shows that globalization and economic developments have led to pressure from stakeholders on companies to report on social responsibility and sustainable development. The origins of accounting for sustainability can be traced back to the 1930s, since when it developed continuously until it became a widely recognized business practice in companies. Accounting for sustainability consists basically of three pillars. It is explained how Human Resource Accounting, Social Accounting and Environmental Accounting were initially developed separately from each other and are now important integrated parts in sustainability reporting. Furthermore, the UN 2030 Agenda describes 17 Sustainable Development Goals that have been enthusiastically received by many actors, including the accounting profession. Finally, Chapter 1 discusses criticisms and challenges with accounting for sustainability. *Chapter 2 Theories of Accounting for Sustainability* provides an overview of various theories that often occur in connection with research on accounting for sustainability. This chapter describes the most important aspects of theories, how they interact, and how they can help to explain some of the phenomena that research on accounting for sustainability is involved in. Accounting for sustainability has a broad approach to what is being studied and includes, among other things, financial information, descriptive reports and how an organization lives up to what is required by environmental standards, ethical aspects regarding sustainability in production and manufacturing, providing information to respond to external pressures or the needs of internal decision-makers that companies and organizations seek to address. Chapter 2 concludes with discussing arguments for and against different theories in sustainability reporting.

Part 2 Accounting for Sustainability in Practice (internal perspective) gives an in-depth overview of sustainability accounting in practice by focusing on the internal perspective. Part 2 contains four chapters. *Chapter 3 Management Accounting and Control for Sustainability* is about an internal perspective that is primarily aimed at the provision and use of information to managers within the organizations to make informed business decisions and assist in the formulation and implementation of an organization's strategy. Therefore, Chapter 3 describes how to design a Management Accounting Control (MAC) system for sustainability. This designing is first and foremost illustrated in four steps, where step three is about planning, implementing, following up and adapting the business in relation to sustainability goals and strategies. A critical reflection on similarities and differences that exist between traditional MAC and what MAC for sustainability is, and what this means for the 'role of management accountants', concludes the chapter. *Chapter 4 Integrating Management Accounting and Control for Sustainability* aims to describe more in detail the major difference between integrating certifications/standards and integrating strategic and significant sustainability priorities for the entire company. Integration is then explained by means of a three-part division, namely cognitive, organizational and technical integration. It is further described how integration can be understood in the light of structuring processes between people and structures. Therefore, it is clarified how technical, cognitive and organizational structures are affected and what is needed to integrate sustainability issues into MAC systems. An overview of today's most well-known MAC techniques and tools for sustainability are presented before the chapter concludes with a discussion on how everything is related and what it means for management accounting for sustainability. *Chapter 5 Towards a more sustainable and integrated performance Management* aims to give the reader an insight into what is required to integrate, for example, sustainability aspects into organizations' performance management processes. The starting point for the chapter is the criticism that the traditional financial management has endured in recent decades and the shortcomings that can be continuously observed in most organizational contexts in relation to traditional financial management. The significance and understanding of, for example, support processes and performance ideals are highlighted as potentially important for a more integrated, sustainable and relevant performance management process. *Chapter 6 Sustainability Management Systems and Processes* provides an overview of the most important international standards regarding quality, environment, occupational health, safety and sustainability issued by an international standardization body. The chapter begins with the emergence and work of the international standardization organization regarding certification processes and standards. The ISO 9000 quality management system is presented. An overview of environmental management systems illustrates ISO 14000 and its scope. Next follows a presentation of ISO 45001, which is a series of standards that form the basis of a management system for work environment issues. A presentation of ISO 26000 shows how this sustainability guideline covers the broad spectrum of organizations' existing activities. The chapter concludes with a reflection on the challenges that organizations face when introducing and using sustainability management systems and their processes.

Part 3 Reporting Sustainability (from internal to external perspective) of the book is about reporting sustainability from an internal to an external perspective. Four chapters present different concepts and frameworks, such as Triple Bottom Line, Global Reporting Initiative, Integrated Reporting as well as how accounting communication is dealt with for sustainability. *Chapter 7 Triple Bottom Line* introduces one of the most influential approaches worldwide to reporting and monitoring of sustainability performance. This tool aims to broaden the focus of managers and investors to a more holistic perspective on organizational performance, introducing three bottom lines: profit, people, and planet that can be used for both managing organizations and reporting performance. The chapter introduces the reader to the development of the approach and the content of the Triple Bottom Line as well as various possibilities of calculation. The chapter concludes with a reflection on the problems that organizations face when introducing and using the Triple Bottom Line. *Chapter 8 Global Reporting Initiative* provides an overview of the most widely used framework for sustainability reporting in the world. The chapter describes the development of the Global Reporting Initiative over the past 20 years, and describes how the evolution from guidelines G3 / G3.1 to G4 to the GRI Sustainability Reporting Standards introduced in 2016. The most important features of the structure of the standards are briefly described, to give an overview of how detail and comparability are sustainability information can be achieved. In the end of the chapter, criticism of GRI and the challenges ahead of GRI are discussed. *Chapter 9 Integrated Reporting* provides an overview of Integrated Reporting <IR>, which has become a new development in sustainability reporting. The chapter describes the development of Integrated Reporting as an organization whose ideas originate from South Africa's work with corporate governance codes, the so-called King reports, for the last 15 years. Furthermore, the chapter briefly presents how the International Integrated Reporting Council works with various organizations to strengthen sustainability reporting. It explains how an integrated reporting framework has been developed and found acceptance for use among companies worldwide. Concisely, the most important features in terms of content and structure of integrated reporting are described to provide an overview of how the method integrates traditional financial information with sustainability information. Finally, criticism and challenges are discussed with integrated reporting. *Chapter 10 Accounting Communication for sustainability* begins with the questions why, to whom and how information about environmental and social aspects of the business is communicated, both internally in companies and externally from company to various stakeholders. Focus is put on the motives, target groups and channels for sustainability reporting and how sustainability information is communicated externally. Communication strategies and linguistic strategies used by companies in sustainability reporting are presented. The chapter also provides an overview of research traditions in area of accounting communication, as well as research methods that can help researchers to study aspects of accounting communication of sustainability.

Part 4 Capital Market and Audit (external perspective) comprises four chapters. *Chapter 11 Sustainability Reporting from a Financial Market Perspective* begins with a presentation of the actors in the financial market as well as their different roles and their relationships with sustainability reporting. A discussion is made how companies and the financial market gradually have increased focus on corporate social responsibility and sustainable business. It is presented how this increased focus has resulted in sustainability rankings and indices, as well as the ongoing development of a new sustainable finance landscape and how various regulations and initiatives aim at enhancing corporate disclosure. Finally, research is presented on the relationship between sustainable business and various financial performance measures.

Chapter 12 Socially Responsible Investment (SRI) presents the emergence of the investment discipline, which is a growing market in the financial industry. The goal of SRI is to combine financial investments with social responsibility to create long-term competitive returns that simultaneously have a positive socio-economic impact. Specific Environmental and Social Governance (ESG) criteria for environmental, social and corporate governance reflect SRI's investment focus. This chapter provides an overview of the historical development of SRI. This chapter outlines basic sustainable investment strategies and tools within SRI and how important organizations within SRI have developed acceptance of SRI. Finally, criticism and challenges are discussed with Socially Responsible Investment. *Chapter 13 Sustainability Audit & Assurance* begins with a description of the growing trend among companies to publish sustainability reports, which started to develop external audits and assurance of sustainability reports. The chapter describes that sustainability audit and assurance is an independent review of the company's internal sustainability processes and increases the robustness, accuracy and reliability of information in sustainability reports. The chapter contains a brief presentation of regulations and standards in sustainability assurance. It describes the three most well-known assurance standards ISAE 3000, AA1000 AS and SA8000. Finally, criticism and challenges are discussed with sustainability audits. *Chapter 14 Critical Reflections and Future Developments* is the final chapter of Accounting for Sustainability. A number of important players in the market for sustainability accounting and how the shift from voluntary disclosure to statutory sustainability reports has gradually changed are presented. The chapter describes a possible turning point for accounting for sustainability, as increased legal requirements for sustainability information have resulted in growing demands on its quality. Then, current developments of sustainability reporting against aggregated reporting frameworks are discussed. Finally, some reflections are presented on the future developments of accounting for sustainability.

This book is aimed at readers who want to get a description of basic accounting conditions and who are interested in getting an overview of different sustainability perspectives, frameworks, standards, processes, and starting points. To facilitate learning, each chapter begins with a brief introduction to the area and concludes with a summary. A starting point is why a particular problem or question is interesting for discussion. Here is also a connection to how the issue or problem affects accounting for sustainability and its various stakeholders. Each chapter has in the end a number of study questions, where the reader can test their understanding of the content. We do not address all details in this book and issues of technical nature are not addressed. For further information and technical questions, we refer to the various organizations, standards and frameworks. In many areas, there are also documents available that cover more technical issues. However, at the end of each chapter we do provide a number of references to academic articles and reports on websites, which makes it possible to delve further into the subject.

The idea is that the book can be used in university education in business administration at different levels of education. For introductory courses in basic accounting, the first part of the book can provide an overview of basic concepts and theoretical problems associated with sustainability accounting. The book is also intended for more advanced courses in accounting and for students who want to write a bachelor or master thesis.

Accounting for Sustainability is a book that reflects the complexity of the subject of accounting, and therefore the book is also interesting for practitioners who want a general overview.

We are aware that each chapter can easily fill all its own books. Readers who want to immerse themselves further can easily do so by the references we have suggested as further readings.

We wish you an interesting read!

The authors

Gunnar Rimmel, Susanne Arvidsson, Peter Beusch,
Berit Hartmann, Kristina Jonäll,
Svetlana Sabelfeld & Matti Skoog

Part I

Background & Theoretical Perspective

1 Accounting for sustainability – historical development of the field

Gunnar Rimmel

Abstract

This chapter provides an overview of accounting for sustainability. Accounting for sustainability reporting has been recognized as an important part of companies' information provision and the financial market has also begun to change its approach and attitude towards accounting for sustainability. The chapter begins with globalization and economic developments that led to pressure from stakeholders on companies to report on social responsibility and sustainable development. Furthermore, the origins of accounting for sustainability can be traced back to the 1930s and developed continuously until it has become widely recognized business practice among the companies. Accounting for sustainability consists basically of three pillars. It is explained how Human Resource Accounting, Social Accounting and Environmental Accounting were initially developed separately from each other and are now important integrated parts in sustainability reporting. Furthermore, the UN 2030 Agenda describes 17 Sustainable Development Goals that have been enthusiastically received by many actors, including the accounting profession. Finally, criticism and challenges are discussed with accounting for sustainability.

Learning outcomes

After reading this chapter, you are expected to be able to:

- Describe the importance of accounting for sustainability;
- Explain differences between the different pillars that play a central role in accounting for sustainability; and
- Account for basic developments related to accounting for sustainability.

1.1 Introduction

Globalization has improved the lives of many people around the world. It has given us access to high technology, information technology and increased trade worldwide. Despite these positive aspects, globalization has contributed to some concerns. Globalization has also led to increased consumption and increased competition, which has followed in the wake of globalized economic development. The increasing level of production and consumption has a major impact on the environment. Raw materials are shipped to consumers worldwide, and research has shown that transportation is responsible for 75 percent of worldwide carbon dioxide emissions (Bebbington & Unerman, 2018). With the unrestrained consumption and industrialization around the world also increased emissions of carbon dioxide and environmentally hazardous substances, deforestation and monocultures, overfishing of the sea and reduction of biodiversity. Increase in temperature on our planet as a result of greatly increased carbon dioxide emissions due to industrialization causes changes in precipitation, rising sea levels and melting of glaciers and snow. These are all clear signs of the ongoing climate change. To reduce climate change, activities such as burning fossil fuels and deforestation must be reduced. Measures against climate change must be taken to ensure sustainable development.

1.1.1 Globalization and its consequences

Globalization and economic development have turned many companies from national companies into large powerful multinational companies, but with great power comes great responsibility. The increased competition as a result of globalization has led companies to move their production of products to countries where workers' wages are lower in order to cope with the pressing global competition. This has meant that in many cases working conditions do not maintain the same level as in European countries, where workers' rights are much more strongly regulated. Many companies that have placed their production of products on subcontractors in low-wage countries such as China, India, Vietnam or Bangladesh have suffered scandals where the subcontractor's workers work in the low-wage factory, so-called sweatshops, with starvation wages and poor health security, without breaks, no access to clean water and risk of life. Today, Corporate Social Responsibility (CSR) is an important factor for successful companies, regardless of the industry in which they operate. The link between CSR and improved business with positive effects has been demonstrated by research (Baboukardos & Rimmel, 2016). Therefore, the practice of corporate social responsibility has evolved from companies that seek to fulfil their obligations to society through philanthropy, to companies that have incorporated the CSR concept and adapted many factors into their business as environmentally friendly manufacturing and improving working conditions to create sustainable development.

1.1.2 CSR's emergence

Corporate social responsibility and sustainable development are two concepts that usually go hand in hand as they aim to describe the same topic. The three main parts (see Chapter 7) of CSR are economic, social and environmental effects that an organization has on society through its operations. The economic dimension aims to describe how companies work on sustainability issues that can arise from their interaction with different types of stakeholders (e.g., suppliers, customers) and how it can affect their market position. This means that accounting information includes sustainability information. The purpose of such gathering of sustainability information is to look beyond the short-term profitability and build on relationships to emphasize the long-term economic development and thus the continuous life of the business. Furthermore, the social dimension of CSR aims to improve health, safety and the well-being of employees, e.g., motivate workforce by offering training and development opportunities. This also enables companies to function as good citizens in the local community. Such actions are reflected, among other things, in the companies' way of producing goods and services in an ethical way with the safety of their workplace. Finally, the environmental dimension of corporate social responsibility suggests that companies should focus on minimizing the ecological effects that their business has on the environment, which might require them to implement environmental management systems (see Chapter 6).

1.1.3 Sustainability reporting

Over the past two decades, sustainability reporting has been recognized as an important part of corporate disclosure (see Chapter 10) and the financial market has also begun to slowly change its approach to accounting for sustainability (see Chapter 11) and provides financial resources through the Social Responsible Investment funds (see Chapter 12). A key factor for this is increased awareness among companies that report on the benefits of taking action on sustainable business operations. Standards and guidelines such as the Global Reporting Initiative (GRI) (see Chapter 8) or Integrated Reporting (see Chapter 9) have emerged to guide companies throughout the process of establishing sustainability reporting with the aim of demonstrating how companies can practically implement sustainability in their operations. Sustainability reporting is voluntary for SMEs, but in accordance with EU Directive 2014/95/EU, it is mandatory for entities of general interest within the EU to carry out sustainability reports for the 2017 financial year (EU, 2014). The directive applies to large companies with an average number of over 500 employees. The directive came into force in 2014, and companies that are subject to the new legislation must publish by 2018 – by the end of 2018 – reports containing relevant information on the environment and society.

The accounting industry has begun to offer services similar to traditional financial accounting by producing verifiable sustainability information. External review and auditing of sustainability reports have begun to develop (see Chapter 13). This has also been made possible by companies changing their financial management (see Chapter 3) towards sustainability by developing sustainability control and control tools (see Chapter 5) and integrated management accounting (see Chapter 5).

Accounting for sustainability reflects a current view of good sustainable business practice. The current view on good practice will undoubtedly change in the future, when new problems may be seen as further important parts of social responsibility. A major positive impact on accounting for sustainability are the Global Sustainable Development Goals (SDGs) adopted by the UN General Assembly at the end of 2015 in connection with the UN 2030 agenda. The 17 sustainable development goals place increased demands on accounting for sustainability and strengthen its position against traditional financial reporting (Bebbington & Unerman, 2018).

1.2 Development of accounting for sustainability

Contrary to the popular assumption, sustainability reporting is not a new phenomenon but has existed for about 70 years. Although its significance has become more known to the public over the past two decades. Social controversies and concerns with the environment have subject to society for centuries. But despite the fact that sustainability issues have existed for centuries, the emergence of sustainability reporting is largely linked to the emergence of the modern company. Maturity of accounting and the development of accounting standards is a slow process. For hundreds of years, accountants have worked to describe the financial practice in companies by developing various forms of external accounting and financial management. Nevertheless, it was only in the last century that accountants began to set accounting standards. Similarly, sustainability accounting, reporting and standardization is also a slow process that is not much more than 60–70 years old.

Although references to similar concepts go back several decades, the concept of corporate responsibility is often referred to by American economist Howard Bowen's (1953) book *Social Responsibilities of the Businessman* as the first definition of sustainability. Bowen writes about the social obligation that business people have to make decisions or follow plans that are desirable conditions for society's goals and values. Social responsibility views on sustainability are the foundation for sustainability research. At the same time, the breadth of the sustainability concept shows that a joint start date to determine when accounting for sustainability began is illusory. The sustainability concept encompasses many different areas such as social interactions, human rights, local and global environments. It has been a successive process that has partly become more visible and highlighted to the public interest when specific cases occurred. Disastrous oil spills such as in Alaska and the Gulf of Mexico or starvation work in Bangladesh's low-wage factories of large multinational corporations lead to the public's demand for increased transparency and disclosure of corporate behaviour.

1.2.1 Sustainability reporting

In contrast, the modern sustainability concept began its development in the 1940s, but can be traced back to at least the 1930s (Carroll, 1999). The importance of sustainability has increased since the 1960s due to increased awareness of sustainability concepts such as environmental destruction and social inequality. It had become important for companies' various stakeholders, such as customers, government institutions or activist organizations, to examine what measures companies are taking on different sustainability issues. This trend was reflected in the content of company reports, which began to add environmental, social and economic reporting as a supplement to companies' financial statements (Delfgaauw, 2000). The reason why companies report on sustainability issues is that society began to demand to a greater extent than before that companies should show more responsibility for their actions.

An important step for the development of sustainability reporting was the Brundtland Report in 1987. The UN World Commission on Environment and Development prepared under the chairmanship of Gro Harlem Brundtland the report Our Common Future, published in 1987 (World Commission on Environment and Development, 1987). Brundtland's report contains a definition of sustainability that is often used: *"Sustainable development is a development that meets today's needs without compromising the ability of future generations to meet their needs (UN, 2015, p. 1)"*. The Brundtland report made the issue of sustainability an important topic and sustainability reporting from companies has increased since the report was released. Sustainability reporting is a way for companies to voluntarily provide non-financial performance information required by their stakeholders (Gray, Kouhy & Lawers, 1995).

1.2.2 European commission and sustainability issues

Another of the most widely accepted definitions of sustainability is the one described by the European Commission in its Green Paper on Promoting a European Framework for Corporate Social Responsibility (EC, 2001, p. 6):

> A concept where companies integrate social and environmental problems into their business operations and their interaction with their stakeholders on a voluntary basis. Being socially responsible not only fulfills legal expectations but also goes beyond conformity and invests "more" in human capital, the environment and stakeholder relations.
>
> (EC, 2001, p. 6)

The European Commission has been pushing sustainability issues to start legislating sustainability information requirements for businesses. In Sweden, state-owned companies have been obliged since 2008 to provide a sustainability report. Since 2016, large companies in Sweden have been required to present a sustainability report and the report will provide information on how the company works with issues relating to the environment, social conditions, employees, corruption and human rights. The new law applies from 1 December 2016 and applies for the first accounting year after 31 December

2016. Furthermore, EU Directive 2014/95/EU has entered into force and large companies must publish sustainability reports by 2018.

Accounting for sustainability has evolved from philanthropy and voluntary information to increased regulated sustainability information as an expression of long-term sustainability thinking that the world will not be polluted and resources will also suffice for future generations to come. Accounting for sustainability consists of three pillars:

- Economic
- Social
- Environmental

The process begins with reporting of employees in Human Resource reporting and then moves on to Social reporting and Environmental reporting. These three pillars and developments are still alive in the current developments that are about to integrate sustainability reporting with traditional accounting.

1.3 Human resource accounting

Companies' tendency to view their employees from a financial perspective as human resources is not a new idea. Human Resource Accounting (HRA) has been on the research agenda for about 50 years with varying degrees of significance. To a large extent, early research within HRA focused on the problems of accounting for investments in human resources (e.g., Hermanson, 1964).

According to Flamholtz (1999), there have been five phases of research in human resource accounting. During the first phase from 1960 to 1966, models were developed that conceptualized and measured human resources efforts from work economics, accounting and psychology. At this stage, it was considered that the traditional financial statements do not adequately reflect the financial position of a company due to the fact that human assets are not included in the balance sheet. Therefore, a method was developed to measure the value of human assets created through recruitment or training. Much of the early research on HRA focused mostly on determining staff metrics for reports that should be utilized by managers and investors. The second phase of HRA was between 1966 and 1971. During this period, researchers attempted to construct and verify their models for human resource accounting theoretically and in practice. The third phase of the development of the HRA from 1971 to 1976 experienced an increased research interest. The American Accounting Association's Human Resource Accounting Committee described HRA as the process of identifying and measuring human resource data and communicating this information to interested parties. Consequently, HRA aims to increase the quality of financial decisions by providing information on human capital to internal and external users of company reports. After

HRA became very popular in the mid-1970s, interest in the fourth phase diminished between 1976 and 1980. This was caused by a widespread notion that HRA was only about considering employees as financial objects. The fifth phase extends from 1980 to the present, when interest in HRA has been revived. According to Gröjer and Johanson (1997), human resource issues have always been topical, but there were no researchers who took the field. With the advent of integrated reporting, interest in HRA has once again risen, as human capital is one of six capital within integrated reporting.

1.4 Social accounting

In a review of 25 years of research on social accounting, Rob Gray (2002) describes that social accounting is often used as a generic term which covers all forms of accounting that go beyond financial. Thus, social accounting is not a precise or definable concept, but complex, versatile and ever-changing. Social reporting from the 1970s and 1980s received a great deal of interest from various organizations and governments that included issues of social responsibility and responsibility for society. During the 1970s, companies' interest in social accounting was a response to activist groups who argued that companies need to take more social responsibility and responsibility for society. It was a period in which various research studies of corporate social accounting were published in academic accounting journals. These studies were about the social activities, performance or influence of the business organization. Social accounting focused on measurement and reporting, both internally within companies and externally, about the company's effects and its activities on society. Significance and interest in social accounting grew at the same time as a clear increase in the interest of activist groups to put pressure on companies regarding issues of ethics, power, social responsibility or ecological destruction. Research on social accounting began to strengthen research on leadership and corporate social responsibility. This meant that new concepts were created such as social audit, social performance, social information and responsibility. There was also an increase in experimental research into corporate practices, such as social performance metrics, which addressed a whole range of issues that were central to understanding the concept of business and society. In the mid-1970s, the accounting profession in parts of Europe also had positive attitudes to social accounting. In France, developments in social accounting led to the introduction of the French social balance sheet, which has been mandatory since 1977 in French companies with 300 or more employees. The French social balance sheet must contain numerical information needed to assess the employment and employment situation within the company and to evaluate changes during the two preceding years. During the 1970s, the development of human resources continued in the financial accounting and reporting paradigm, causing the continued development to end until the mid-1980s (Roslender & Dyson, 1992). Since the mid-1980s, the complexity of the company increased and with social reporting started to be reinforced through environmental report-ing. Today, this practice of social accounting can be considered common in the company's reporting as it is still an important part of accounting for sustainability.

1.5 Environmental accounting

Since the late 1970s, the interest in social accounting began to slowly di-minish and partly be combined with environmental accounting that had just emerged. Environmental accounting has become a growing and dy-namic area that gained momentum during the 1990s. Environmental ac-counting is aimed at companies identifying and clarifying the resources that were consumed and the costs incurred for the environment through the companies' operations. Environmental accounting is about making environmental-related costs more transparent with the help of companies' accounting systems and reports. In other words, environmental accounting is a system that tries to make a quantitative assessment of the costs and benefits for a company because of the various environmental protection measures the company chooses. Environmental protection measures may involve, for example, switching to more environmentally friendly manufacturing processes or materials for production. To a large extent, environmental ac-counting involves identification, measurement, calculation and distribution of environmental costs. Finally, data from environmental accounts can be communicated to the company's various stakeholders as part of the annual report. Thus, the purpose of environmental reporting is also that a company informs its stakeholders about the company's environmental performance. Information on environmental performance includes: environmental im-pact, performance in managing these impacts, and contributions to ecolog-ical and sustainable development.

The development of environmental accounting over time can be described as follows:

1.5.1 1970–1980: Emergence

The emergence of the first environmental accounting studies, which had a more descriptive nature.

1.5.2 1981–1994: Content debate

Debates on the role of accounting in providing companies with information about their environmental impact. During this period researchers' interest in this area is increasing. Corporate management and auditors are also begin-ning to pay more attention to environmental issues. The number of research-ers in environmental accounting is also increasing at the expense of research on social accounting.

1.5.3 1995–2001: Maturity of environmental reporting

The importance of reported environmental information is beginning to be taken into account and environmental audits are launched. Environmental reporting, both theoretically and practically, is beginning to be extensively discussed, especially in industrialized countries. The studies and researchers in this area are beginning to receive increased attention from companies and government organizations. The number of research studies is beginning to grow significantly and the environmental reports are still the main sub-areas that the researchers focus on.

1.5.4 2002: Guidelines and standardization

Around the turn of the millennium, a number of guidelines and regulations on environmental accounting and environmental information reporting are being issued, which are largely voluntary and developed by private organizations and initiatives. The number and quality of articles on environmental reporting continue to grow. Studies in environmental accounting are beginning to address the complexity of the subject and make important contributions to the development of this research area.

Public awareness of environmental issues such as environmental pollution, environmental protection and environmental development has grown tremendously from the 1970s when the first environmental protection laws came into force. Environmental impact assessment, which shows the costs associated with the environmental impact of manufacturing, has during the last decade become an important part of environmental reporting. Since the end of the 1990s, there has been an increase in the spread of social information and the environment in both companies' annual reports and independent sustainability reports. Sustainability reporting has included the previously separate tracks of human resource accounting, social accounting and environmental accounting. This contributed to the increase in research studies that analyze the social and environmental data that companies report on which should form the basis for the preparation and implementation of guiding principles and companies' practice of accounting for sustainability.

1.6 Sustainable development goals (SDGs)

Research on the roles of accounting to promote sustainable development has expanded and become more sophisticated. Over the past three decades, the concept of sustainable development, where the Brundtland report has been an important milestone for developing guiding principles for addressing environmental and human development problems. Now it has reached a new milestone that will have major consequences for the development of the field of accounting for sustainability. In the latest renewal of the Global Sustainable Development Agenda, the UN adopted the *2030 Sustainable Development*

Agenda (UN, 2015). The 2030 Agenda includes 17 Sustainable Development Goals (SDGs) that connect all states to eradicate poverty and hunger, reduce inequalities, ensure good education, better health, worthy jobs and sustainable growth. The UN's intention with the 17 SDGs is to stimulate action by states and corporations over the next 15 years in areas that are crucial to humanity and the planet. These 17 SDGs are increasingly referred to as "Global Goals" and the website, www.globalgoals.org contains comprehensive information on the 17 SDGs and their specific content and measures. Since the global targets were launched in 2015, they have gained tremendous traction from a wide range of actors ranging from NGOs, the public sector to many companies. The accounting profession is also among the players who have enthusiastically joined the SDGs. The accounting profession sees a key role for auditors and accounting to support companies implementing the SDGs (Bebbington & Unerman, 2018).

Although a list of global goals (see Table 1.1) provides an indication of the aspects that are considered important, they do not illustrate how these goals can relate to each other or the underlying drivers of the consequences that SDG seeks to address. Here, sustainability reporting can play an important role in achieving the SDGs. Existing research in social, environmental and sustainable development can inform how accounting research is relevant to specific SDGs. There are knowledge and skills of accountants that can enable measurement areas, valuation methods, reporting and results management. In the academic world, SDG-related research has begun to emerge. The SDGs and their potential, ability will put further focus on accounting for sustainability and will employ accounting research in the future.

Table 1.1 UNDP's global goals for sustainable development

Goal	Focus
1	No poverty
2	No hunger
3	Health and well-being
4	Good education for everyone
5	Equality
6	Clean water and sanitation
7	Sustainable industry, innovations and infrastructure
8	Decent working conditions and economic growth
9	Sustainable industry, innovations and infrastructure
10	Reduced inequality
11	Sustainable cities and communities
12	Sustainable consumption and production
13	Fight climate change
14	Life under water
15	Ecosystems and biodiversity
16	Peaceful and inclusive communities
17	Implementation and global partnership

1.7 Criticism and challenges with accounting for sustainability

Until the past five years, there has been some great opposition to accounting for sustainability. It is not that accounting has made attempts many times before. Since HRA, social accounting and environmental accounting do not follow the tradition of financial accounting. Given the voluntary nature of sustainability reporting that it has long enjoyed, it seems that there was no incentive for companies to provide information that also shows a lack of progress in, for example, reducing carbon dioxide and greenhouse gas emissions. Without incentives for companies to track environmental performance, one wonders why a company would invest in collecting data that may not be available or easily accessible. For a smaller company, collecting such data can be financially difficult. Accounting for sustainability can increase accountability and transparency. At the same time, criticism has been made that similarly, the reporting mechanisms can be used to obscure declining performance by changing metrics, omitting information or simply focusing on other aspects of corporate social responsibility. However, the latest developments in regulating accounting for sustainability through new legal requirements have begun to take the same path as we see for financial accounting. If financial accounting laws are not complied with by companies, there are legal opportunities to determine penalties. The same is now available for accounting for sustainability. Accounting for sustainability is here to stay. They have become commonplace in corporate reporting. Transparency and sustainability information are high on the corporate agenda. However, sustainability accounting is not just for companies, but for a wide range of stakeholders ranging from investors, customers, suppliers, employees, governments to society. Accounting can play an important role, since information in sustainability reports needs accurate stories about the companies' sustainability activities. There is a growing demand for sustainability reports. Therefore, the information in sustainability reports must be credible, reliable, robust and include material issues for stakeholders. The latest developments regarding regulation, standardization and implementation of accounting for sustainability will continue to lead to greater maturity of sustainability reporting. In view of the SDGs, sustainability reporting will be integrated to a greater extent with financial accounting to achieve the global goals.

1.8 Summary

This chapter provides an overview of accounting for sustainability. Today, Corporate Social Responsibility (CSR) is an important factor for successful companies, regardless of the industry in which they operate. Therefore, the practice of corporate social responsibility has evolved from companies trying to fulfil their obligations to society through philanthropy, to companies that have incorporated the CSR concept and adapted many factors into their activities as environmentally friendly manufacturing and improvement of working conditions to create sustainable development. This chapter describes the development of accounting for sustainability. Contrary to the popular assumption, sustainability reporting is not a new phenomenon but has existed for about 70 years. Although, its significance has become more known to the public over the past two decades. Accounting for sustainability consists of three pillars: economic, social and environmental. The process started with reporting of employees in Human Resource accounting and then went on to social reporting and environmental reporting. These three main parts and developments are still alive in the current developments that are about to integrate sustainability reporting with traditional accounting. The development of human resource accounting is briefly presented. Subsequently, a brief overview of social accounting is given. Since the late 1970s, the interest in social accounting began to slowly diminish and partly be combined with environmental accounting that had just emerged. Environmental reporting has become a growing and dynamic area that has gained momentum since the 1990s. Research on the roles of accounting to promote sustainable development has expanded and become more sophisticated. The UN 2030 Agenda contains 17 sustainable development goals, which have been enthusiastically received by many actors, including the accounting profession. Finally, criticism and challenges are discussed with accounting for sustainability.

Study questions

1 What role does globalization play in the development of sustainability reporting?
2 In what way does sustainability accounting reflect a current view of good sustainable business practice?
3 Why is sustainability reporting not a new phenomenon?
4 What did EU Directive 2014/95/EU mean for sustainability reporting?
5 What are the three pillars for accounting for sustainability?
6 How has human resource accounting developed?
7 What are the five phases of research in human resource accounting?
8 How has the concept of social accounting been described?
9 What caused the continued development of human resource accounting until the mid-1980s?
10 What is the purpose of environmental reporting?
11 How can the development of environmental accounting over time be described?
12 What role can sustainability reporting play in achieving the UN's sustainable development goals?
13 What criticism was made against sustainability reporting?
14 What are the future challenges for accounting for sustainability?

References

Baboukardos, D. & Rimmel, G. (2016). Relevance of Accounting Information under an Integrated Reporting Approach: A Research Note, *Journal of Accounting and Public Policy*, Vol. 35 (4), pp. 437–452.

Bebbington, J. & Unerman, J. (2018). Achieving the United Nations Sustainable Development Goals: An Enabling Role for Accounting Research, *Accounting, Auditing & Accountability Journal*, Vol. 31 (1), pp. 2–24.

Bowen, H. R. (1953). *Social Responsibilities of the Businessman*. New York City, NY: Harper & Brothers.

Carroll, A. (1999). Corporate Social Responsibility, *Business and Society*, Vol. 38 (3), pp. 268–295.

Delfgaauw, T. (2000). Reporting on Sustainability Development: A Preparers View, *Auditing: A Journal of Practice & Theory*, Vol. 19, pp. 67–74.

EC (2001). *Green Paper: Promoting a European Framework for Corporate Social Responsibility*, DOC/01/9, http://europa.eu/rapid/press-release_DOC-01-9_en.htm.

EU (2014). *Europaparlamentets och rådets direktiv 2014/95/EU: Tillhandahållande av icke-finansiell information och upplysningar om mångfaldspolicy*, http://data.europa.eu/eli/dir/2014/95/oj.

Flamholtz, E. G. (1999). *Human Resource Accounting: Advances in Concepts, Methods and Applications*. Boston, MA: Kluwer Academics Publishers.

Gray, R. (2002). The Social Accounting Project and Accounting Organizations and Society Privileging Engagement, Imaginings, new Accountings and Pragmatism over Critique?, *Accounting Organizations and Society*, Vol. 27 (7), pp. 687–708.

Gray, R., Kouhy, R. & Lavers, S. (1995). Corporate Social and Environmental Reporting: A Review of the Literature and a Longitudinal Study of UK Disclosure, *Accounting, Auditing & Accountability Journal*, Vol. 8 (2), pp. 47–77.

Gröjer, J. E. & Johanson, U. (1997). Current Development in Human Resource Costing and Accounting: Reality Present, Researchers Absent?, *Accounting, Auditing & Accountability Journal*, Vol. 11 (4), pp. 495–505.

Hermanson, R. (1964). *Accounting for Human Assets*. East Lansing: Michigan State University.

Roslender, R. & Dyson, J. R. (1992). Accounting for the Worth of Employees: A New Look at an Old Problem, *British Accounting Review*, Vol. 24 (4), pp. 311–329.

UN (2015). *Transforming Our World: The 2030 Agenda for Sustainable Development*, https://sustainabledevelopment.un.org/content/documents/21252030%20Agenda%20for%20Sustainable%20Development%20web.pdf.

World Commission on Environment and Development (1987). *Our Common Future*, Report of the United Nations World Commission on Environment and Development, Oxford: Oxford University Press.

2　Theories of accounting for sustainability

Gunnar Rimmel and Kristina Jonäll

Abstract

This chapter provides an overview of various theories that often occur in connection with research on accounting for sustainability. This chapter describes the most important aspects of theories, how they interact and how they can help to explain some of the phenomena that research on accounting for sustainability is involved in. Accounting for sustainability has a broad approach to what is being studied and includes, among other things

- financial information
- descriptive reports and how an organization lives up to what is required by environmental standards
- ethical aspects regarding sustainability in production and manufacturing
- providing information to respond to external pressures or the needs of internal decision-makers that companies and organizations seek to address
- arguments for and against different theories in sustainability reporting.

Learning outcomes

After reading this chapter, you are expected to be able to:

- Explain different types of theories used in research in accounting for sustainability.
- Explain differences in the basic approaches between different theories and be able to illustrate their starting points.
- Explain basic concepts related to different theories.

2.1 Introduction to theories of accounting

Theory is a tricky thing, it's something we use all the time, usually implicitly. Cooking, going to the store, commenting on football or discussing yesterday's television programs involve theories, although we would usually not bother to identify and consider them. Theory is, very simply explained, a perception of the relationship between things. The theory refers to a state or framework and determines, among other things, how we view and perceive things, what things we think are related and what we see as "good" or "bad".

You have probably already encountered a lot of theories in different contexts. When it comes to sustainability reporting, we need the theory to support observing, organizing and explaining a number of things. These may include, but need not be limited to, the following issues:

- What is and what is not sustainability reporting?
- Why do companies and organizations engage in sustainability reporting, or why don't they?
- Why does sustainability accounting practice look the way it does?
- Why and how does it change over time?
- What effects does sustainability reporting have on the organization, interests and environment?
- What makes a good or bad sustainability accounting practice?

Problems and solutions vary depending on how broad or narrow our perception and theoretical framework are allowed to be. In this chapter we will present some theories that are often used in sustainability reporting. Our selection of theories is selective and incomplete because all theories that can be used would fill a book of their own. The selection therefore does not provide a complete theoretical approach but is rather comprehensive. The theories presented in this chapter are not for closing or simplifying the debate about whether or not the sustainability report is. On the contrary, we try to provide a theoretical framework that can serve as a starting point for initiating the discussion on sustainability reporting. With this in mind, we will now examine some of the theoretical frameworks that have been used in research on sustainability reporting.

2.2 Principal-agent theory

Principal-agent theory is a commonly used theory in accounting research. It is often used in studies that focus on managers' incentives to voluntarily provide information to the organization's stakeholders.

The principal-agent theory assumes that in every relationship there is a principal and an agent (Jensen & Mecklin 1976). The principal is usually the person who gives an assignment. The person who receives the assignment is called the agent. The principal often wants to direct the agent in a certain way to get what the principal wants out of the assignment. A basic assumption in principal-agent theory is that people always want their own best and try to maximize their own benefit. According to the theory, there are two ways to control agents. One way is to reward the agent, if the agent acts in a certain way. The other way is to use control to check that the agent behaves in the way wanted by the principal. Often both reward and control are used.

The inherent problem in principal–agent theory is that the agent almost always has more knowledge about the business status quo and how it can be optimized than the principal (Akerlof 1970). This is called information asymmetry (Healy & Palepu 2001). The point of departure for the principal–agent theory is thus that in an organization we have principals who must ensure that the agent meet their needs. However, the agent always puts self-interest and self-maximization first, while at the same time sitting on information that the principal does not have but need to have. If you do not control the contractor, he will use his information transfer to his own advantage. The principal–agent theory's solution to this is to use contracts that make the agent motivated to work for the principal's best.

The principal–agent problem can be illustrated with the following example. Shirin and Clara and are both students. Shirin has a car that she doesn't need because she usually bikes everywhere she goes. Shirin has a loan on her car of € 18,000, which she quickly needs to get rid of as her finances as a student do not really allow the payments. Clara works extra at a car company in the afternoons and weekends. Shirin asks Clara for help. She knows absolutely nothing about cars and sales and asks Clara to sell her car. Clara will receive € 1,000 in commission. Clara sells the car the following day for € 15,000, even though she knows that the value is at least double. However, she gets the car sold quickly and receives her commission. To avoid the principal–agent problem, Shirin should have signed a contract with Clara. This contract could have stated that said that Clara receives ten percent of the selling price and that the minimum Shirin wants for her car is € 20,000. This would have made that Clara would have tried to get as much as possible paid for the car. In this way it would have benefited both Clara and Shirin.

The principal–agent theory may partly explain why organizations provide sustainability information. Organizations have an incentive to report as much positive information as possible to differentiate themselves from competitors. Accounting for sustainability can serve as a signalling tool in the stock market, assuming that undisclosed information is disadvantageous and that the share is overvalued (Ljungdahl 1999). Investors are also increasingly weighting sustainability factors in their assessments. Analysts have to be able to assess the risks that a company has incorporated in their operations, as well as how well the organization handles these risks. Several financial analysts have realized that environmental risks, poor employee relations or unethical business practices can have a major impact on organizations' operations and thus on the value of the organization. Organizations that do not report environmental impact and not take responsibility for social issues are considered to include a higher investment risk. Voluntary reporting of sustainability information can therefore be a way of drawing attention to the fact that organizations take this type of risk seriously.

2.3 Stakeholder theory

Stakeholder theory is based on a theoretical model that assumes that organizations have various stakeholders (Donaldson & Preston 1995). Freeman (1984) defines a stakeholder as a group or individual who is influenced by decisions made by the organization, or who themselves are able to influence the organization's agenda and decisions. Stakeholders consist of many different groups and individuals, for example, employees, customers, suppliers, shareholders, banks, environmental activists or government authorities. All of these stakeholders can help or harm an organization. The number of stakeholders can vary from organization to organization, depending on the type of organization or in which market they operate. The stakeholder model can be used to map the organization's relationships with its various stakeholders (see Figure 2.1, Stakeholder Model).

The arrows in the model go in both directions. At a first glance, there are no indications that priorities are being made between stakeholders' interests and benefits over others. This would mean that all stakeholder relations are equally important. From the organization's perspective, the role of accounting is a tool for managing and meeting the requirements of various stakeholders and thereby legitimizing the organization's operations (Deegan 2002). Since there are different stakeholder groups who all have different views on how organizations should be managed, stakeholders theory allows for many different social contracts with different stakeholder groups instead of just one contract with society at large. This means that there will be some stakeholders that have greater influence than others and thus these are considered to be

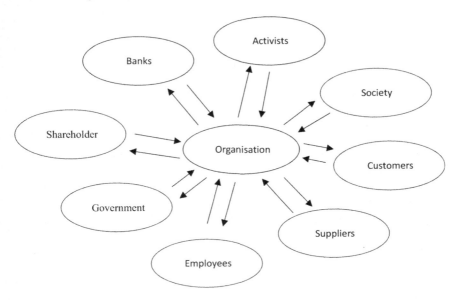

Figure 2.1 Stakeholder model.

more important for the organization (e.g., shareholders). A mapping of who these stakeholders are is often done by the organization to make it easier to communicate with the most important stakeholders. Such mapping examines the specific requirements and interests of each stakeholder.

In order for the organization to be able to achieve its own strategic goals, it is important that it can retain its stakeholders. A basic condition for stakeholders to remain with the organization is that the organization meets their requirements. By voluntarily satisfying the needs of the most important stakeholders, the organization can gain competitive advantages over other organizations.

Stakeholder theory can be divided into two perspectives, a normative and a positive perspective. The point of departure from the normative perspective is that all stakeholders should be treated fairly by the organization, which means that organizations must meet stakeholder requirements regardless of how it affects the organization (Hasnas 1998). This means that all stakeholders have the right to know how the organization's activities affect them. Examples of such information may be; what emissions the organization produces, what initiatives are taken for employee safety or how the organization works with fair working conditions regardless of the type of employment (Deegan & Unerman 2011). In the normative perspective, it is not relevant for the organization to differentiate between stakeholders based on importance. The organization's management thus needs to give all stakeholders equal attention and consideration. If conflicts arise between the interests of different stakeholders, the organization should handle these conflicts in such a way that there is as even balance as possible between the requirements of the different stakeholders. Research within this perspective of stakeholder theory often answers the question of how an organization should act in given situations.

The point of departure from the positive perspective is that there are situations where management must differentiate between different interests. In this perspective, stakeholders are identified based on what power and influence they have on the organization. The degree of power and influence will be decisive for which stakeholder the organization will take into account first (Deegan & Unerman 2011). This means that the organization's management ensures that the organization meets the expectations of specially selected stakeholders. Usually those that are most important to the organization. Only the most important stakeholders have great influence on the organization. This perspective differs significantly from the normative branch, where all stakeholders are equally important. An important part of the organization's work is to assess the importance of meeting stakeholder demand in order to achieve the strategic goals set by the organization. Stakeholder demands, requirements and expectations change over time. This means that the organization must constantly adapt its business and information strategies. The more important the organization believes the stakeholder is, the harder the effort the organization must make to retain the stakeholder. Research within this perspective seeks to provide answers on how organizations should act towards their stakeholders to make their business work. A successful organization is the one that can satisfy the requirements of several important interest groups.

According to Clarkson (1995), stakeholders can be divided into two groups, primary and secondary stakeholders. The primary stakeholder group includes those stakeholders that the organization is completely dependent on. Without these stakeholders the organization cannot survive. Thus, there is a strong dependency relationship between the primary stakeholders and the organization. Primary stakeholders are predominantly shareholders, employees, investors, customers, suppliers but also the state and municipalities, as these provide infrastructure and ensure that laws and regulations are followed. The success of the organization depends on the extent to which the organization can create value and satisfy the primary stakeholders.

The group of secondary stakeholders includes stakeholders who are affected by the organization's activities, even though they have no direct transactions with the organization. Thus, the organization's conditions for survival or success are not affected. Secondary stakeholders may, for example, be environmental organizations, environmental activists, or mass media who have nothing directly to do with the organization, but who try to influence the organization's image and production behaviour. Information is a very important factor that can be used to inform the organization's stakeholders about the business in order to gain acceptance and support. Sustainability information can be a great way to create relationships with stakeholders to communicate the organization's sustainability efforts.

There is criticism of stakeholder theory, as the stakeholder model puts the interest of the organization at the centre. The critics believe that this violates the stakeholder theory, as by placing the organization in the middle it indicates that the company is more important than other interests that are placed around the organization. The stakeholder model suggests that the organization is given a more important position, as it can decide on stakeholders and stakeholder relations. Stakeholder theory serves as a collective concept and represents different approaches when addressing issues associated with the relationship between organization and stakeholders. This includes stakeholder rights, stakeholder power or effective stakeholder management. This opens up for further criticism of the theory. Since stakeholder theory is explained, interpreted and used in many different ways, the evidence and arguments presented for its use are sometimes contradictory. Nevertheless, in the last 30 years, a growing number of researchers have used stakeholder theory to illustrate the complexity and challenges that organizations face when reporting sustainability.

2.4 Legitimacy theory

The foundations of legitimacy theory originate from political economic theory. In this, all forms of accounting reports are regarded as economic, political and social documents. The basic idea is that economics, society and politics cannot be distinguished and that the economic issues cannot be examined objectively in the absence of the political and social context of the organization's economic activities.

The theory of legitimacy is based on the idea that organizations constantly strive to act within the boundaries of rules and norms set by society (Dowling & Pfeffer 1975). The basic assumption is that organizations are constantly trying to gain legitimacy where they operate. Legitimacy is the condition that arises when the organization's value system and values are consistent with what exists in the context in which the organization operates. Norms, limits and values are not fixed but change over time. If there are differences between the values of society and the organization, a threat to the legitimacy of the organization arises. Because values change over time, but also differ among stakeholders, it is difficult to say exactly what is legitimate at any given time. An organization can only survive if the society in which it is operating experiences that the organization adds value that is consistent with the value system of the society. As a result, organizations need to respond over time to changes occurring in the outside world, otherwise the organization may lose its legitimacy even if the organization is unchanged. If expectations change, the organization must report how they have changed or explain why they choose not to change.

Legitimacy theory rests on the basic assumption that there is a *social contract* between an organization and society, where society accepts the organization's actions as long as the benefits outweigh the disadvantages. The social contract forms the basis of how society considers the organization to conduct its business. The survival and existence of the organization can be jeopardized if society considers that the social contract between them has been broken, for example, if the organization is utilizing child labourers or producing environmentally hazardous products and if this is not accepted within the surrounding society. According to the legitimacy theory, the organization will always try to ensure that its activities and achievements are accepted by the environment. Especially, this becomes clear if the environmental interest in the organization increases. If society does not consider that the organization is acting in an acceptable manner, sanctions can be imposed that will prevent the organization from continuing its operations. Examples of sanctions are that suppliers eliminate the supply of raw materials or labour, or that the government imposes higher taxes on certain goods and services. Introducing laws and fines are other ways in which society can act to prevent activities that do not align with society's values and expectations.

Many believe that legitimacy can be a resource that the organization relies on to operate and survive. However, the organization can both influence and/or manipulate the resource. Often, one talks about identification strategies when such impacts are discussed. Lindblom (1993) has identified four such strategies. To maintain or create legitimacy, organizations can:

1   educate and inform about the organization's activities and results;
2   try to change the environment's view of the organization without changing behaviour itself;

3   pay attention to any other problem to hide their own, or
4   work to change the external expectations to the benefit of the organization.

Other researchers have looked at strategies that help organizations to increase their legitimacy. If an organization adjusts its goals and production so that they conform to environmental standards, the organization can gain increased legitimacy. The same applies if the organization through communication with the environment manages to change values so that they correspond to the organization's norms and values. A third way is that organizations through communication make sure that the organization is associated with symbols and institutions that already have great legitimacy in the environment in which the organization is located.

Accounting and information can thus be used to strengthen society's perception of an organization, its products and manufacturing and the management's image. Sustainability reporting is, to a large extent, not statutory but voluntary, which means that there are other reasons why organizations choose to produce a sustainability report than they are forced to. Legitimacy theory is often considered to be the theory that best explains why organizations voluntarily publish sustainability reports. With a sustainability report, an organization can show its responsibility to society, for example, by informing society how the organization tries to minimize environmental impact in production through new manufacturing processes.

2.5 Institutional theory

It has become increasingly common to use institutional theory as a theoretical framework when studying sustainability issues. Institutional theory has a close relationship with both stakeholder theory and legitimacy theory. There are some scholars who even argue that legitimacy theory is a special part of institutional theory, see for example, Bebbington, Larrinaga-González & Moneva-Abadía (2008). Institutional theory also has a close relationship with several other theories, such as, the resource-based theory and the contingency theory, which are not addressed in this book.

The central idea behind the institutional theory is that institutions are a result of how people construct their social reality. When people interact with each other, different ways of acting are created. Such behaviours are passed on between cultures and over time these behaviours eventually become accepted ways of acting or relating. When a behaviour is repeated enough times it becomes a habit and eventually often an unwritten law. An example of such behaviour is the Swedish custom of taking off your shoes and walking in the socks indoors even when you are a guest at someone's home. For an American this would seem to be a very strange and odd phenomenon, while a Swede would be offended if a visitor did not take off his shoes before stepping into the living room.

An institution is thus a valuation, a norm or a culture that has arisen through repetition over a long period of time and which has become a kind of "unwritten law", something mutually agreed and not questioned (Berger & Luckman 1967).

Institutional theory is about how organizations adapt to the values, norms and cultures that exist to give them legitimacy in the environment in which they are located. In the outside world there is a more or less general idea of how organizations should look and how they should act in given situations. If the organization adapts to the institutional requirements, it receives support, such as legitimacy, and thus ensures its survival. Different types of institutional influence (or isomorphism) are usually discussed (DiMaggio & Powell 1983). A compelling institutional impact is based on laws and regulations that exist in the environment in which the organization is located. The organization must comply with laws and regulations, pay taxes and other fees. The mandatory rules are enforced by the fact that there are systems that punish breach of rules. Normative institutional influence is often based on cultural expectations, what is desirable and how things should be done according to current norms. Norms are often different for different roles, and what is appropriate and correct behaviour varies between different actors or organizations. If the organization does not comply with norms, there is a risk of losing one's reputation or trust from the surroundings. This risk is often greater than being affected by the formal sanction system (Tengblad 2006). There is also a mimic institutional impact that is based on the organization's desire to be similar to other organizations, often ones that are considered good or best.

Institutional theory can thus give us an understanding of how organizations interpret and respond to both social change and traditional pressures and expectations. The theory is often used in research on accounting and reporting, where the motive has been to create an understanding of why and how accounting and reporting has become what it is, or is not. Examples of such research are Dillard, Rigsby & Goodman (2004), which shows that the application of the Global Reporting Initiative (GRI) is accepted by society, and thus the legitimacy of organizations is maintained.

2.6 Disclosure theory

In accounting research, disclosure research encompasses a broad spectrum ranging from analysis of financial and narrative information, both mandatory and voluntary, to presentation of the organization in printed reports or via the Internet. That is, everything from figures in financial statements to descriptions in annual reports or sustainability reports. In an attempt to formulate a comprehensive theoretical basis for the financial reporting of organizations, accounting researchers have developed various disclosure theories that explain different approaches in financial disclosure. Disclosure research may explain the variations in organizations 'information provision between countries, by describing how external factors are behind differences between organizations' sustainability information in written reports and on the Internet in different parts of the world. The different starting points also determine the relationship between different theoretical aspects and how these relationships can address the weaknesses of theories. In addition, theories serve as explanatory tools for differences between corporate information levels and general information practices. Disclosure means that the organization provides an overall picture of the business through its information to the outside world. This information can vary and includes everything from financial information in the form of figures to narrative information describing how companies live up to environmental regulations and other regulations. Many studies in disclosure research analyze how organizations use voluntary information to respond to external pressures, internal needs or what is needed for investor decision-making (Meek, Roberts & Gray 1995). Thus, organizations' information covers a large number of communication channels that are based on different causes and dynamics to provide information to stakeholders. Accounting researchers have studied this dynamics and the various causes in a large number of previous studies (Rimmel 2003; Nielsen 2005; Jonäll 2009; Sabelfeld 2013).

There are a number of studies that use legitimacy theory to explain the level of voluntary information in sustainability reporting. One assumption that legitimacy theory makes is that organizations strive to ensure that their actions are within the framework of society. This means that organizations voluntarily communicate their activities in the form of information in various company reports, so that the outside world can make an assessment of whether the company meets their expectations. Often, there are many different expectations from different directions on how organizations should behave (Milne 2002). Such multifaceted expectations can lead to voluntary disclosure of the organization's desire to show that it adheres to the framework of external expectations, for example, because production that the organization has in other countries complies with laws, standards and rules that the outside world considers important, even if the production country may have other or lower requirements. In practice, such reporting is done using various voluntary elements in the organization's various reports, such as annual reports or special sustainability reports.

It may be important for organizations to have specific strategies for managing risks, as risks may lead to reduced legitimacy. Voluntary information in financial reports can then play a significant role for the organization to legitimize its activities vis-à-vis third parties. Many studies show that voluntary information is often used by organizations to strengthen their legitimacy.

2.7 Signalling theory

The signalling perspective emerged as a response to the problem of information asymmetry that exists today between many organizations and their owners. Signalling theory, just like the principal-agent theory, is basically about describing behaviour between two parties when they have access to different amounts of information. Those with more information need to communicate this to those who have less or no information (Connelly, Certo, Ireland & Reutzel 2011). Signalling theory is based on how open an organization is to its stakeholders, that is, what kind of information the organization chooses to communicate outward.

The motive for organizations to provide, especially voluntary information, is that the organization wants to demonstrate its ability to meet the needs of stakeholders and show how they stand out from other organizations located in the same market. By providing voluntary information, the organization exhibits greater transparency and can therefore attract more investors and create a better reputation in the market. Providing information can also lead to the organization being able to charge higher fees and more secure access to work or assignments (Hooghiemstra 2010). The organization will, in the future, increase its voluntary information in order not to be perceived as inferior to its competitors and to ensure that the organization is not undervalued. Due to the high costs that voluntary information entails, most organizations will primarily emphasize what they are better at than their competitors in the same industry.

Voluntary information provided by organizations increases transparency and reduces information asymmetry between organization, management and stakeholders. Voluntary supplementary information from the organization can attract new shareholders, which means that the organization's shares are sought after in the market. An effective signal is when the receiver of the signal can judge whether the information is reliable and at the same time understand the meaning of the signal.

Studies show that organizations that are open and generous with additional information to external stakeholders signal an effective corporate governance. An organization that does not conceal or hold information to its surroundings signals the credibility and quality of the organization. An organization that prepares sustainability reports signals outwardly that the organization is governed in a healthy way. If the organization also allows an external review of the sustainability report, the organization signals that it is credible. Signalling theory can be used as a starting point when you want to understand why an organization decides to prepare a sustainability report and for what reason they choose to have it reviewed. The publication of voluntary information need not only have positive consequences. Critics believe that communicating certain information can be a disadvantage as it can damage the organization. This is especially true if external users, such as competitors, get hold of sensitive information.

2.8 Summary

This chapter provides an overview of a number of theories that are relevant when examining sustainability reporting. This chapter describes the most important aspects of theories, how they work together, and how they can help explain different levels of information and information in companies and organizations. There are similarities between many of the theories presented in the chapter. Many theories also overlap. This means that many researchers use more than one theory to explain how an organization reports sustainability.

Principal-agent theory is a common theory that explains what incentives organizations have for providing sustainability information.

Stakeholder theory is based on a theoretical model of thinking that is based on the organization's various stakeholders.

The legitimacy theory is based on the idea that organizations constantly strive to act within the boundaries of rules and norms set by society. Sustainability reporting is to a large extent not statutory, but voluntary, which means that there are other reasons why organizations choose to produce a sustainability report than they are obliged to do.

Institutional theory is often used in research on sustainability reporting and reporting where the motive has been to create an understanding of why and how accounting and reporting has become what it is, or is not.

Disclosure theory try to explain the variations in organizations' information provision of sustainability.

Finally, the signalling theory is discussed, which, like the principal-agent theory, is basically about describing the behaviour between two parties when they have access to different amounts of information.

Study questions

1   What role does accounting information play in principal–agent theory?
2   What is the point of departure in stakeholder theory?
3   What does institutional theory consist of?
4   What role do external factors play in disclosure theory?
5   What is the point of departure of signalling theory?
6   How do voluntary and statutory disclosures differ?
7   What is the meaning of principal–agent theory for sustainability reporting?
8   What role does legitimacy theory play in sustainability reporting?
9   How does legitimacy theory explain different levels of voluntary disclosure?
10   Why can sustainability information reduce information asymmetry?
11   What role does institutional theory play in accounting for sustainability?

References

Akerlof, G. A. (1970). The market for 'lemons': Quality uncertainty and the market mechanism, *Quarterly Journal of Economics*, Vol. 84 (3), pp. 488–500.

Bebbington, J., Larrinaga-González, C. & Moneva-Abadía, J. M. (2008). Legitimating reputation/the reputation of legitimacy theory, *Accounting, Auditing & Accountability Journal*, Vol. 21 (3), pp. 371–374.

Berger, P. L. & Luckmann, T. (1967). *The social construction of reality: A treatise in the sociology of knowledge.* London: Penguin Books.

Clarkson, M. (1995). A stakeholder framework for analyzing and evaluating corporate social performance, *Accounting, Auditing & Accountability Journal*, Vol. 15 (3), pp. 113–124.

Connelly, B. L., Certo, S. T., Ireland, R. D. & Reutzel, C. R. (2011). Signaling theory: A review and assessment, *Journal of Management*, Vol. 37 (1), pp. 39–67.

Deegan, C. (2002). Introduction: The legitimizing effect of social and environmental disclosures–A theoretical foundation, *Accounting, Auditing & Accountability Journal*, Vol. 9 (2), pp. 282–311.

Deegan, C. & Unerman, J. (2011). *Financial accounting theory*, European edition, 2 suppl. Maidenhead: Mc Graw-Hill Education.

Dillard, J. F., Rigsby, J. T. & Goodman, C. (2004). The making and remaking of organization context: Duality and the institutionalization process, *Accounting, Auditing & Accountability Journal*, Vol. 17 (4), pp. 506–542.

DiMaggio, P. J. & Powell, W. W. (1983). The iron cage revisited: Institutional isomorphism and collective rationality in organizational fields, *American Sociology Review*, Vol. 48 (2), pp. 147–160.

Donaldson, T. & Preston, L. E. (1995). The stakeholder theory of the corporation: Concepts, evidence, and implications, *The Academy of Management Review*, Vol. 20 (1), pp. 65–91.

Dowling, J. & Pfeffer, J. (1975). Organizational legitimacy: Social values and organizational behavior, *The Pacific Sociological Review*, Vol. 18 (1), pp. 122–136.

Freeman, R. E. (1984). *Strategic management: A stakeholder approach*. Boston: Pitman.

Hasnas, J. (1998). The normative theories of business ethics: A guide for the perplexed. *Business Ethics Quarterly*, Vol. 8 (1), pp. 19–42.

Healy, P. M. & Palepu, K. G. (2001). Information asymmetry, corporate disclosure, and the capital markets: A review of the empirical disclosure literature«, *Journal of Accounting and Economics*, Vol. 31, pp. 405–440.

Hooghiemstra, R. (2010). Letters to the shareholders: A content analysis comparison of letters written by CEOs in the United States and Japan, *The International Journal of Accounting*, Vol. 45 (3), pp. 275–300.

Jensen, M. C. & Meckling, W. (1976). Theory of the firm: Managerial behavior, agency costs, and ownership structure«, *Journal of Financial Economics*, Vol. 3, pp. 305–360.

Jonäll, K. (2009). *VD:n har ordet: Bilden av det goda företaget–text och siffror i VD-brev.* (The CEO has the word: A picture of the good company – text and numbers in CEO statements) Göteborg: Bokförlaget BAS.

Lindblom, C. K. (1993). The implications of organizational legitimacy for corporate social performance and disclosure«, *Critical Perspective on Accounting Conference*, New York.

Ljungdahl, F. (1999). *Utveckling av miljöredovisning i svenska börsbolag–praxis, begrepp, orsaker (Development of environmental accounting in Swedish listed companies – Practice, concepts and causes).* PhD thesis, Lunds universitet. Lund University Press.

Meek, G. K., Roberts, C. B. & Gray, S. J. (1995). Factors influencing voluntary annual report disclosures by US, UK and continental European multinational corporations, *Journal of International Business Studies*, Vol. 26 (3), pp. 555–572.

Milne, M. J. (2002). Positive accounting theory, political costs and social disclosure analyses: A critical look, *Critical Perspectives on Accounting*, Vol. 13, pp. 369–395.

Nielsen, C. (2005). *Essays on business reporting: Production and consumption of strategic information in the market for information.* København: Copenhagen Business School.

Rimmel, G. (2003). *Human resource disclosures: A comparative study of annual reporting practice about information, providers and users in two corporations.* Göteborg: Bokförlaget BAS.

Sabelfeld, S. (2013). *Investor relations on the web–Interpretations across borders.* Göteborg: Bokförlaget BAS.

Tengblad, S. (2006). *Aktörer och institutionell teori (Actors and institutional theory),* GRI-rapport 2006:10, Göteborgs universitet Handelshögskolan.

Part II

Accounting for sustainability in practice (internal perspective)

3 Management accounting and control for sustainability

Peter Beusch

Abstract

This chapter describes management accounting and control (MAC) for sustainability. Compared to the external (or financial) accounting perspective, which primarily focuses on the needs of external stakeholders, MAC is about an internal perspective that is primarily aimed at the provision and use of information to managers within the organizations to make informed business decisions and assist in the formulation and implementation of an organization's strategy. The chapter therefore describes how to design a MAC system for sustainability. This designing is first and foremost illustrated in four steps, where step three is about planning, implementing, following up and adapting the business in relation to sustainability goals and strategies. This step is the main area of MAC and is therefore broken down into four sub-steps, which are described more in detail in the chapter. A critical reflection on the similarities and differences that exist between traditional MAC and what MAC for sustainability is, and what this means for the 'role of management accountants', concludes the chapter.

Learning outcome

After reading the chapter, the reader is expected to be able to:

- Understand what is meant by the term 'management accounting and control' for sustainability; what it includes and how it is reflected in companies.
- Specify the difference between a performance improvement perspective and a transparency perspective in terms of accounting and sustainability.
- Illustrate the designing of a MAC system for sustainability and what the most important steps then are, and how they are connected.
- Describe in more detail the content of the core area of MAC for sustainability (plan, implement, follow up and adapt the business in relation to (sustainability) goals and strategies).

- Explain the similarities and differences that exist between traditional MAC and what MAC that is required for sustainability, and what this means for the new 'role of management accountants'.

3.1 Introduction

In the field of accounting and sustainability, it has mainly been studied what is reported in external reports. We know, however, much less about how companies really account, manage and control for sustainable value creation internally. This and the next two chapters are primarily about this internal work with designing and using management accounting and control for sustainability, and how it relates to the external accounts provided. The reason for the imbalance between the frequencies of the internal versus the external academic discourse probably is that it is easier to examine the content of external reports than to get access to study how the management accounting and control practices for sustainability within firms are. Before we delve deeper into this subject, however, we first display how we define and look at this subject.

Primarily, the term *management accounting* and the term *management control* are in the academic literature used for about the same and for different things. In this and the next chapter, these two terms are applied together as 'management accounting and control' and abbreviated as MAC. This connected way of writing is supposed to illustrate the interrelated and often exchangeable nature of them, especially when discussed together with sustainability. According to IMA (2008, p. 1), "management accounting is a profession that involves partnering in management decision making, devising planning and performance management systems, and providing expertise in financial reporting and control to assist management in the formulation and implementation of an organization's strategy".

This is about in line with popular definitions of management control, which includes the "design and use of controls to formally and informally ensure that the behavior and decisions of employees are consistent with the organization's objectives and strategies" (as provided in Maas, Schaltegger & Crutzen, 2016, p. 242). Seal, Rhode, Garrison and Noreen (2019, p. 3), in their sixth edition of their Management Accounting textbook, describe in an appealing and compelling way the work of managers to include four major activities, that is: planning, directing and motivating, controlling and decision making. Thus, the key issue with both areas, management accounting and management control, in contrast to external (financial) accounting is that information is:

- designed and intended for use by managers and other employees within the organization, instead of being intended for use by shareholders, creditors, public regulators, etc.;
- primarily forward-looking, instead of historical;
- usually rather confidential and used by management, instead of publicly reported;

- computed by reference to the needs of managers, often using management information systems, instead of by reference to general financial accounting standards.

Therefore, management accounting and control (MAC) here is about an internal perspective that is primarily aimed at the provision and use of information to managers and employees within the organizations to make informed business decisions and assist in the formulation and implementation of an organization's strategy. In Sweden, and probably in many parts of the world, there are people who view MAC as topics that deal quite exclusively with financial issues and financial goals. These individuals are likely to find it difficult to get used to something else and would probably keep the word 'financial' in front of the word goals in the above description. The fact is, that from the beginning of the 20th century until around the 1980s, it was mainly financial goals and measures, e.g. cost-effectiveness, profits, and profitability measures, which were at the center of almost all calculations and management techniques used to manage operations. This has characterized several generations of financial and accounting officers, which in turn seems to also have affected how adaptable and flexible finance departments within companies are today.

What MAC for sustainability is and should be bears great resemblance to the 'relevance lost' debate in the 1980s and 1990s in general. In Sweden, and probably many parts of the world, it was only during the 1980s and 1990s that radical changes in the form of new ideas on how to manage operations came about. The dominant logic of profitability, for several decades (Jannesson & Skoog, 2013), was then considered to have lost relevance in the increasingly complex and multinational companies, where different goals and objectives would have to be fulfilled simultaneously (see relevance lost debate in Johnson & Kaplan, 1987). Since then, there has been a tug of war between traditionalists, who are afraid that too many different dimensions and goals would blur the strongly needed financial focus, and the financial managers who believe in a more balanced and multidimensional MAC system.

Norton and Kaplan's (1993) balanced scorecards, which began to circulate worldwide during the 1990s, were probably the first and most important of their kind to restore relevance within MAC processes rather than to focus on financial consequences of past activities. The authors considered US corporate management to be too much financially and short-term oriented. This was considered to be the reasons behind the lost competitiveness of US companies particularly compared to Japanese firms. What was needed was a more balanced approach with more business-oriented tools and measures, namely the balanced scorecard. This scorecard, with cause-effect linkages, focused on four interrelated areas:

1   Customer needs – the customer perspective;
2   the internal processes – the process perspective;

3   internal development and learning – the development and learning perspective; and

4   the traditional financial perspective.

More about the balanced scorecard is presented in the next chapters. Today's discussion of MAC and sustainability, which has been led primarily by academics, but increasingly is applied by business leaders themselves, has great similarities with the relevance lost debate, and the question is whether we have reached the beginning of a new paradigm shift. During recent years, a quite significant amount of research has been published that accounts for problems, but also solutions, in the area of MAC and sustainability. Primarily, these results come from qualitative case studies of individual companies and describe in detail how MAC needs to be changed or expanded in order to meet the new demands that society, and other parts, imposes on the firms involved. In the following presentation, an introductory summary is provided on the topic of MAC for sustainability where the content is based on some of the most important research from recent years.

Companies have an enormous important role and function in society as they create resources, employ people, pay taxes, construct infrastructure, etc. and with all that enable social development and welfare. However, companies are also accused of having a negative impact on environmental, social, and economic aspects in society. It is then often the state and the other public institutions and non-profit organizations that need to take care of these unfavorable factors, the so called 'negative externalities'. With tax revenues, they should then not only redistribute resources from rich to poor so that communities function without major disruption, but they are also expected to clean up in nature and solve all unprofitable problems that companies do not want to work with.

However, in total, private companies have around ten times greater purchasing power than states and public institutions together and they are, in total, in possession of much greater knowledge and expertise (Porter, 2013). Therefore, in the field of economics and strategy highly respected economists, such as Michael Porter, consider that it is best if private companies try to push with positive social development right from the beginning on a broad front with something they call 'shared value creation'(Porter & Kramer, 2011). Creating shared value (CSV) is according to these advocates distinctively different to corporate social responsibility (CSR) as it is supposed to be a win-win situation where the company instead of simply doing good (CSR) is creating economic and societal benefits relative to costs (CSV).

Porter (2013) further argues that the leverage effect (ten times the purchasing power) benefits the positive development of society much more than what has been the case so far with a much divided system (private and public). On this issue, however, one can see major differences in different countries and regions. If you compare, for example, the US with Sweden by looking at the division into private and public and how companies, the public institutions, but also the political system works, and how the cooperation between them takes place, you quickly understand that Sweden's companies, in most cases, operate in a societal context that puts them differently than they do in the United States.

That is why it is important to see companies as value creators that goes beyond the financial dimension only. Companies are central to all development within societies and therefore need to be managed and controlled for such (positive) means. From this perspective, one moves from a shareholder value focus to a more balanced and wider stakeholder value focus. Creating shared value is supposed to be integral to competition and even, according to Porter and Kramer (2011), to profit maximization (the word 'maximization' probably can be debated) and is realigned with the company's short- and long-term plans and internal processes rather than with external reporting activities only.

3.2 Sustainability and the internal and external perspective on a company

Society's demands on companies have increased significantly in Sweden, and in other parts of the world, compared with the 1990s, which is evident in the public debate and in the reporting of companies. This is clearly visible in all kinds of goals and strategies companies mention in their annual reports and on their websites. Companies nowadays need to master an increasingly complicated everyday life with demands from more and more stakeholders compared to before. This becomes even more obvious when companies need to break down overall goals and strategies into sub-goals and sub-strategies. In summary, one can say that there are today more stakeholders who have a stake in what the companies do, and how they do it, than was the case previously (see the discussion in Chapter 2).

These increased demands affect the way how companies need to manage their businesses and how they have to deal with information not only externally but above all, in case they really want to make a difference, internally. Internally, this applies to the subject of MAC; externally this area is mostly dealt with under the topic of external (financial) accounting. The reason why we here apply both the terms, external and financial, in the parentheses is the following. With external, we mean providing information from the organization to outside stakeholders as opposed to the internal use, thus use for MAC purposes. The term financial, on the other hand, signals a more academic discourse where financial accounting (as opposed to management accounting) is the specialized branch of accounting that deals with (recording, summarizing, presenting) financial transactions according to guidelines, laws, etc.

The difference between the internal and external way of looking at, and working with, accounting and sustainability, however, is a problem. This is summarized in Figure 3.1 with an internal and an external perspective, which is an own and simplified interpretation of what Maas et al. (2016)

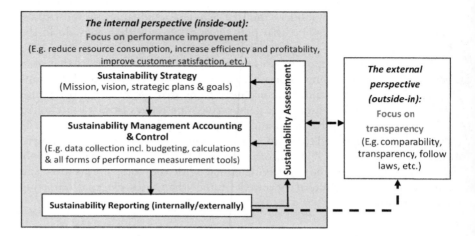

Figure 3.1 The internal and external perspective on accounting and sustainability (simplified interpretation of Maas et al., 2016).

have presented in their research. Figure 3.1 first illustrates the internal or '*inside-out*' perspective, where the relationships are shown with the solid lines, which represents the typical MAC perspective. Main focus here is to improve performance (e.g., reduce resource consumption, increase efficiency and profitability, improve customer satisfaction, etc.). That is why Maas et al. (2016) call this perspective the *performance improvement perspective*.

This perspective begins with clear sustainability strategies and objectives (mission, vision, strategic plans and objectives) that must be implemented or put into practice in the company with the help of MAC tools where focus is on data collection and internal reporting for decision making. In Chapter 4, we write more in detail about these tools (e.g., budgeting, different calculation techniques, performance measurement tools in general). Internally, sustainability reports are then generated that are used to get a picture of how the business and its various parts have performed, which is summarized in the *sustainability assessment* box, and to provide a basis for new improvements. Some information from the internal sustainability reporting then is provided to external parts (external reporting), according to the transparency criterion, which is the next perspective. This is shown in Figure 3.1 with the dashed line.

The external or '*outside-in*' perspective, on the other hand, is not about internal performance improvements but the outside pressure and impact on firms and their behaviors. The focus here, above all, is on transparency and comparability issues, and to see that the company complies with accounting laws and standards. In this case, it is especially important that the company can be compared with, e.g., similar companies in the industry or other companies in general. First and foremost, it is important that the external reporting contains everything that is essential for a good assessment of the company's results and position.

Of course, this is very important especially for investors and lenders who risk their invested money, but also other external parties who have an interest in the company (suppliers, tax authorities, the state, customers, etc.). The more that is at stake for an external stakeholder, the greater the transparency requirements for what the company really does, how they do it, and what this means for the result, the tied-up capital and, if the company is listed, the share price.

For family-owned and unlisted companies, there is less of a dividing line between external and internal, and thus no strictly separated way of thinking. In listed companies, on the other hand, important investors, but also analysts and other stakeholders, require regular updates of company management at a more detailed level precisely to better understand what is happening internally (see the discussion of agent theory in Chapter 2). This way, one tries to avoid information asymmetry, that is, the difference between providing information to an internal party and to an external party. In addition, laws are in place to prevent insider offenses by prohibiting employees' trading in shares in their own company if they have more (market price-affecting) information than is published outside.

However, a major problem regarding information about companies' work on sustainability in the current situation is that many companies have poorly designed and/or insufficiently integrated MAC mechanisms that generate and deal with all information required for decision-making internally. In Figure 3.1, one must understand that the solid lines between Sustainability Strategy, Sustainability Management Accounting and Control, and Sustainability Assessment and Sustainability Reporting are indicating an ideal picture but not reality. Research shows that these areas, in practice and in academia, are managed like isolated islands rather than integrated (Maas et al., 2016). Thus, there is a lack of a holistic picture. In addition, when dealing with sustainability issues compared to traditional (financial) managerial work, the lack of sufficient and detailed enough information creates problems with informed decision-making. Sometimes tools and techniques are also missing to control the activities and processes involved, and to make a proper evaluation of the performance achieved.

This will be discussed in more detail in Sections 3.4 and 3.5, which specifically deal with MAC for sustainability. There, we will use the term MAC systems precisely because many in the field of accounting, academics in particular, look at all the steps – and the tools, mechanisms and processes that this includes – from a structural or system perspective. That one can, and also should, see it from other perspectives as well is discussed in Chapter 5. Before that, however, the next section will highlight some special features that characterize the development, and partly the lack of such development, of the internal practices of MAC for sustainability.

3.3 Norms and standards guiding (internal) sustainability work

Contrary to the area of external (financial) accounting where there today exist national and global requirements from legislators, regulators and different standard boards to facilitate, first and foremost, comparability and transparency, all managerial work internally, thus with MAC within the company, is voluntary. Thus, such MAC practices therefore are not at all global practices but rather company specific and situationally/contextually. Thus, laws and regulations in the area of sustainability reporting might have an impact on the information provided in company external accounts; however, in order for company performance in the area of sustainability to really progress and achieve sustainable outcomes, other forces are (also) required. Legitimacy, efficiency, resource consumption, reputation, and other competitive advantages must justify that corporate management is changing its traditional (financial) course toward more sustainability. This new course then includes a changed company vision, changed strategies, and in addition to financial goals and targets also social and environmental sustainability goals. Such an approach is often called a Triple Bottom Line (TBL) approach and is described in more detail in Chapter 7.

In several countries, mainly Anglo-Saxon, there exist non-profit organizations that act as norm and standard setters in the field of management accounting. These organizations have also sought to interpret and adapt to the new demands of society regarding sustainability. Examples of such organizations include ACCA (Association of Chartered Certified Public Accountants), CIMA (Chartered Institute of Management Accountants), AICPA (American Institute of Certified Public Accountants) and the new CGMA (Chartered Global Management Accountants). Also, within the European Union there is a forum for the accounting area, FEE (Federation of European Accountants), which today offer advice and information on how to go about when implementing sustainability aspects in companies. In addition, HRM Prince Charles in 2004 started a project called A4S, which stands for Accounting for Sustainability, which today has a great influence on many other frameworks (such as those from CIMA) mainly in designing work processes and decision support systems for financial managers and other financial key positions.

In Sweden, on the other hand, there is no such organization and the forums that exist today (e.g., Ekonomistyrningsforum) have so far shown little interest in really pushing the sustainability issues in organizations forward. In Sweden, the most active player in sustainability, linked to mostly external (financial) accounting, consists of the Industry Organization for accountants, accounting consultants and tax advisors (FAR) and is featured in articles in their journal *Balans*. In addition, the Swedish Corporate Governance Board has also assisted with the translation of mostly European and global ideas on sustainability and how to deal with corporate governance. Industry organizations also appear to be another force, e.g. SWESIF – Sweden's Sustainable Investment Forum – brings together banks, funds, law firms, etc. to see improvements in this area.

The large accounting firms that have a global presence (KPMG, EY, PWC, Deloitte) are also at their best to find possible approaches to not only influence the external accounting domain, but also to provide new concepts and frameworks for how the internal sustainability work can be managed and improved. KPMG's true value creation methodology is one such approach

(KPMG, 2014). It seeks to include externalities in the accounts in accordance with the TBL principle. An externality is an external effect, often negative (e.g., waste, water or air pollution, etc.) that affects the benefits of third parties, but arises as a result of financial transactions by a company.

At the end of 2016, the Swedish government introduced a legal requirement for sustainability reporting (see Chapter 1) that applies to companies of a certain size (FAR, 2016) with the aim that this also will increase the pressure on companies to really work more with sustainability internally (Damberg & Johansson, 2016). Increased demands for transparency (outside-in-perspective) should therefore also lead to better performance (inside-out-perspective) so that we get rid of the problems within the dashed lines in Figure 3.1.

In Sweden, where there is no real active norm and standard setter in the field of MAC, this legal requirement can mean a lot to drive improvements in the area of sustainability. It is also possible that external requirements will lead to Swedish' educators in the area of MAC waking up and joining the international discussion in the area. The next section will present a summary of the mostly international picture of how companies can go about when creating a MAC system for sustainability. In addition, Swedish examples from practice and how far these companies have come will be briefly illustrated.

3.4 Designing a MAC system for sustainability

This section will demonstrate how some respected researchers in the field view the creation of a MAC system for sustainability. This is summarized in four steps, where *Step three* is the core of MAC in general, namely planning, implementing, following up and adapting the business in relation to sustainability goals and strategies. This step is therefore broken down into *four substeps* which are described in more detail.

Perhaps the most common, but not at all the only and not automatically the best way of seeing MAC, is to see it as a system that includes a variety of parts or sub-systems that should be connected in an appropriate way to achieve the goals you want to achieve with the strategies you have in place. Such a system then includes various means of controls (e.g., formal, structural, and non-formal) and techniques (e.g., budgeting, costing, etc.). The closest one probably can come to a holistic picture of such a MAC system is what by Malmi and Brown (2008) has been summarized as a '*Management Control Package*', which includes five different types of controls. These are then:

1 Cultural control – e.g. clan controls, values, symbols
2 Planning – e.g. long-range planning and action planning
3 Cybernetic controls – e.g. budgets, financial and/or non-financial measurement systems, and hybrid measurement systems
4 Reward and compensation systems
5 Administrative Controls – e.g. governance structures, organizational structures and policies and procedures.

According to the authors, such a package is a collection or set of controls used together to influence individuals' behaviors to achieve the organization's goals (Malmi & Brown, 2008). No matter how you think about MAC, e.g., as a collection of systems in the form of a package or as a system with different parts (or something else, as discussed in Chapter 5), sustainability requires thinking in larger terms than until now. In simplified terms, it is first and foremost that a company and its MAC structure must be seen in this larger context. Such a structure must then enable the inclusion of not only traditional economic goals oriented toward mainly shareholders, but also the social and environmental goals of other stakeholders. However, exactly what these goals are, how they have to be dealt with, and what this means for the company and the work of its management must first be identified.

Table 3.1 summarizes how to create a MAC system for sustainability as a four-step process, where *Step 3* is the typical core of the MAC area, linked however strongly to the other steps. The four steps, and also the four sub-steps, are in many ways similar to what traditional management accounting textbooks think is important for achieving the traditional profitability goals and they are thus nothing new. That is why the word 'sustainability' in most cases is written in parentheses only. The word could nevertheless be omitted. The reasoning for this is as follows: in order to be a sustainable

Table 3.1 Four steps to create a MAC system for sustainability

Internal and external accounting for sustainability	Step 1: Identify stakeholders and their interests/stakes.	Strategy-level Top management from different areas included
	Step 2: Define strategic (and tactical) (sustainability) goals and strategies to achieve them.	
	Step 3: *(Sustainability) Management accounting and control focus area*	*Sub-step 3.1* *Break down strategic to business-related (tactical and operational) goals and plans.*
	Plan, implement, follow up and adapt business in relation to (sustainability) goals and strategies.	*Sub-step 3.2* *Integrate (sustainability) objectives into existing management accounting and control systems or create new systems if necessary.*
		Sub-step 3.3 *Analyze and follow up achieved (sustainability) achievements.*
		Sub-step 3.4 *Report internally and suggest measures for improvement.*
	Step 4: External (sustainability) accounting	Report externally on (sustainability) performance

company, that is to say, a company that lives for a long time, it must probably contribute to a positive development in society overall, and today even
more so than before. This requires companies to meet the needs of most
important stakeholders and perform well over a longer period of time in all
three areas: the environmental, the social, but also the financial area. The
difference, however, seems to be that the list of important stakeholders has
become much longer and their demands varies much stronger than what has
been the case previously.

In addition to Table 3.1 that illustrates the four *Steps* and the four sub-steps
that constitute *Step 3*, a visualization thereof is illustrated in Figure 3.2. In
summary, this shows two surfaces, one white and one gray, where the gray
is within the white. *Steps 1* and *Step 2* are the steps that include external
stakeholders (customers, suppliers, etc.) and precede and affect the inner
and gray highlighted core of the MAC, which are summarized in *Step 3*.
Also *Step 4* is illustrated in the white part that is outside the typically gray
part precisely because the reporting to external parts is supposed to follow
the four internal steps that include the design and use of the MAC systems.
Now, however, this communication is oriented toward external stakeholders rather than internal ones.

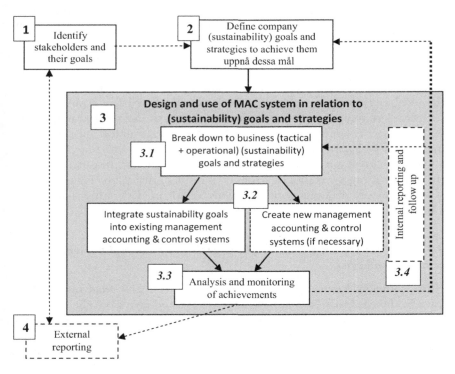

Figure 3.2 A visualization of four steps to design a MAC system for sustainability.

The white and gray areas are not at all separate parts but have, or should have, great interaction. For example, *Step 1* and *Step 2* can be counted as starting points for typical MAC functions, even if they are at a more strategic level and therefore include top-level managers from a variety of areas, e.g. strategy, marketing, finance, production, and in more and more companies, even sustainability managers.

However, in *Step 3* (sub-steps 3.1–3.4), there are traditionally finance and accounting people, ranging from CFOs to controllers and accounting assistants, that dominate the work done and decisions made. It is in these areas, where the interaction with the other functions, which are discussed in more detail below, are very important. The dashed line in Figure 3.2 between *Step 1* and *Step 4* also illustrates that external reporting is directly affected by stakeholders' interests and goals. Below follows a more detailed presentation of the steps and sub-steps.

3.5 The four steps in more detail

3.5.1 Step 1: *Identify stakeholders and their interests*

Identifying company stakeholders and their goals sounds easier than what it is in reality. Many companies, for several decades, have focused primarily on the owners and the return to them (shareholder focus and shareholder value) with profitability measures. Only during the last 15–20 years has the debate turned around and more focus has been placed on including a broader stakeholder focus beside the traditional key stakeholders (e.g., customers, suppliers, lenders and employees) toward more indirect stakeholders such as the state, the local environment, the public, NGO's and other participants of larger society. Here, opinions differ which stakeholders to include and not and for what reason, which of course is a crucial issue. First and foremost, management must be aware of who the stakeholders are, what interests they have, and how to go about meeting these interests, or why not. In order to obtain this information, a stakeholder dialogue is needed, that is, the company must have a two-way dialogue with the involved stakeholders rather than just do a survey.

3.5.2 Step 2: *Defining (sustainability) goals (long and medium long term) and strategies*

If the company has well identified the stakeholders and what interest they have in the company, it is important to define and formulate the new goals the company wants to achieve, but also what strategies will be used to achieve these goals. How to then divide, weight and possibly even rank the stakeholders and their goals in more or less important groups is a very crucial element, which does not infrequently involve the entire management and sometimes even the board. The reason for this is that such an evaluation must be in line with the whole company's business concept and the strategic priorities that a company always has to make.

Having to prioritize and focus on what is best for a company and for society, thus to see the whole picture that sustainability requires, is precisely the difficult thing. First of all, this is reflected in an increasing number of goals and measures that companies need to include and manage at the same time. In addition, these goals can compete with each other and one needs to either let them compete and deal (struggle) with the tension that this brings with it or one needs to prioritize one over the other. Both approaches have their pros and cons. The struggle might be worth it when the outcome of it is satisfying. Avoiding the struggle might be better if the price to pay with all tussle gets too high. However, to avoid working with tensions often leads to a marginalization of sustainability issues in companies rather than to better sustainability performance. Moreover, different goals can be contradictory but also have completely different time dimensions as a basis, which contributes to uncertainty in decision making (e.g., when making investment decisions). Also, there can be so many goals that it becomes difficult to maintain a good overview and to know what is most important.

3.5.3 Step 3: *Design (and use) of MAC systems in relation to (sustainability) goals and strategies*

If *Step 2* has been completed, it is important to design and use MAC systems in relation to (sustainability) goals and strategies. This important step is summarized in the gray box in Figure 3.2 and, as mentioned earlier, can be considered as the main area of the responsibilities of the traditional MAC function (including CFO and other accounting stuff), and what the new (sustainability) MAC is all about. And again, with the risk of repeating, we would like to emphasize the following: MAC for sustainability is for the most part nothing new compared to traditional MAC. The new thing is that we need to include more stakeholders' interests in the traditional MAC mechanisms. Of course, in the absence of such mechanisms and tools, they need to be introduced. The new interests are expressed in new goals and new strategies are needed to achieve these goals. *Step 3* can therefore be divided into at least four sub-steps (3.1–3.4).

3.5.3.1 *Sub-step 3.1: Breaking down to business-related (tactical and operational) goals and strategies*

Sub-step 3.1 is about breaking down the strategic goals into more business-related, i.e., tactical and operational, goals and strategies. In MAC, plans often become materialized and formalized in budgets, which can extend over several years at a more strategic level, and between one and three years at a tactical level. However, the most common are budgets and plans that extend over a year and are broken down to even shorter time intervals (quarterly and monthly budgets). There are, of course, individual companies that do not use formal budgeting, but these companies also set goals in terms of key figures. What also happens in 'beyond budget' companies is that these firms use to set benchmarks, e.g. to perform better than the other companies in the same industry, etc. and they often intensify their forecasting. So, there will always be planning.

3.5.3.2 Sub-step 3.2: Integrate sustainability goals into existing MAC systems or create new systems if necessary

Sub-step 3.2 illustrates that such implementation can be achieved by directly integrating the sustainability goals into existing MAC systems (e.g. budgets, calculations, entire scorecards, etc.) if this is seen as possible. In case the existing systems are not sufficiently well designed or for the purpose appropriate, new MAC systems need to be created. How the integration itself should go ahead and what problems may arise are very important issues in most companies and are discussed in more detail below.

3.5.3.3 Sub-step 3.3: Analysis and follow-up of achieved (sustainability) achievements

Sub-step 3.3, which is still the core of the MAC area, is about analyzing and following up the achieved (sustainability) performance to see how well they are in line with the set goals. This can be done with, e.g. deviation analyses comparing budgeted values with actual outcomes. Furthermore, the size and causes of the deviations are investigated, and data and information regarding environmental factors (e.g. liters, CO_2, etc.) and the social area (e.g. sick days, accidents, etc.) have then to be included. In the area of sustainability, this typical management accounting task still applies, but it is often necessary to supplement further analyses of more qualitative nature (quality, customer preferences and purchasing behaviors, trends) to find out why, for example, sales targets of new sustainability products and services are not reached.

3.5.3.4 Sub-step 3.4: Report internally and suggest actions/corrections

Reporting takes, frequently and in a special format, place externally but, for MAC purposes, primarily internally. As previously indicated, external reporting (*the transparency perspective*) does not fulfill the same purpose as the company's internal reporting, where *performance improvement* is at the center. Therefore, it is not only the purpose and content of the reports that are compiled differently internally compared to external, but also the frequency. Internally, it is normal for employees (or the systems via automation) to report more frequently, sometimes weekly or even daily on transactions, activities, processes and achievements. Internally, a report with greater detail also applies, often broken down to individual customers, customer segments and geographical areas or linked to specific products/services precisely to achieve close monitoring and control effects. Internal reporting must first and foremost provide decision-makers in the company with the basis for following up (sustainability-related) decisions and for improving performance (*the performance perspective*).

3.5.4 **Step 4:** *External reporting*

Step 4 now applies to the external reporting where real practice has been extensively researched, and which is also described in detail in this book in several chapters. The external reporting of what the company does, through annual, sustainability or integrated reports and other channels (e.g. via webpages, year-end or quarterly annual communications, etc.), should first and foremost be done in the format, with the content, and in the frequency required by laws and regulations and, in the best cases, also in the way the main stakeholders want it to be presented. Of course, there are also norms, standards and other institutional forces that determine how companies choose to provide their external accounts of their (sustainability) work and performance.

The differences in the external and internal reporting of all work done in general, and sustainability work in particular, are therefore usually large in most companies without this having to do with *green-washing* or *window-dressing* issues. Still, such problems might contribute to differences because in reports to outside stakeholders, companies have the opportunity to tell for them favorable things whereas such stories do not really help increase performance internally. This is visible in, e.g., annual reports, where fine pictures and favorable accounts of companies on positive societal contributions make up a large part of all material that is reported. The negative stories, on the other hand, are more seldom or even absent at all.

3.6 **Similarities and differences and what this means for the management accountant**

Collecting, compiling, interpreting, reporting and communicating data and information is at the heart of traditional MAC and this is still at the heart of the new MAC for sustainability. Furthermore, one should be able to internally investigate the causes of various deviations from sustainability goals and strategies and to be able to propose improvement measures. All of this should lead to enhanced business processes and activities related to overall sustainability performance. Such improvements may, e.g., be environmental improvements, energy savings, etc., which will also, in the best of cases, lead to better performance in the traditional financial areas, e.g. increased revenues, reduced costs and lower the capital tied up. This is what Porter & Kramer (2011) call a win–win solution.

What is new, however, is that one must apply a more holistic framing that automatically includes more goals and measures (sustainability goals and sustainability measures) as companies today act in a more complex context with more stakeholders involved. The complexity is not least visible in the list of all metrics and measures recommended by today's most accepted Global Reporting Initiative (GRI) framework, which now even is called a standard that is presented more in detail in Chapter 8. Managing, controlling and creating value in more and more new areas, and to think broader, requires that company's management has even better control of what the leading and the lagging indicators are and how all this fits together. In the area of sustainability, relationships are often even more difficult to outline and, in addition, rarely easy to measure in monetary terms. You can also say that companies' area of interest or value chain seems to be extended up-streams and down-streams through sustainability elements, as companies need to look more closely at who their suppliers (and the suppliers' suppliers) and their customers (and customers' customer) are and how they deal with sustainability issues.

Today's managers within accounting and finance need to be able to understand and work with more areas than has previously been the case. In addition, there are often areas that are not as easy to measure and translate into monetary terms. Employee satisfaction is, e.g., a measure of social sustainability that is considered very important. However, it can be difficult to measure how satisfied an employee is. It is even more difficult to see the relationship between an employee index, or another metric that expresses this satisfaction, and other performance measures, such as efficiency and profitability. However, it is exactly such data and even more complicated (e.g. measuring social benefits, reputation, legitimacy, goodwill) that is increasingly the value of company's balance sheet. Here you see a clear link between what MAC for sustainability requires and IIRC's new capital concept, which includes six capital (IIRC, 2013), and which is discussed in more detail in Chapter 9.

3.7 Summary

In summary, in order to achieve a greater and faster transition to society's overall sustainable development, similar to what Michael Porter (2013) emphasizes, companies need to have a MAC system in place that includes and embraces not only financial aspects but also social and environmental ones. To achieve this, research advocates that it is first and foremost important that companies express clear mission and visions connected to sustainability and transform this into sustainability goals and strategies that show what the company wants in practice to achieve and what priorities it therefore wants to make. If these explicit goals and strategies are in place, the next step is to support the company's work by translating these goals and implementing these strategies at all levels and within all functions, which is precisely the overall purpose that MAC traditionally always had.

What is important about sustainability, and which differs from the traditional role and function of MAC, is that the CFO's/management accountant's/controller's need to act more clearly as advisors and boundary crossers in questions about the interface between traditional (and financial) MAC and more sustainability-oriented issues. This, in turn, requires that these employees understand better what sustainability is and what it means for the company than has been the case so far.

Study questions

1　What is meant by the term 'management accounting and control' (MAC) for sustainability and how does the concept's meaning differ from the traditional definition of MAC?

2　Why is the current discussion in the field of MAC and sustainability similar to the debate that took place around 1985 to 1995 and which led to the emergence of, among other things, the balanced scorecard? What do you think is different and why?

3　What do you think is the role of companies in society today and has it changed over time, and if so, how has this change been? What goals should companies then set to achieve the value in society, and how do you think companies will go about achieving those goals?

4　What does Michael Porter (2013) mean by the leverage effect and how can this have a positive impact on society? What does this leverage effect mean for the area of MAC for sustainability? What do you think of the real leverage and the opportunities this provides? Is it realistic? Why or why not?

5　Who is driving forward the development of the MAC area in your country and what does this mean for the development and adaptation of sustainability issues?

6　What are the differences between the 'performance improvement perspective' and the 'transparency perspective' regarding MAC and sustainability? Can you see other typically external or internal factors that affect how MAC for sustainability is designed and used?

7　In what way do different perspectives (including those you yourself came up with in the question before) affect the design and use of MAC for sustainability? Can you give examples of what this means for the companies in question but also for its stakeholders?

8　The essence of MAC for sustainability is to plan, implement, follow up and adapt the business in relation to sustainability goals and strategies, but how is all this related and what is needed for these things to be successful?

9　What are the main steps and most important work issues required to achieve such a MAC system? Who will then perform these steps and with what methods?

10　In summary, what are the similarities and differences between the traditional MAC and MAC for sustainability and what does this mean for the role of the management accountant and related job positions (e.g. CFO, controller)?

References

Crutzen, N. & Herzig, C. (2013). A review of the empirical research in management control, strategy and sustainability, in: Songini, L., Pistoni, A., Herzig, C. (Eds.), *Accounting and control for sustainability (Studies in managerial and financial accounting, Volume 26)*. Bingley, UK: Emerald Group Publishing Limited, pp. 165–195.

Damberg, M. & Johansson, M. (2016). *Nu ställer vi krav på hållbarhet för företag*. www. svd.se/nu-staller-vi-krav-pa-hallbarhet-for-foretag (Assessed 28-03-2017).

FAR (2016). Hållbarhetslagen – så slår de nya kraven. Balans, 23 maj 2016. www.tidningenbalans.se/nyheter/hallbarhetslagen-sa-blir-den (Accessed on 17-08-2017).

IIRC (2013). Integrated reporting. https://integratedreporting.org/ (Assessed on 24-02-2020).

IMA (2008). Statements on management accounting. www.imanet.org//-/media/ 6c984e4d7c854c2fb40b96bfbe991884.ashx?as=1&mh=200&mw=200&hash= 4E6AF697C021AA3EB0C358AE6FE2AEB1BCA992DE (Assessed on 24-02-2020).

Jannesson, E. & Skoog, M. (2013). *Perspektiv på ekonomistyrning*. Liber: Stockholm.

Johnson, H. T. & Kaplan, R. S. (1987). *Relevance lost – The rise and fall of management accounting*. Boston: Harvard Business School Press.

Kaplan, R. & Norton, D. (1993). Putting the balanced scorecard to work. *Harvard Business Review, 71* (5), pp. 134–140.

KPMG (2014). "A tool to connect corporate and society value creation", KPMG International Cooperative. www.kpmg.com/AU/en/IssuesAndInsights/ArticlesPublications/Documents/new-vision-of-value-2014-executive-summary.pdf (Assessed on 15-12-2015).

Maas, K., Schaltegger, S. & Crutzen, N. (2016). Integrating corporate sustainability assessment, management accounting, control, and reporting. *Journal of Cleaner Production*, Vol. 136, pp. 237–248.

Malmi, T. & Brown, D. A. (2008). Management control systems as a package —Opportunities, challenges and research directions. *Management Accounting Research*, Vol. 19 (4), pp. 287–300.

Porter, M. E. (2013). *Why business can be good at solving social problems* (Filmed in June 2013 for TEDGlobal 2013 (16 Minutes), TED-talk: www.ted.com/talks/ michael_porter_why_business_can_be_good_at_solving_social_problems/transcript?language=en (Assessed on 24-02-2020).

Porter, M. E. & Kramer, M. R. (2009). The big idea – Creating shared value. *Harvard Business Review*, Vol. 89 (1–2), Jan-Feb 2011, pp. 62–77.

Seal, W., Rohde, C., Garrison, R. H. & Noreen, E. W. (2019), *Management accounting*, Sixth Edition, London: McGrawHill. ISBN 978-0-0771-8553-4.

4 Integrating management accounting and control for sustainability

Peter Beusch

Abstract

This chapter aims to describe more in detail how companies can integrate management accounting and control (MAC) for sustainability. First, the major difference is illustrated between integrating rather simple certifications/standards and integrating strategic and significant sustainability priorities for the entire company. Integration is then explained by means of a three-part division, namely a cognitive, an organizational and a technical integration. It is further described how integration can be understood in the light of structuring processes between people and structures. Therefore, it is clarified how technical, cognitive and organizational structures are affected and what is needed to integrate sustainability issues into MAC systems. Since technical structures are not infrequently the core of traditional MACs, major focus is then placed on the description of the technical structures and the technical integration required for sustainability. An overview of today's most well-known MAC techniques and tools for sustainability (e.g. budgeting, calculations, hybrid control and measurement systems, etc.) is then presented before the chapter concludes with a discussion of how everything is related and what it means for (management) accounting for sustainability.

Learning outcome

After reading the chapter, the reader is expected to be able to:

1 Describe the difference between integrating a simple certification in the field of sustainability and integrating large and comprehensive sustainability strategies within a company.
2 Understand what can be meant by the term 'integration' in the field of management accounting and control (MAC) and sustainability, and how it can be related to structuring processes in general.
3 Describe what constitutes cognitive, organizational and technical structures within companies, and how these structures are affected and what is needed to achieve sustainability integration within each and one of these structures.

4   Describe in more detail the typical technical structures that often form the core of the area of MAC and how they can be linked to sustainability.
5   Describe how all this is related and what it means for (management) accounting for sustainability.

4.1 From simple certifications to strategic sustainability priorities

In the last chapter, *Step 3* was presented as the most important and perhaps also the most comprehensive step for accounting and finance managers and other employees in this domain within organizations to design a management accounting and control (MAC) system for sustainability. *Step 3* was about planning, implementing, following up and adapting the business in relation to (sustainability) goals and strategies. This was divided into four parts, where Part 3.2 consisted of integrating sustainability goals into existing MAC systems or, in case there are no existing systems for this purpose, to create new MAC systems for these new goals and objectives that one wants to achieve.

What is meant by the word 'integration' can be illustrated in many different ways. One way to see integration is to look at it as if we are bringing together two different systems, where the usual and traditional (often financially oriented) MAC systems already exist. Because new requirements from (new) stakeholders come up, you either have to add them to the original (financially oriented) systems or you have to design new systems for the specific purpose. Such new requirements may have their beginnings in a relatively simple certification. The word certification means that something complies with a requirement specification, norm or standard.

Sustainability standards and certifications are voluntary, usually third party-assessed, norms and standards relating to, e.g., environmental, social, ethical or safety issues that can be adopted by companies to demonstrate the performance of their organization or products in specific areas. Standards are normally developed by a range of stakeholders and experts in a particular sector and they are accompanied by a verification process to evaluate that the company complies with that particular standard. The connection between internal work and external verification on behalf of certifications can be compared with the overall sustainability issues firm internally and the external reporting thereof (as discussed in the previous Chapter 3).

Today, many companies use different certificates as proof of compliance, but certifications can range from having a very small to having an excruciating impact on a company and the management systems used. For example, ISO 14001 is an environmental certification that requires the organization to have a quality management system where the focus is on planning, control and monitoring of environmental issues within the companies. OHSAS 18001, on the other hand, aims to prevent accidents and illnesses and then mainly looks at the work environment and health of the staff. Both mentioned certifications are large and require many organizational tasks to get 'certified' and 'verified'.

Certifications are often time-limited and in many areas and industries, certain certifications are required in order to become supplier to other companies (B2B). The link between certifications and the area of sustainability is very clear today in society as a whole, and not just in the corporate world with, e.g., labels such as FSC (forest products), Fairtrade (mostly for small producers and farmers) and Organic (organic farming).

Most certifications require that you company internally work with planning, monitoring, controlling and reporting on the issues the certification includes. The problem is, however, that many of these new work tasks are outside the usual tasks and systems that accountants and finance people use. The HR department mainly handles the social issues, e.g., the employees' wages, health, satisfaction, efficiency, etc. The environmental issues, on the other hand, can be found in many different departments and levels, in manufacturing companies, however, mainly in the factories, i.e. at the operational level, and they are coordinated, often to a much lesser extent, at the higher levels in organizations.

A further problem is that environmental and social issues usually use other than financial measures, e.g., water consumption in liters, air pollution in tones of CO_2, or noise in decibels, etc. When there is for accounting and finance related people no common value, namely measures in financial terms, i.e. in Swedish crowns, Euro or USD, it is not easy to work for them, as most traditional calculations and other accounting templates, for products and services, require a monetary format. It is not always possible to have truly quantitative measures, but social issues can often only be measured with different scales, where the scales might well be numerical but cannot be compiled in a mathematical way. For example, a five on a scale where you fill in whether something is satisfactory or not is not automatically five times better than a one on the same scale.

Economic issues are traditionally the issues that always come high on the agenda in many companies. The great risk with environmental and social goals that cannot be grasped by accounting and finance people, or cannot be translated into financial goals and dimensions, then is that such issues become marginalized. Thus, the introduction of a new certification in a company might rather become a thing beside rather than attending the most important meetings at the top management level. The consequence is that they become less prioritized than the traditional financial issues.

If it only applies to the introduction of a rather small certification, it may not appear to be a major problem for a company when not everything is connected and fully integrated. However, the problems arise when companies deliberately choose sustainability as a strategic priority, which more and more companies are doing today, not only in Sweden but also globally, and yet they plan, manage, control and follow up these sustainability priorities alongside the traditional MAC systems. Then, the risk with sustainability issue to become marginalized is major. Below we will explain the reason for this and what can be done to avoid such problems.

4.2 Structuration processes and sustainability integration

To walk the talk, thus to integrate sustainability issues at all levels of a company, and in MAC systems, rather than to provide external information about it only is today perhaps considered the most important puzzle piece to bring about a faster transition to a sustainable development of companies and society. As previously discussed, integration can be seen in many ways, mainly depending on what you consider to be the subject of MAC. In this chapter, we account for a three-part integration division that has received attention recently. In several MAC articles (e.g. in Gond, Grubnic, Herzig & Moon, 2012; Rodrigue, Magnan & Boulianne, 2013; Battaglia, Passetti, Bianchi & Frey, 2016), a framework has been used that focuses on integration mainly based on three characteristics. These are:

1   A cognitive integration
2   An organizational integration
3   A technical integration

These researchers have investigated the integration between traditional MAC systems, which usually have a financial focus, and control systems that focus on environmental and social issues, here so-called sustainability MAC systems. We use the three-part integration division in own research (Beusch, Dilla, Frisk & Rosén, 2020). Below, however, we first illustrate how integration can be looked at in a larger context that shows how things in the world might be structured in general, and in companies in particular. Own research results, from a large international company, show that all integration is reflected in a larger process that takes place in reality, namely something we here call a "structuration process" that includes the two main dimensions of structure and agency.

The division is similar to the long academic discourse on structuration processes that determine how things in organizations and societies are shaped and embodied. This is most evidently described in Anthony Giddens many works (especially in his writings from 1979 to 1984), in which he summarizes the two dimensions with the concepts of structure and agency. Below is a brief simplified summary and interpretation of what has been written in Giddens' work connected to the MAC literature. However, we apply a more pragmatic approach to the whole reasoning.

Figure 4.1 summarizes the *structuration processes* where we have agency (human beings/agents/actors) on one side and the structures they create on the other side of a common field. In the text here, for simplicity's sake, we only use the concept of agency for the three concepts of human beings/agents/actors although literature, with its different frameworks and interpretations, can use

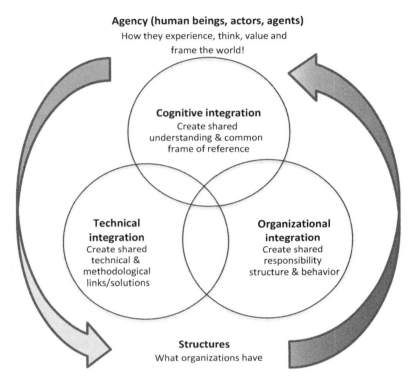

Figure 4.1 Ongoing structuration process, control integration and practice development.

different or the same names to describe slightly different discourses depending on the field of research (e.g., in Englund, Gerdin & Burns, 2011). In summary, however, this agency and structure concept can be seen as reaction to almost 'people-free' functionalistic research, where technical efficiency is in focus, then often disconnected from values, culture, politics and history.

As in Giddens' (1979 and 1984) works, agency can in reality hardly be totally separated from the structures they themselves create, consciously and unconsciously, because precisely the interaction between them, the structuration process, as illustrated in Figure 4.1 with the two large arrows, determines the design and characteristics of each. Two core assumptions of structuration processes are important to mention here. First, these processes apply the concept of *duality of structures*, rather than dualism, to illustrate that "structure works as both the medium for, and outcome of, social systems" (Englund et al., 2011, p. 495). Second, this includes the problem with "the paradox of embedded agency" that is: "if social structures are so powerful an influence on behaviour how can they change and if agents have free-will why is their behaviour constrained by social structures at all?" (Englund et al., 2011, p. 506).

In Figure 4.1, we place, in the middle of the structuration process, the three above mentioned types of integration between traditional and sustainability MAC systems (e.g., in Rodrigue et al., 2013; Battaglia et al., 2016) in three circles. Full integration can then be imagined in the middle of the three circles where we have a technical, cognitive and organizational integration simultaneously, which we will describe in more detail below.

Knowledge plays a key role in all structuration processes as it provides the basis for the rules and structures that people create around them. In this way, people are knowledgeable, reflexive, cognitive persons who, through their activities, create structures, which often become real and lasting institutions (institutional structures). As these institutional processes continue, parts of these structures are reproduced and transformed. Institutional becomes a structure if it forms a permanent part of organizations or society that influences the behaviours and values of individuals and collective groups. This is done by the existence of norms for action, cognitions, emotions and values. If you deviate from these norms, it is assumed that this leads to some kind of disadvantage or cost.

In the case of MAC and sustainability, one can imagine a situation where the company's employees try to integrate strategic sustainability priorities into their traditional, usually financially oriented, MAC systems and tools. Figure 4.1 therefore shows, in the lower part of the figure, the structures or what the company has and consists of. These structures have been created or produced by employees over generations, and are reproduced, in most cases, all the time. Such reproduction can either go slow or fast, depending entirely on the situation, the context, the people involved, internally and externally. The strength of the institutions and, on the one hand, the propensity to retain the structures as they are, is placed against a willingness to continuously adapt to changing conditions. In literature, this is sometimes described as the *'stability and/versus change'* or *'continuity and/versus change'* (Englund et al., 2011) dilemma.

The sustainability issues that currently require companies to mobilize and thus also adapt their agency and structures can be considered to be of a nature that requires organizational and institutional change. The extent of the changes required seems to determine how the interaction between the structures and agency advances and how long this takes. Anyone who looks around at daily work, or when studying at university, understands that the structures can have all sorts of shapes and peculiarities. One type of structure that includes much of the human component is social and cultural structures. On the other hand, almost as an opposite, we have natural and material structures, which, theoretically in any case, can exist without humans. Apart from the planet and nature itself, however, everything else has been materially and physically structured, constructed and produced by humans. Factories and assembly lines, computers, products, papers etc. are such constructed and man-made things.

Entirely physical or material structures that constitute MAC mechanisms are relatively rare in companies, although one could count access cards, barriers or even the access to everything else that constitutes a company as this kind of structures. Departments, for example, may constitute physical structures, and even the hierarchy within a company constitutes some form of almost physical structure that affects the way MAC mechanisms work, or are intended to work, although this 'physical' is usually only visible on paper in the form of concepts or drawings (e.g. organizational charts) and not as tangible/physical artefacts, which is described in more detail later.

Gond et al. (2012), Rodrigue et al. (2013) and Battaglia et al. (2016) emphasize that integration is primarily required in the cognitive, technical and organizational area in order for traditional MAC systems to be successfully combined/integrated with the new sustainability MAC systems. In their studies, the researchers have used Simons' (1995) Levers of Control (LOC) framework, which is also the framework we have applied in own research, which we will refer to below. In the following discussion, we further refer to two other popular MAC concepts when describing this integration. First, this is Malmi & Brown's (2008) management control package concept, which we already introduced in Chapter 3 as a holistic management control typology that includes five groups of controls. Second, we link the three-part integration concept to other popular MAC literature (e.g. Merchant & van der Stede, 2017).

4.3 Cognitive structures and MAC integration

Integrating cognitive structures is considered a basic prerequisite for a company to successfully work towards sustainability (Gond et al., 2012; Rodrigue et al., 2013; Battaglia et al., 2016). A bit simply put, cognitive structures are people's attitudes, ways of thinking, mindsets, values and beliefs. In the MAC literature, these structures are often referred to as social or cultural controls, sometimes also as people controls (Merchant & van der Stede, 2017) where social norms, values and cultural habits, etc. form the structures that hold the whole control system together. In Simons' (1995) LOC framework, one can most clearly see value-based control in what he calls belief systems, which then include formal control mechanisms such as mission and vision statements, and other credos to affect employee's behaviour. In Malmi & Brown's (2008) control package, cognitive structures are largely within cultural control, namely within clans, values and symbols, i.e., formal and informal forms of control, where social norms are considered to affect not only thoughts, but also action.

Cognitive integration, or the integration of cognitive structures, requires working towards achieving a common approach regarding/view of what MAC and sustainability means and how to relate to it. Here, it is primarily about getting employees to gain a more similar understanding of how the connections between economic, social and environmental sustainability aspects look like and what this means for the company. In this matter, there are mainly two cognitive types of people (Hahn, Preuss, Pinkse & Figge, 2014). The first type only makes sustainability investments if these pay off according to the business case principle, thus are paying pay-back within the (short) time limit that is common for traditional investments. The second cognitive people type accepts the fact that many of today's sustainability investments require a different (new) approach where the profitability aspect, which is the typical *business case approach*, must be partially or completely overridden in order to address important issues for society.

Within the domain of sustainability, there are many times when you either do not know what return the investment will generate or you do not know when this will happen. Therefore, the *paradoxical view* has it that one should not make a traditional business-case for such issues, precisely because profitability goals can be contradictory compared to social and/or environmental goals according to the criteria used by today's governing mechanisms (Hahn et al., 2014). Thus, from a *business case* approach, most things still centre on financial returns, the pay-back. Sustainability issues can be included, and taken into account, in cases where they do not conflict with this economic logic or the *business case*.

However, demonstrating positive causality is often difficult in the field of sustainability due to measurement problems and because the areas have different formats (monetized or not). Submitting proof of a *business case* is not easy then. Often a logical connection can be sensed by the involved but not statistically or mathematically proven. This is, for accounting and finance people, a problem as budgets, calculations and most other accounts overall have to total exactly. This can be regarded as one of the main explanations why sustainability initiatives have not been more successful in accounting and finance dominated areas and that development there has been slow.

On the other hand, *paradoxical thinking* accepts, according to Hahn et al. (2014), different logics and do not latch on to just the economically rational. Here, social or environmental issues may be in focus and prioritized despite the fact that they may run counter to financial returns as other, non-monetary values, are included into the (e)valuation. Therefore, you do not need to compile a *business case* to be able to proceed with, for example, strategic investment decisions. Also, conflicts between different stakeholders are accepted to a larger extent and you focus on what the company contributes to society and not just the organizational contribution, and this also in other than just financial terms.

Sustainability managers often, probably due to their education, background and personality, have often such a *paradoxical view*. Traditionally trained financial managers, controllers and accountants more often think in terms of the *business case*, however. Business cases are thus their preferable cognitive approach because they are trained to think so. It has, for decades, also been the logic they have been expected to work on. It can be considered that these people do not even do their job well in case they think differently – which is important to keep in mind when trying to improve cognitive integration for sustainability. Accounting and finance peoples' cognitive way of thinking is probably still mostly a *business-case mindset*, everything else is almost strange.

4.4 Organizational structures and MAC integration

Organizational structures can best be understood by looking at Malmi & Brown's (2008) administrative controls, which includes governance structures, organizational structures, and an organization's policies and procedures. In Simons' (1995) LOC framework, boundary systems might, at least to quite some extent, cover the aspects of organizational structures (e.g. rules, limits, prescriptions). Organizational integration is the type of integration that Gond et al. (2012) describe least clearly in their integration framework. However, the authors emphasize that organizational integration is basically about support processes for enabling a common practice of employees who work with MAC issues and employees who work with sustainability issues. Organizational integration therefore means above all ensuring that you practice work in an integrated manner, which requires, in relation to sustainability goals and strategies, to:

*   structure and define organizational responsibilities and determine which individuals get to participate in which decision-making;
*   set up policies and procedures;
*   determine how information flows between functions and levels are; and
*   define other task allocation, coordination and supervision directed towards the achievement of organizational aims.

Together, this assumes that the company creates shared responsibility units and includes organizational structures and processes that enable social adaptation (socialization) across the traditionally often functionally divided boundaries (e.g. R&D, purchasing, production, HR, sales, etc.), which often also consist of specific skills. Information and knowledge about sustainability issues should then not only be with some experts, but also with those who have the accounting and financial areas as their main responsibility. In order for organizational integration to lead to better sustainability work within companies, a systematic approach is needed to consider how these organizational structures, or administrative control systems (Malmi & Brown, 2008), are designed. The important thing is that clear links are created between the traditionally different practice areas and that socialization takes place.

4.5 Technical structures and MAC integration

4.5.1 Technical structures are often at the heart of traditional MAC literature

Probably most MAC literature that has been written over the last 40 years has focused on what could be assigned to technical structures as it, first and foremost, is about the infrastructure within a company that enables the (similar) structuring, collection, processing and reporting of accounting information.

The technical structure is thus a composition of material, technical, social and knowledge-based structures. What can be included here is all forms of *system-technical infrastructure* (e.g. accounting system, IT system, ERP system, etc.). It is also about the methodological links and concepts that are built into the various technical structures that form the basis for how such accounting infrastructure ultimately is designed and used. The methodological concepts in turn have often been developed for several decades in society in general (such as the double-entry bookkeeping system) and in companies more specifically, with, e.g., formalized and standardized calculation models, specific budgeting processes and various types of specific arranged and designed management concepts and scorecards.

For example, technical structures are illustrated in three of the five parts of Malmi & Brown's (2008) management control package. They are represented by planning (long rang and action planning), cybernetic controls (budgets, financial measurement systems, non-financial measurement systems, hybrid measurement systems) and reward and compensation systems. In terms of Simons' (1995) LOC framework, it is first and foremost diagnostic controls that constitutes the technical structure, since diagnostic controls' main task is to monitor, communicate and correct for critical target variables and deviations.

The technical structures in the field of MAC usually are thought of as more 'material' or physical substance opposed to the cultural or social structures described above, which are usually of a more intangible and informal nature, although some sort of formalization is often present. Therefore, technical integration means that traditional MAC systems, and the tools and techniques associated with them, e.g. budgeting, different types and preferences of calculations, or a balanced scorecard, must also include the new sustainability goals (Gond et al., 2012), which then are primarily system interface and infrastructure issues.

Design issues are also important because the accounting systems, and other information flow mechanisms and tools used within the company, must be interconnected to support a common management of all data, information and decision-making. Thus, the main purpose of the technical integration is to create information channels and systems that enable the collection, analysis and follow-up of common (financial and sustainability-oriented) data for performance measurement, variance analyses and as a decision-making basis in general.

4.5.2 An overview of today's most well-known MAC techniques and tools for sustainability

The following overview (Table 4.1) of traditional and sustainability-oriented MAC techniques and tools summarizes some of the most commonly mentioned concepts that can be counted to be part of the technical structural area. Thus, there are technical structures that exist in companies with the main aim to achieve integration in Part 3.2 (integrate (sustainability)

Table 4.1 MAC techniques and tools & sustainability

(Traditional) MAC techniques & tools	*MAC techniques & tools for sustainability*
Budgeting and Planning (short and long term)	• Environmental Budgets & Planning • Social Budgets & Planning • Sustainability Budgets & Planning
Cost accounting and calculation techniques	• Full Cost/True-cost Accounting regarding environmental issues • Full Cost/True-cost Accounting regarding social issues • Lifecycle Costing (LCC) and Lifecycle Management (LCM) • Circular Economy • Activity-Based Costing for Sustainability
Hybrid performance measurement systems/ Integrative tools and techniques	• Eco-Efficiency Analysis • Sustainable Balanced Scorecard • Sustainability Reporting • Multicapital-Scorecard
Reward and Compensation systems	• Sustainability oriented Reward and Compensation Systems

objectives in existing MAC systems or create new MAC systems, if necessary) in Figure 3.2, as discussed in Chapter 3.

The following overview is based on a number of publications in an international and a Swedish perspective (e.g. Passetti, Cinquini, Marelli, & Tenucci, 2014; Carlsson, 2017). It is important to note, however, that there has been quite some *talk* about these tools and techniques in recent years. In reality, however, this does not mean the same as if they are *applied and used* to the same extent. On the contrary, some research shows that there still is no particular systematic and fully conscious work done today to include and integrate social and environmental goals and metrics into the traditional (usually financial) MAC concepts.

The parts in Table 4.1 are, in many ways, similar to three types of Malmi & Brown's (2008) management control systems, namely 'planning, cybernetic control, and reward and compensation systems'. The biggest difference, however, is that we also focus here on specific cost accounting and calculation techniques, which is an important element of real MAC practices in firms and, in addition, includes much tutoring on the basic courses in management accounting at many universities. Sometimes, these courses are even called *Cost Management* or *Cost Accounting* or *Management and Cost Accounting*. However, cost management/cost accounting may be less relevant in the more theoretical and academic discourse, which Malmi & Brown (2008) also mention in their article. In terms of sustainability, however, a lot revolves around costs, which we illustrate below. We, however, start with budgeting and planning.

4.5.3 Sustainability budgeting and planning

Budgeting and planning is an important element in most companies, as it is often the largest formal process involving future planning. Simply put, one can say that there are three types of special budgets for sustainability. The first type consists of environmental budgets, the second type of social budgets and the third type summarizes both together as a sustainable budget, then either separate from the traditional financial budget or together with such financial planning. In addition, of course, these areas can be placed directly in the traditional and usually financially oriented budgets so that they do not get their own name. Such a budget can be seen as including a Triple Bottom Line (TBL) thinking, which theoretically probably is the best way to push sustainability issues into MAC tools.

A real TBL budget simply includes both social and environmental budgets, and at best also the financial budgets, side by side. Environmental budgeting refers to the budgeting of future environmental outcomes and is a forward-looking planning tool that determines available resources for environmental issues for a future period. This tool also helps determine the size of environmental targets. Of course, it is important that you also decide what the important environmental goals and objectives are that should be in focus. Here you can see a clear difference between a company's internal and external approach. A company, internally, focuses on own environmental improvements where targets/goals and strategies are directly linked to the company's income/loss statement and have a fairly clear impact on (lost/increased) revenues and (saved/increased) costs. This area is normally under control of the company precisely because it is about 'internal affairs'. For example, use of 'green energy' or 'non-fossil fuel' within production and transports are internal performance metrics that measure environmental issues that can be planned for rather easily. These measures are often numerical but rarely of a monetary nature, and need to be translated/converted first in order to be included in typical accounting information systems.

The external environmental goals and dimensions, on the other hand, are more difficult to define and measure, and often less visible. This is the case because they are 'external' to the company, thus so-called externalities, which is an external effect of what the company does. These externalities can be positive or negative, but above all the negative ones are a problem from a sustainability point of view because these are things that, at present, are often outside the company's area of responsibility, yet they are the result of what the company does or produces, e.g. greenhouse gas emissions, water pollution, noise, land use, etc. External environmental factors can, however, also be the factors that the company would like to include in their calculations and managerial decisions, but is not able to really do this simply because they have no control over them. Environmental budgeting and monitoring, and thus a formal planning for environmental goals and measures, with using financial and non-financial data can contribute to less environmental impact but also lower costs and increase revenues.

Social budgeting, on the other hand, refers to the budgeting of future social outcomes and is a forward-looking planning tool that determines available funds for social issues for a future period. This tool also helps to set social goals and metrics and expresses the aspirations, expectations and commitments of an organization regarding social impact for an upcoming period. Here, too, one can reason the same way as above for the environment domain because one can think of an internal perspective within the social field (the own employees) and a company external perspective (external community and society in which the company operates). Measurement systems and structures that deal primarily with internal issues are, e.g., those intended for measuring social issues related to employees' health and safety and employment conditions and satisfaction, career development paths and rewards.

Externally, on the other hand, it is more difficult to define what you mean by the social dimension and how to incorporate all this into a structured MAC process such as budgeting. Here it can be about human rights in more general terms than just the employees, it can be about social activities, or the social assessment of products that the company sells. In this area, the Global Reporting Initiative (GRI) standards offer a large number of focus areas and metrics (see Chapter 8) that can be applied by companies who really want to make a difference externally with the help of (internal) budgets and planning. What is important is that the budget process leads to a systematic approach that delivers information on what activities can be regarded as socially efficient and effective. Numerical metrics are here normal and some things even expressed in monetary terms. However, perhaps the most common are non-monetary measures and not infrequently those of the most subjective nature.

4.5.4 Cost accounting and calculation techniques for sustainability

Full-cost accounting, or even *true-cost accounting*, are terms that have specific meaning when linked to the area of sustainability. Traditionally, full-cost accounting simply means to include all direct and indirect costs (and revenues) incurred to carry out the business operations. This, however, has not included social and environmental costs and benefits of two kinds. First, when such costs were not measurable due to e.g. non-monetary format. Second, when such costs were caused to external parties to the firm who did not choose to incur that cost or benefit (again the so-called 'externalities). *Full-cost* or *true-cost accounting*, according to the TBL concept, therefore means to consider, collect, include and present information about the environmental, social and financial costs and benefits for each proposed product, service, activity or alternative overall, and this company internally (in the first case) and for real sustainability matters to become effective, also company externally (in the second case). Normally, a full-cost is the sum of all the environmental and social costs of a product/service/activity/alternative until it is delivered and paid.

First, you can create *product calculations* or also *activity-based calculations* (ABC), which are calculations that make extensive use of activities and cost drivers to reduce current costs. This can focus on reducing, e.g., waste, energy use, land use, decontamination, by-products, noise, odour, transportation costs, fuel costs, etc. It simply means that you need to make sure that you get the right information about precisely these environmental and social costs and include them in the usual calculations, so that the whole, i.e., including the negative impact of the company's products/services/activities/ alternatives, is more clearly visible. Based on this more holistic picture, other more far-reaching and long-term decisions can be made than with just the traditional financial calculations.

The next step is to try to reduce future costs by calculating on better technology, increased recycling, reduced energy use, reusable packaging, better transportation solutions, a better waste sorting system, etc. This is then mostly about investment calculations where you look at the whole (manufacturing) processes and how it can be improved. In addition, you can also expect increased revenues by investing in sustainable products that can be sold (more expensive) to (new) conscious customers. In this way, all parts of the income statement are included and also, in many ways, the link to the balance sheet through new (green) investments.

4.5.5 *Life cycle costing and cost management for circular economy*

A concept that has gained momentum and, e.g., been erected as the number one priority of the upcoming European Green Deal to achieve net-zero carbon emissions by 2050 is *circular economy* (Simons, 2019). For companies, it is essential to look at this from a *Life Cycle Costing* or *Circular Economy* perspective, which means to do business in a more circular (and re-invest, re-create, re-use, re-cycle) rather than linear way that simply followed the idea of 'take, make, waste'. A *circular economy* model aims at redefining growth and focusing on positive society wide benefits. Thus, all calculations therefore must be based on reduced environmental (and social) impact through increased collection and reuse, but also through e.g. sharing economy. The calculations focus on, and serve to, remove environmentally hazardous substances, to redesign the products for as little waste as possible; to use renewable energy, to return materials, and to share products or equipment, to rent instead of procure, or to lease instead of owning.

Life-cycle calculations and analyses are the compilation and evaluation of inflows to, and outflows from, a product system over its entire life-cycle, as well as the evaluation of the potential environmental (and social) impacts of a production system over its entire life-cycle. We here use the social dimension of sustainability in parentheses as the main focus of *Life-cycle costing* and *circular-economy* so far mostly has been on the environmental dimension. More and more, however, especially since the introduction of SDG's 17 sustainability goals, social issues have become strongly linked to these two concepts.

From a cost accounting and calculation perspective, employees might apply quite similar techniques and tools as before but they need to, first and foremost, expand the time span, backwards and forwards, to include all the time it takes from the beginning of the product/service to its actual end, and include more factors that might be important (e.g. 'externalities'). Life-cycle calculations have started to take off, especially in the areas that require a lot of energy and large natural resources. The manufacturing of cars is a typical example of this where you can find an illustrative case that also shows the difficulties that can arise and why specific cost accounting techniques and calculations for the entire life-cycle are strongly recommended to really contribute to sustainability.

Electric cars seem to be the type of cars of the future and have become increasingly popular with buyers. South African Elon Musk, who stands behind the Tesla cars, can be considered a revolutionary in the field. However, the most recent debate, that also concerns him, is that it is not certain that today's production of electric cars is good from a life-cycle perspective. In a report compiled by researchers commissioned by the Swedish Transport Administration and the Swedish Energy Agency (Dahllöf, Romare & Larsson, 2017), the authors state that the production of the battery for a Tesla Model S leads to emissions corresponding to eight years of operation of a petrol driven car. Elon Musk rejects this claim via Twitter that the study is naïve and at the same time emphasizes that Tesla's battery factory, Gigafactory, is powered by renewable energy.

Nonetheless, the manufacturing of batteries today is still very energy intensive and can therefore have significant emissions. The Swedish study's conclusions say nothing about whether electric cars are good or not overall. However, it says that electric cars are good because they have zero emissions in the local environment and therefore, there is a reason to invest in them. However, the study also says that one must take an active grip on production and not just its use. The study therefore finds that better data from the manufacturers is needed to make accurate comparisons of the total impact on the entire life cycle of the cars. The authors clearly state that future instruments need to take into account emissions even in the production phase (Dahllöf et al., 2017). For a real analysis, and e.g. to be able to help from a state-wide level via subsidies, you need to have data, environmental and financial (in terms of costs and revenues) on the entire life-cycle of battery production, use, and probably also what happens to the batteries thereafter.

4.5.6 Hybrid control and measurement systems/integrative tools and methods

4.5.6.1 A sustainability balanced scorecard (SBSC)

A sustainability balanced scorecard (SBSC) is an extended variant of a conventional balanced scorecard (BSC) that also includes environmental and social aspects. The main advantage of the original BSC, developed by Kaplan & Norton (1993), is considered to be based on the idea that a financial focus is insufficient to manage companies and that additional stakeholders, with a balanced approach, had to be taken into consideration. Three other perspectives, which also derive from Kaplan & Norton, are often mentioned in this context, namely internal processes, customers and markets, and learning and development (see Chapter 3). The important thing is that companies that use a BSC design the dimensions according to their own preferences and according to what they consider to be important goals to achieve and with strategies that should be designed accordingly. Therefore, there are many different types of BSC and also many different ways to include the new sustainability goals.

An SBSC is a tool that identifies, systematizes, visualizes and measures strategically important economic, environmental and social goals. One can thus say that it usually follows a 'triple bottom line' (TBL) logic. There are several possible ways to design an SBSC structure. The first variant is to add the new sustainability goals of the social and environmental areas to the already existing dimensions where they seem to fit best. Another alternative is to create your own sustainability dimension, which then includes both areas, the social and the environmental, or you add two new sustainability dimensions, one for the social and one for the environmental area. One last option, which is sometimes mentioned, is to use two different balanced scorecards, the traditional BSC already in use, and a new BSC alongside, which then only includes the new sustainability goals. The big disadvantage of the last alternative, when you do not combine all dimensions in the same BSC, is that you do not see the whole picture at ones and how things work together. Thus, there is a risk that the separate BSC, including sustainability specific metrics, will get marginalized and loose significance over time.

A major advantage with the SBSC idea is that it is based on a very well-known and well-used concept (BSC) and applies a similar logic regarding integrating and balancing different components within a company in order to implement and support the strategy/ies. This logic implies that several different dimensions must be brought together and that this is organizational reality that cannot be avoided. In many ways, this is the reason why companies with BSC's also (should) choose to build on this to achieve improvements in the sustainability area.

There are, however, two disadvantages with the use of an SBSC compared to e.g. Simons (1995) LOC methodology. These two problems are similar as with the traditional BSC, but may become even more evident when combined with sustainability issues. Since no company has unlimited resources, it always means that you have to prioritize certain things over others. Thus, you cannot fully satisfy the interests of all stakeholders and in all situations. It is important to balance these interests and that is why some authors (e.g. Sundin, Granlund & Brown, 2010; Hahn & Figge, 2016) argue that it is precisely the process of balancing, i.e., in verb form, that should be the focus of everything that has to do with sustainability, rather than thinking that one should be able to get a balanced result in all dimensions and in all situations. Such balancing processes, however, is not what traditional finance and accounting structures support.

The second challenge of an SBSC is that it mostly deals with the diagnostic, and to some extent even interactive, control function in companies when talking e.g. Simons' (1995) LOC concept. The more value-based and from a cognitive integration dimension very important belief and boundary controls (Simons, 1995), on the other hand, have little effect.

4.5.6.2 A Multi-Capital Scorecard

A Multi-Capital Scorecard is perhaps one of the newest TBL-based methodology to increase sustainability performance and simplify its reporting (Thomas & McElroy, 2016). This is done by companies focusing and counting on all capital that is included as input and until it is transformed into output but above all outcome (according to the six capital concept from IIRC, see Chapter 9). In addition, in everything companies do, they must see themselves in their context with obligations and opportunities. Thus, this scorecard is combining a stakeholder perspective with a context-based multi-capitalism performance and reporting approach. This scorecard applies a systems-based philosophy, including all capitals, and sets context-based targets in order to transform organizations in a way that is supposed to make them more ecological. Benchmarking, within the industry and within certain regions, and above all within planetary boundaries, is the main driver for all improvements within MAC practices then.

4.5.6.3 Eco-efficiency analysis

Eco-efficiency has, primarily within the industrial area, been proposed as one of the main tools to promote a transformation to 'do more with less', hence to produce more goods that require as little energy and material as possible, in both manufacturing and use. The analysis develops and optimizes the properties of products as well as the operational activities around products regarding the relationship between its economic added value, the use of natural resources and the company's (often financial) goals. The major advantage of this tool is that eco-efficiency can be calculated by extending the typical, and in companies' finance and accounting departments very well-known, *Du-Pont formula* that measures economic profitability (Return on Assets, ROA), with the resource use required in relation to the financial value created. Thus, such an analysis measures capital efficiency and ecological efficiency simultaneously.

Figge & Hahn (2013) report, e.g., in their study how eco-efficient certain car brands in the car industry are by looking primarily at CO_2 emissions in relation to the capital base, on the y-axis, and on the traditional measure of return on total assets (ROA), on the x-axis. The great advantage of their study is that it is based on an old and very well-known model (the *DuPont formula*). The disadvantage is that the analysis is a strong simplification. It does not show all the factors that are part of the ecological impact of car manufacturing. This problem could be avoided with more sophisticated calculation and data gathering methods. However, the bigger problem that remains is twofold. First, eco-efficiency is focusing merely on the environmental dimension together with the financial dimension of sustainability, thus, omits the social dimension. Second, the total growth of production can still erase all efficiency gains made, leaving societal impact in total negative.

4.5.7 Sustainability reward and compensation systems

In short, reward and compensation systems that meet the requirements for sustainability must be based on multidimensional measures and not just financial measures that the company achieves. This means that when building such a systems, the focus is to a lesser extent on the traditional financial measures (e.g. profitability measures, share-price increase, etc.) as the basis for rewards, but more on how well you manage to achieve environmental and social goals.

So far, there is not much research that has investigated precisely the link between compensation and reward systems and sustainability. Own research, however, shows pros and cons with this. Simply applying the same methodology as with traditional reward systems to compensating how well you achieve goals might, however, not be enough. For example, if trying to ensure that no accidents happen and rewarding the responsible managers based on the number of accidents can mean that one simply does not report accidents, which of course counteracts reduced accidents in reality (Beusch et al., 2020).

Another example, however, is bonuses for selling sustainability products. Sellers in a company investigated still got their bonuses based on a traditional 'turnover' measure. It is, in such a case, easy to calculate that these salespeople first and foremost are interested in selling the products that can easily be sold to increase turnover rather than working extra hard to sell the more environmentally friendly products, which then also are more expensive, and in addition, or exactly due to that, much more difficult to sell. It is precisely in such a situation that the company must have a long-term sustainability commitment and plan. This includes to 'sustainability' educate employees, especially the salespeople, and ensure that knowledge, attitudes and behaviours change. These salespeople must become better at selling the more expensive but energy-efficient and environmentally less harmful products. If they succeed with that, bonuses for such achievements might be the right way to go.

4.6 Summary and how everything is connected

Malmi & Brown's (2008) management control package, divided into five parts, which summarizes 40 years of MAC research, can be seen as a fairly good compilation of control issues that can be involved during structuration processes needed for sustainability integration. The design of planning, cybernetic controls and reward and compensation systems is strongly influenced by the administrative control systems (governance structures, organization structures, and policies and procedures) and by cultural and social forms of control (clans, values, symbols). The key message from Malmi & Brown (2008, p. 291) is that different systems often are introduced by different interest groups at different times and that this is the reason why one should look at all this as a package of systems, thus holistically, rather than single systems. To include sustainability matters into traditional MAC systems might exactly be such a situation. This way, a logical control package, including technical, organizational and cognitive integration, is supposed to be created that generates organizational meaning for the involved agents and best possible MAC for sustainability.

Own research in the field clearly shows that cognitive integration still seems to be one of the major obstacles to achieving a faster transition towards sustainability (Beusch et al., 2020). First of all, managers in the field of finance and accounting often lack knowledge about what sustainability means and what such integration takes to get translated into positive contributions beyond nice external reporting that sometimes even includes 'window dressing' and 'green washing'. Many managers still today see sustainability issues mostly as a cost and not a source of increased revenues or important aspects to gain the license to operate (legitimacy) and due to responsibility matters.

When cognitive integration does not exist, or only partially works, in a company or at different departments of a company, it seems to be very difficult to compensate with a possible integration within the other two dimensions (technical and organizational) precisely because cognitive awareness and understanding is important to create meaning in all organizational work, and thus in all sense-making and ultimately decision-making. For things to develop towards sustainability, a basic requirement that employees and managers seem to be interested in working towards more sustainability at all is needed.

Own research further shows that for such cognitive integration to happen, intensive use of interactive control systems (Simons, 1995) is needed within companies (Beusch et al., 2020). This then includes meetings, face-to-face debates and challenges, non-invasive facilitating and inspirational involvement, focus on strategic uncertainties, and knowledge sharing and learning. However, it is not important that everyone at once thinks and values business in a paradoxical way (Hahn et al., 2014). To reach feasible solutions, a pragmatic mix of paradoxical and business-case thinking is considered to be enough in reality as one cannot stop doing business during the time when this translation has to go on.

Of course, all of this, in a company, is created by real agents, and all structural work also influences how these agents think and value things, and how they act. This also affects/is affected by the culture within the company. For this very reason, an organizational culture can be regarded as the result of a structuration process, which is the ongoing process between agency and structure. In addition, agents always have to deal with the fact that they are influenced and shaped by the very same structures, which refers to the so-called 'paradox of embedded agency' (Englund & Gerdin, 2018).

More research is needed in the future to gain more clarity in the relationships between the different integration dimensions and what this means to agency and structures. We assume that full integration, i.e. in the middle of Figure 4.1, where all three circles overlap, can be achieved when, e.g., managers and employees think and value sustainability and finance issues equally high (cognitive integration), use system-technical solutions that enable full technical integration of sustainability and financial information while also working, in reality, integrated (organizational integration) with sustainability and financial issues in practice. This in turn requires the company to provide technically integrated (system) solutions and tools.

The circle diagram also shows that many different alternative combinations can exist that do not mean full integration in all three dimensions, namely where, e.g. only two of the circles overlap. It is not even entirely certain if all dimensions must be integrated for all sustainability issues or if certain dimensions are sufficient within certain time frames and in specific situations. More research is needed in this area to clarify the links between MAC changes and sustainability. What theoretically seems to be the best does not automatically have to be the best in reality.

Study questions

1   Describe different types of sustainability certifications that you know of and discuss how you think they are incorporated into different companies.
2   Check out some major companies' annual reports (or go to the investor relation links on the company's website) and look for the accounts of the company's mission, vision, but also how they formulate their strategies and goals. What do you find in terms of sustainability? How is this formulated? What do you think this says about the company work internally with management accounting and control systems to achieve what they report about externally?
3   Describe what a 'structuring process' is that includes people and structures. Can you see the results of such processes around you? Can you see your own role in structuring processes?
4   Describe what is meant by the term 'integration' and what the separation into cognitive, organizational and technical integration means.
5   Discuss, preferably in pairs or larger groups, similarities and differences in the cognitive structures (e.g. attitudes, ways of thinking, values) that you yourself have or that your friends or colleagues have, or simply the environment that you are surrounded by. What does cognitive integration mean to you, as a couple or in a group?

6   Similarly, please discuss, in pairs or larger groups, similarities and differences in the organizational structures (e.g. organizational units of responsibility, policies, and procedures) that surround you. What changes would organizational integration for sustainability require?

7   Finally, also discuss, in pairs or larger groups, similarities and differences in the technical structures (e.g. financial management tools, models, concepts, etc.) that you work with, either at school, in the workplace, or in everyday life. Do you see sustainability issues included in these technical structures?

8   Do you see a situation in your life, at school, or in your workplace where the cognitive, organizational and technical integration for management accounting and control and sustainability overlaps completely (i.e. where you are in the middle of the three circles)?

References

Battaglia, M., Passetti, E., Bianchi, L. & Frey, M. (2016). Managing for integration: A longitudinal analysis of management control for sustainability. *Journal of Cleaner Production*, Vol. 136, pp. 213–225.

Beusch, P., Dilla, W. N., Frisk, E. & Rosen, M. (2020, February 5). *Management control for sustainability: Towards integrated systems* (under review at MAR, Management Accounting Research).

Carlsson, J. (2017). Tools for sustainability management accounting – A survey of the frequency and purpose of using tools for sustainability management accounting in Swedish listed companies. Master thesis 2017, Göteborg University.

Dahllöf, L., Romare, M. & Larsson, M. O. (2017). www.ivl.se/toppmeny/pressrum/pressmeddelanden/pressmeddelande-arkiv/2017-05-29-ny-rapport-belyser-klimatpaverkan-fran-produktionen-av-elbilsbatterier.html (Accessed on 18-1-2018).

Englund, H. & Gerdin, J. (2018). Management accounting and the paradox of embedded agency: A framework for analyzing sources of structural change. *Management Accounting Research*, Vol. 38, pp. 1–11.

Englund, H., Gerdin, J. & Burns, J. (2011). 25 years of Giddens in accounting research: Achievements, limitations and the future. *Accounting, Organizations and Society*, Vol. 36 (8), pp. 494–513.

Figge, F. & Hahn, T. (2013). Value drivers of corporate eco-efficiency: Management accounting information for the efficient use of environmental resources. *Management Accounting Research*, Vol. 24 (4), pp. 387–400.

Giddens, A. (1979). Agency, structure. In *Central problems in social theory* (pp. 49–95). London: Palgrave.

Giddens, A. (1984). *The constitution of society: Outline of the theory of structuration*. Los Angeles: University of California Press.

Gond, J. P., Grubnic, S., Herzig, C. & Moon, J. (2012). Configuring management control systems: Theorizing the integration of strategy and sustainability. *Management Accounting Research*, Vol. 23 (3), pp. 205–223.

Hahn, T. & Figge, F. (2016). Why architecture does not matter: On the fallacy of sustainability balanced scorecards. *Journal of Business Ethics*, Vol. 150 (4), pp. 1–17.

Hahn, T., Preuss, L., Pinkse, J. & Figge, F. (2014). Cognitive frames in corporate sustainability: Managerial sensemaking with paradoxical and business case frames. *Academy of Management Review*, Vol. 39 (4), pp. 463–487.

Kaplan, R. & Norton, D. (1993). Putting the balanced scorecard to work. *Harvard Business Review*, Vol. 71 (5), pp. 134–140.

Malmi, T. & Brown, D. (2008). Management control systems as a package—Opportunities, challenges and research directions. *Management Accounting Research*, Vol. 19, pp. 287–300.

Merchant, K. A. & Van der Stede, W. A. (2017). *Management control systems: Performance measurement, evaluation and incentives*. Harlow: Pearson Education.

Passetti, E., Cinquini, L., Marelli, A. & Tenucci, A. (2014). Sustainability accounting in action: Lights and shadows in the Italian context. *The British Accounting Review*, Vol. 46 (3), pp. 295–308.

Rodrigue, M., Magnan, M., & Boulianne, E. (2013). Stakeholders' influence on environmental strategy and performance indicators: A managerial perspective. *Management Accounting Research*, Vol. 24, pp. 301–316.

Thomas, M. P. & McElroy, M. W. (2016). *The multicapital scorecard: Rethinking organizational performance*. White River Junction: Chelsea Green Publishing.

Simons, F. (2019). Circular economy erected as 'number one priority' of European GreenDeal. www.euractiv.com/section/circular-economy/news/circular-economy-is-number-one-priority-of-european-green-deal/ (Accessed on 20-2-2020).

Simons, R. (1995). *Levers of control: How managers use innovative control systems to drive strategic renewal*. Boston, MA: Harvard Business School Press,.

Sundin, H., Granlund, M. & Brown, D. A. (2010). Balancing multiple competing objectives with a balanced scorecard. *European Accounting Review*, Vol. 19 (2), pp. 203–246.

5 Towards a more sustainable and integrated performance management

Matti Skoog

Abstract

This chapter aims to give the reader an insight into what is required to integrate, for example, sustainability aspects into organizations' performance management processes. The starting point for the chapter is the criticism that the traditional financial management has endured in recent decades and the shortcomings that can be continuously observed in most organizational contexts in relation to traditional financial management. The significance and understanding of, for example, support processes and performance ideals are highlighted as potentially important for a more integrated, sustainable and relevant performance management process.

5.1 Performance management and management control

Modern performance management can be said to be both a reaction to financial management and an attempt to answer the criticism directed at financial control. Unfortunately, traditional financial management has often been about over-calculation, over-documentation and short-termism (Johanson & Skoog, 2007, 2015). Modern performance management is a very broad and complex concept. In some way, control always takes place in companies and organizations. Ideally, this happens consciously and is coordinated in line with the organization's visions and strategies. But more often than not, control is only partially coordinated, is to some extent unconscious and does not always align with visions and strategies. Whether ideally or imperfectly, it signals values and accountability – or lack of accountability. Control involves exercising accountability as well as exercising power, and it is also influenced by accountability and power. It both influences and is influenced by organizational culture and societal trends. Thus, management controls functions both as a mirror of existing conditions and as a tool for change. It is based on the past, but intends to influence the future. It balances stability and change. Management control aims to achieve both external efficiency, that is to do the right things, and internal efficiency, that is to do things the right way. To achieve this, simplicity, relevance, comprehensibility, accessibility, participation and acceptance are important elements.

If traditional financial management uses mainly monetary units, financial metrics, the business–oriented management control advocates choose to supplement financial metrics with non–financial metrics. Many believe it can be difficult to capture the significance of non–material resources through measurements and figures. To express complex phenomena and relationships, stories of different kinds can be important complements. Bjurklo and Kardemark (2003) showed in their research from the forest industry how stories about certain critical events for the business play a controlling role in the business. They believe that managers use both "hard" information (numbers) and "soft" information (stories) to understand, make judgements and manage the business, especially in situations where the organization is facing radical change. The use of these stories is an example of how important informal elements can be in the management control of an organization. It can therefore be stated that traditional financial management needs to be expanded to modern management control and it should also be integrated (see later in the chpater for what is meant by integrated in this context). Measurement, control, order and clarity are important, but the primary role of integrated performance management is communicative and educational. That is, the purpose is to promote understanding and mobilize future action. The latter means that we most often have to admit that the formulation of certain problems and alternatives to action is based on subjective constructions of reality. If the purpose is to mobilize action, it can often also be that measurement precision can and should give way to communicability, and perhaps simplification. The results from these goals is an ambition for operational relevance in control and measurement, where acceptance for a reasonable measurement precision in most cases is high, but where the communication requirements are even higher to create interest, commitment and understanding of the control signals that are given. An integrated performance management process should therefore not be "silent" but be characterized by "sound".

Business–oriented management control can be said to include both reporting/accounting and management. The concepts of control and management can have roughly the same meaning (Samuelson 2008). One difference, however, is that management (and above all leadership) is more associated with personal relationships than is the case with the concept of control, which focuses on processes, systems, structures and routines. Although management is part of control, I will not deal with leadership in this chapter.

Like the concept of performance, the concept of company and organization is complex. This is complex, partly because the boundaries of a company and an organization are now increasingly diffuse. At the beginning of industrial society, a company was often the same as a workplace. The legal form, the building and the workplace were often the same as a factory. Employees, managers and owners lived around the factory. Today, many companies and organizations are more intangible. Several legal entities are part of a network, and parts of the production chain can be "outsourced". Some companies and organizations have no, or very limited, tangible assets; intangible ones are in the form of, for example, patents and trademarks (intellectual property), employees' competence and health (personnel-related), databases (structure-related) and assets such as customer relations and image (market-related). The complexity of the corporate concept also has consequences for and emphasizes the need for what can be called integrated.

By integrating, we believe that control needs to be developed and brought together in order to become a whole. For example, non-financial indicators, which are of great importance, need to be integrated with the more traditional financial management. That is, non-financial management needs to be integrated with financial management. The choice of the word integrated also aims to emphasize the importance of the reporting being well integrated with the management of the business. Reporting and management also need to address both tangible and intangible resources (for example, competence, health, customer relationships and sustainability). Furthermore, historical events need to be integrated with current and future conceivable events and effects. Finally, the term integrated means that both management and reporting intend to handle the requirements and needs of several different stakeholders. The integrated control process addresses both economic and social and sustainability issues in order to meet not only the management's, but also the owners' (the principal's), the employees', the financial market's, customers' and society's needs. More on integrated performance management and what is meant by this concept will be presented later in the chapter.

5.2 Integration restrictions in traditional financial management

In recent decades, traditional financial management has been subjected to quite extensive discussion and criticism from both researchers and practitioners. Let's start with some views from a practical perspective and phenomena labelled "unnuanced cost thinking". We then move on to summarize the extensive criticism from both researchers and practitioners.

A major and widespread problem today, as well as several decades ago, is the general view on costs and how they are interpreted in relation to decisions about the future. Are costs something that should always be minimized, or can spending be necessary for future income, quality and sustainability generation? Since costs, but not future potential revenues, quality levels or sustainability effects, can be accounted for and registered in the systems, there is a high probability that the focus on (short-term) costs can be counterproductive.

If we allow a traditional accounting manager and a sustainability manager to represent the different perspectives, the accountant will usually act on the basis of a cost minimization thinking under the motto that it is about "managing with scarce resources", while for the sustainability manager, it is often about seeing costs as enabling different initiatives from a sustainability perspective. This is, perhaps, to focus less on cost-minimization in order to manage more with the sustainability-related resources in focus. Accounting managers often pursue their agenda according to the precautionary principle, according to which costs cannot or should not be calculated too low and revenues too high, while sustainability managers often think that costs are key enablers for generating future sustainability and thus applying a "sustainability precautionary principle". Accounting managers are often also "verification-oriented", that is, anything that is uncertain about the future, such as potential revenue, is counted as zero before it is realized. It should also be added that the accountant most often supports her/his actions in existing accounting legislation and accounting practice. Sustainability managers, on the other hand, are often more vision-, market- and ideology-driven: potential future revenues must be related to the sustainability vision for the organization and which relationships with the market exist or should be created in order to sustainably conduct operations far into the future, regardless of whether they can be verified at present or if they are specified in any normative or statutory document.

From an accounting perspective, it is rarely good if costs increase, regardless of the type of cost involved. What is then ignored is that there are a number of costs that are "investment like", that is, they will play a strategic role in a longer time perspective than the current fiscal year. The risk of a "unnuanced cost thinking", in which you treat all costs in the same/similar way, is that you do not evaluate and assess the different logics and importance of the costs for the business's ability to deliver sufficiently high income and/or quality and sustainability levels in the future.

One of the reasons for the widespread problem of balanced cost-thinking is that many organizations manage their operations on an annual basis and always have to adhere to the annual budget established the previous year. The risk, then, is that as an organization (or unit within the organization), in order to get the budget to balance, you will forgo a strategically important resource consumption that is not classified as an investment in traditional accounting and calculation logic.

Another example of a situation where an unconstrained cost thinking often expressed is when the organization should invest in competence development. Competence development costs should be expensed immediately according to accounting standards and routines. The problem with this is not only that they may postpone or forgo these skills investments because there is no room in the budget, but also that they do not control, evaluate and follow-up these costs, which are often of a long-term investment nature. Competency development costs are often distributed to a certain number of individuals and apply to a certain amount and/or a certain number of days per unit or individual. When these individuals have received their course, or what it is all about, and the course cost is paid, you are simply ticked off as being implemented. If one had instead made some form of investment calculation for these competence investments, it would have been natural, as for most other investments, to follow-up and evaluate the cost and the investment.

For example, the need to differentiate between "pure" costs and what may be regarded as "investment like" costs was one of the reasons behind the emergence of human resource accounting in the 1960s in the USA, and personnel accounting and calculation in the 1980s in Sweden. In the EU, in the mid-1990s, the issue of whether skills investment should be included as an asset in the balance sheet was discussed (Johanson & Henningsson 2007). There are examples of companies that have actually done this, at least internally. One of these was a consulting company that wanted to promote the need for constant competence development in order to maintain its market dominance (Johanson et al. 2001a). Thus, the cost of skills development was not expensed in the year in which it arose but was distributed as other investments over the probable economic life of the investment.

Another phenomenon linked to cost thinking and cost analysis is that it is very seldom that limits are set for how low different types of costs may/should be in an organization or unit. However, defining upper limits for different types of costs is very common. The nuance of this boundary practice is that organizations generally seem to ignore or simply fail to understand the link between cost, revenue, quality and sustainability. That is, without a certain (lowest) level of costs, you, as an organization/manager, limit the opportunities for revenue, quality and sustainability generation. One of the reasons for this problem is that traditional accountants are trained in cost control, and not in the relationship to revenue, quality and sustainability generation. They often receive and take on the role of "cost police" in the organization, and it is very seldom that they communicate and signal that the costs are too low to meet the quality or sustainability goals of the organization or the surrounding community.

Although most organizations have the ambition to survive in the long term, as the accounting principle is usually referred to as the going concern principle, and thus not only focus on the current year, in some organizations, there is a too strong orientation towards strict cost minimization combined with an excessive focus on the current financial year. This can have undesirable consequences later on both financial profitability and the sustainable development for the organization.

5.3 Scientific criticism of financial management

Financial management is often considered to not provide a sufficient information basis for making the right decisions – indeed, some even claim financial management to have lost its relevance (Johnson & Kaplan 1987). Johanson et al. (2006) summarize the criticism that financial management, rather than being a support tool for management, risks separating management from the organization in general because it has become too abstract, too short-term and too money-oriented. It has also been accused of being too historically oriented, too focused on measurement precision and unable to provide adequate and satisfactory information on the significance of intangible resources (Johanson & Skoog 2007). The basic idea of achieving transparency and representing an objective and measurable reality through the economic description of an organization has also been criticized (ibid.). Johanson and Skoog (ibid.) also criticize the focus on formal elements in the control process. Control takes place in many different ways, both formally and informally.

Financial management is institutionalized as a result of many years of development and application. This has contributed to the establishment of different forms of habits or rituals, both at the organizational, unit and individual levels. One such example is the long history of double entry book-keeping and the large number of associated instrumentally trained economists and accountants who monitor that the rituals are followed. This has contributed to creating stability, security and comparability, but it can also entail a risk that you will not have time to adapt the control system to new conditions. Control can even be an obstacle to organizational and business development, not to mention the organization's sustainability development. In order to avoid the latter, control interactivity and integration are important.

The hierarchical idea has been described as an ideology based on "command and control" and has also been criticized by reasoning that the "command and control" ideology can lead to dysfunctional behaviour in the organization. Another problem with control based on "command and control" is that the metrics used to a large extent are linked to activities, that is, to the actual resource conversion, rather than to the purpose of the operation, that is, the result/performance, and, in extension, the effect of these results from, for example, ethical and environment-oriented perspectives.

An important area for criticism has been the overly reductionist focus on financial figures. This has contributed to an overly short-term focus on reducing costs rather than ensuring the long-term survival and sustainability of the business. The focus on financial key figures is also considered to have created a gap between the people who are in decision-making positions and the operational activities. Johnson (1992) describes the time from 1950 to the end of the 1980s as "the managerial gospel of the dark age", based on the fact that the financial accounts during this time increasingly functioned as a filter between different actors within an organization, and abstract accounting, to a greater extent, actually replaced the knowledge of the business conducted. The ability to visualize and understand the organization's long-term value creation was thereby significantly reduced. This – combined with the fact that traditional accounting-based control was strongly top-down oriented, that is according to the command and control ideology – contributed to the control and measurement processes not creating motivation and commitment to development, improvement and action, but rather was seen as a formal requirement in order to satisfy those who did not understand either the organization or the surrounding market and society.

5.4 Support processes

At the beginning of the 2000s, a study was conducted that analysed how management control works in ten large Swedish companies (Johanson et al. 2001a, 2001b). Among these were Swedbank, NCC and Telia Sonera. For several years, approximately for over 20 years, these companies had systematically and continuously measured and taken into account various intangible resources in their formal control processes. In addition to using financial and productivity metrics, regular attitude measurements were made among customers and staff. The purpose of the measurements was to try to understand, for example, the importance of leadership, motivation and competence for customer loyalty, productivity and profitability. Because the measurements were conducted regularly and for so many years, there were opportunities for extensive statistical studies of influential relationships. Broadly speaking, it can be said that there was a strong connection in the direction indirectly stated earlier: productivity, customer loyalty and profitability were strongly influenced by employees' perceptions of leadership and their competence and motivation.

The companies studied had also, over the years, developed a system for handling the data that were produced. In the studies of the ten companies, we tried to understand how the actions of managers and other employees interacted with structures and processes within the companies. We were able to identify a number of processes that were important to support the acceptance, understanding and use of the measurements of productivity and profitability, as well as customer and staff surveys. These processes, which we call support processes, are about creating awareness, mobilizing commitment, contributing to learning and ultimately influencing action. The processes support the basic measurement and control process, which is based on objectives (strategies), reporting, analysis and follow-up of the objectives before formulating new objectives for the organization and its units. Some of the support processes have been created, planned and started consciously, while others have arisen and developed without conscious intention or planning. They have been developed gradually and were integrated into the control when the study was done. It can be said that the support processes are a prerequisite for what I call in this chapter integrated performance management. They help to give the control system long-term visibility and stability. All processes are formal in the sense that we have previously put into the concept, that is, they have been developed into permanent practices. In our analysis, we identified the following seven processes:

- *Measurement processes.* Through surveys among customers and employees, systematic and continuous measurements of perceptions about the business and the intangible resources are made.
- *Marketing processes.* The very existence of employee and customer surveys, as well as data from these measurements, is marketed both internally

and externally in order to draw attention to both the control instrument and the importance of the non-material resources. The core of these processes is to create acceptance and understanding of the results of the customer and staff surveys.

- *Reporting processes.* The information collected is systematized and reported regularly, as is financial reporting. In some of the companies, reporting on non-material resources is integrated with financial reporting and is addressed to both senior management and to managers and employees throughout the organization.

- *Evaluation processes.* Large amounts of data are collected via the financial accounting system, productivity measurements and surveys. These data are continuously evaluated through various forms of statistical analysis.

- *Motivational processes.* In the same way that senior management seeks financial information, it also seeks information on survey results. This demand, as well as organized dialogues between managers at different levels, is motivating. The motivation is also affected by the measurement results being linked to the reward systems. Another factor that influences motivation is that the measurement results are systematically compared with both other units within the organization and other companies in the industry.

- *Contracting processes.* Each measurement, every questionnaire, is linked to a goal and thus also to an action plan. In order to strengthen the link between survey results and action, a dialogue (more or less formally) is concluded on how an undesirable result should be addressed. The contract processes are thus an expression of decentralized responsibility for vision, strategies and measurement results.

- *Monitoring processes.* The entire control system is continuously monitored in various ways, for example, by analysing response rates to different questions and by how the use of the system affects answers to different questions.

During the years that have passed since we conducted the study, we have been able to analyse and discuss performance management with close to 200 companies in various contexts. All these conversations and projects have further confirmed the importance of the support processes. However, it should be noted that we have in no way created a complete list of possible support processes. Some organizations may well need to add something that we have not captured, and others may also need to deduct some of the processes we identified in our studies. However, we believe that the support processes we identified in the ten companies have a certain universally valid integration relevance – also for dimensions, objectives and follow-up regarding sustainability of various kinds.

In summary, the support processes presented and discussed here aim to create a long-term acceptance and understanding of the corporate governance that the organization practices in order to "play a role" and actually be used, that is, integrated in the organization both strategically and operationally, and not only formulated in the strategy or reported to external stakeholders.

5.5 Performance ideals

Control is never ideological, but as Hofstede emphasized in 1978, the underlying ideology of control has not been sufficiently problematized. However, it is not just Hofstede who highlights the importance of the underlying ideology for control. So does Hood (1995) as well as Hasselbladh et al. (2008). They link their reasoning to new public management but use the word governance/control ideal instead of ideology. Wessén (1960) gives "ideal" the meaning of future goals. Inspired by Dean (1999), Hasselbladh et al. (2008) also used the concept of regime. By that they mean a constant way of organizing a business. A regime consists of a business regime and a control regime. An operating regime defines them as "organizing elements of daily professional practice, such as continuously applied methods, routines and professional norms" (ibid. p. 29); a control regime is defined as "configurations of ideals, knowledge and management practices" (ibid. p. 27) which frame a business regime and "which, at a certain point in time and in a certain context, constitute a dominant form of standardizing and directing the purpose and direction of the work" (ibid. p. 29). The control regime thus states what is "natural, desirable and what is considered to be good performance" (ibid. p. 27). In order to more clearly distinguish between the two different regimes, the following text replaces the concept of business regime with the concept of practical regime.

The two regimes fix the behaviour patterns of the employees (or others who are the subject of the control) and the relevance criteria of the business. That the boss is the one who decides can be said to be a practice born out of a control regime that states that this is how an organization should be organized, which is often hierarchical. This, in turn, is expressed in the practice regime in terms of, for example, routines that involve employees being controlled or themselves expected, by others and by themselves, to make themselves controllable by reporting their activities to their manager.

The two regimes are held together by a performance ideal, that is, a logic that is intentional and oriented towards a certain set of goals and modes of action (Hasselbladh et al. 2008). The performance ideal is not an expression of what prevails at a given time, but is stable and coherent. Often the ideal is obscured by the measurement or imaging tools. It is quite common to "not see the forest for all trees", that is, what is measured is given too much importance at the expense of the basic management ideal. At worst, those involved are unaware of the basic performance ideal. Coupled with Ferreira and Otley (2009), it can be said that unless the different parts of a control system are interconnected and are based on a coherent management ideal, there is a great risk that the other parts of the control system will not contribute to meeting the organization's vision, strategies and goals. However, the performance ideal as well as the performance content and the control support processes are contextually dependent. For example, what is relevant in a bank may not be as relevant in a municipality.

Let me illustrate the importance of using the concept of performance ideal. Mouritsen and Johanson (2005) discuss the consequences of newer control and measurement models, such as intellectual capital. These models aim to push the boundaries of what is measured and are intended to be subject to control. The idea is that the new management model will release employees' creativity and creativity to the company, but therein lies a paradox. In exchange for their ideas and actions, the employee wants to be seen. She needs to be seen as she wants to recognize herself, in her full complexity, not as reduced to a number or as part of a routine. But this can be expressed, understood and contained in the routine measurements and reports. Behind routine measurements and reporting is a governance ideal based on reductionism. The full complexity of each individual can hardly be captured in these measurements and reports. Another example is Anderssons' (2014) analysis of home service control. She shows how two different performance ideals end up in conflict: the care ideal and the financial/administrative ideal. The latter ideal is based on command and control, that is, management through detailed directives for action. Despite a politically stated ambition that care should be the most important, the latter ideal dominates. Unit managers and staff who represent the care ideal try to argue against it, but the care work, which is about close and long-lasting relationships to achieve good quality, will still often fall short. It is the ordering committee that controls its operations through its budget control.

Similar types of challenges are apparent in a variety of organizations and industries. Most clearly, the "cracks" appear in organizations and industries that have one or more strong professional ideals linked to them, such as technology, health care and education organizations (Grossi et al. 2019). In the university world, there are usually at least three different control and evaluation ideals linked to research, teaching and collaboration plus the purely administrative which is about keeping the budget "in balance". However, even in organizations such as DHL that for many years have not only emphasized the importance of sustainability and which systematically controlled and followed up sustainability at the verification level, it is possible to identify tensions between ideals of profitability and sustainability.

5.6 Integrated performance management

Integrated performance management is about something much more extensive than what financial management represents. It is the criticism of financial management that has led us to think further about what factors and structures are important for what we call integrated performance management (Johanson et al. 2019). For example, integrated performance management is not the same as integrated reporting (IR), although similarities exist. One similarity is that both emphasize the importance of integrating financial and non-financial aspects. Both integrated performance management and integrated reporting emphasize the context, that is, how different factors that contribute to the organization's value creation are linked. Another similarity is the quest to satisfy the information needs of different stakeholder groups.

But there are also differences. Integrated performance management is primarily about an internal process (in which reporting is part of the control process), while integrated reporting is primarily about an external report (although the link to the control process is also included). The target group for integrated performance management is primarily corporate management, managers, trade unions and employees, while integrated reporting is primarily aimed at financial markets and customers as well as the surrounding community. Integrated performance management is about mobilizing (Mouritsen et al. 2001; Johanson et al. 2001b): to mobilize employees at different levels in a direction that is in line with the management ideal and vision. Integrated reporting is meant to be mapped. Imaging ability is important. It is important that it gets "right" at this point. Of course, it is important that integrated performance management also contains "right" information, but internal relevance and usability are more important. Thus, in integrated performance management, it is not the imaging precision but the ability to mobilize in combination with the internal relevance that is central. This includes that integrated performance management must handle both formal and informal communication aspects (Simons 1995) of control. The integration of these aspects is partly shown by the extent to which communication and impact discussions are conducted in the organization before and after certain decisions have been made. This is whether the decisions are based on financial or non-financial information or whether the effects are mostly financial or non-financial in nature. These may include, for example, questions such as the following: What possible effects can one expect from a reduction of a sustainability-related cost item in the budget? How do you interpret and act on different types of outcomes and effects of decisions?

Thus, relevance and mobilization are important keywords for integrated performance management, while imaging and transparency to demonstrate the responsibility regarding a company's financial and sustainability management are important keywords for IR. Behind these differences is a significantly different view of how reality can be understood, an ontological difference. IR assumes that factors, relationships and phenomena can be understood objectively, depicted and thus made visible in order to achieve transparency. When the transparent information is communicated to a stakeholder, he or she can make rational decisions. This idea is based on the idea of "economic man", that is, all actors search for complete information regarding different options for action and then make rational decisions. My view of integrated performance management has a fundamentally different starting point: that control processes are about social constructions where reality does not exist from an objective perspective. It is constructed by us humans as we observe and participate in the social interaction.

Another important part when it comes to integrated performance management is that governance is not something that lies "alongside" all other organizational activities. It is not handled by any or a few within the organization by these "pushing the send button" to get the report out in the timely way and then hoping for the best. Controlling integration is to make it clear to all organizational members that everything they do, say and think has a signal value, and that control, if it is truly integrated, is the very core of the idea of why the organization exists, that is, the organization's ideal, vision and eligibility. The fact that everyone in an organization contributes to the governance of the organization in different ways does not mean that integrated operations management means that everyone has equal responsibility in and for the governance. Of course, management responsibility differs depending on what function and position the individual has and what formal organizational and / or personnel responsibility he has. However, if enough people within the organization know this responsibility, it will ultimately enable the governance to be better integrated into the organization's various practice regimes.

In order to be considered integrated, performance management must also continuously take into account not only internal issues but also what is happening in the industry and in society. Communication with many different stakeholders must be carried out. Different stakeholders have different knowledge needs about what is happening in the organization. To satisfy this, external accounting is not sufficient as a source of knowledge. Integrated performance management also takes into account that there is a time dimension linked to governance. The past, present and future are important, and integrated governance involves both historical consideration and current day-to-day pragmatics as well as visionary acceptance of future change needs. It takes away from an overly large and prolonged focus on any of these time dimensions. A one-sided focus of this kind can lead to distortions and incorrect priorities of the business.

Thus, control of organizations is not just about reports containing numbers. It is about a complex interaction between people and social structures. The concept of control is highly value-laden and is based on basic perceptions of how we can perceive the world and about what people want and are capable of. For example, some argue that this leads to a far too much focus on measurability. Power and Laughlin (1992) have summarized this development with the term "accountingization", and Lapsley (2009) has used terms like "tick box mentality", where the most important thing is that organizational aspects can be quickly and efficiently followed up and revised from a numerical perspective. According to Power (1997), it is a new profession of "accountocrats" that dominates this audit community. The ambition to highlight values and simplify follow-up has therefore not infrequently contributed to the fact that what is more difficult to measure is in the cloud.

5.7 Summary reflections and challenges

When discussing control and performance, content is often focused only on the basis of a function and structure perspective regarding strategy formulations, target levels, choice of and number of key figures and analysis of these in relation to set goals. However, we should also emphasize the importance of not only this type of functional content but also more contextually oriented management ideals, support processes and evaluations. For a business to have any chance of achieving its basic governance ideal, its visions, strategies and goals, governance must be coherent, that is, integrated. Achieving an integrated performance management is complex and is about integration between so many different dimensions. A basic premise is that the management ideal, content, support processes and evaluation are coherent and continuously related to the content aspects. But the following should also be noted and cohesive to come closer to a more integrated and sustainable performance management:

- Control should address both material and non-material resources (for example, competence, health, customer relations, sustainability aspects), and non-financial indicators should be integrated with traditional financial management. That is, non-financial management needs to be integrated with financial. This is in order to create a governance that is more proactive since many of the initial non-financial components will have a financial impact later on.
- In the integrated control, both economic and social and sustainability issues are addressed in order to meet not only the management's but also the owners' (the principal's), the employees', the financial market's, customers' and society's needs. That is, corporate governance has a distinct and multidimensional stakeholder responsibility that is much more extensive, and not only short-term cost-effectiveness and / or profitability in relation to owner requirements.
- Measurement, control and order and clarity are important, but the primary role of integrated performance management is communicative and pedagogical in order to be more relevant. The purpose is to promote understanding and mobilize future action. The latter means that we sometimes have to admit that the formulation of certain problems and alternatives to action is based on subjective constructions of reality. If the purpose is to mobilize action, it can often also be that measurement precision can and should give way to communicability and simplification in order to create a clearer relevance, not least in terms of sustainability.

References

Anderssons, M. (2014) *Välfärdssektorn, en arena för makt och motstånd: Studier av sjukvård och hemtjänst.* Västerås: Mälardalens Högskola.

Bjurklo, M. & Kardemark, G. (2003) *Händelsredovisning: En bok om redovisning av kompetens.* Lund: Studentlitteratur.

Dean, M. (1999) *Governmentality: Power and rule in modern society.* London: Sage.

Ferrerira, A. & Otley, D. (2009) The design and use of performance management systems: An extended framework for analysis, *Management Accounting Research*, Vol. 20 (4), pp. 263–282.

Grossi, G., Kallio, K., Sargiacomo, M. & Skoog, M. (2019) "Accounting, performance management systems and accountability changes in knowledge-intensive public organizations: A literature review and research agenda", *Accounting, Auditing & Accountability Journal*, Vol. 33 (1), pp. 256–280.

Hasselbladh, H., Bejerot, E. & Gustavsson, R. Å. (2008) *Bortom new public management: Institutionell transformation i svensk sjukvård*. Lund Academia Adacta.

Hofstede, G. (1978) The poverty of management control philosophy. *Academy of Management Review*, Vol. 2 (3), pp. 450–461.

Hood. C. (1995) The new public management in the 1980s. Variation on a theme. *Accounting, Organizations and Society*, Vol. 20 (2/3), pp. 93–109.

Johanson, U., Almqvist, R. & Skoog, M. (2019), "A conceptual framework for integrated performance management systems", *Journal of Public Budgeting, Accounting & Financial Management*, Vol. 31 (3), pp. 309–324.

Johanson, U. & Henningsson, J. (2007) The acheology of intellectual capital: A battle between concepts. In C. Chaminade & B. catasus (ed.) *Intellectual capital revisited: Paradoxes in the knowledge intensive organizations*. Cheltenham: Edwar Elgar, pp. 8–30.

Johanson, U., Mårtensson, M., Skoog, M. (2001a) Measuring to understand intangible performance drivers. *European Accounting Review*, Vol. 10 (3), pp. 407–437.

Johanson, U., Mårtensson, M. & Skoog, M. (2001b) Mobilising change by means of the managment control of intangibles. *Accounting, Organizations and Society*, Vol. 26 (7–8), pp. 715–733.

Johanson, U. & Skoog, M. (2007) *Verksamhetsstyrning: För utveckling, förbättring och förändring*. Liber: Stockholm.

Johanson, U. & Skoog, M. (2015) *Integrerad verksamhetsstyrning*. Lund: Studentlitteratur.

Johanson, U., Skoog, M., Almqvist, R., & Backlund, A. (2006) Balancing dilemmas of the balanced scorecard. *Accounting, Auditing and Accountability Journal*, Vol. 19 (5), pp. 842–857.

Johnson, H. T. (1992) *Relevance regained: From top-down control to bottom-up empowerment*. New York: Free Press.

Johnson, H. T., & Kaplan, R. S. (1987) *Relevance lost: The rice and fall of management accounting*. Boston, MA: Harvard Business School Press.

Mouritsen. J., Larsen, H. T., & Bukh, P. N. D. (2001) Intellectual capital and the "capable firm": Narrating, visualising and numbering for managing knowledge. *Accounting, Organizaitons and Society*, Vol. 26, pp. 735–762.

Mouritsen, J. & och Johanson, U. (2005) Managing the person: Human resource costing and accounting, intellectual capital and health statements. In S. Jönsson & J. Mouritsen (ed.) *Accounting in Scandinavia: The northern lights* pp. 559–564. Liber: Malmö.

Lapsley, I. (2009) New public management: The cruellest invention of the human spirit? *Abacus*, Vol. 45 (1), pp. 1–21.

Power, M. (1997) *The Audit Society: Rituals of verification*. Oxford: Oxford University Press.

Power, M. & och Laughlin, R. (1992) Critical theory and accounting. In M. Alvesson & H. Willmott (ed.) *Critical management studies*. London: Sage. pp. 113–135.

Samuelson, L. A. (2008) Ekonomistyrning – en översikt. In N. G. Olve & L. Samuelsson (ed.) *Controllerhandboken*. (9 rev suppl), p.28. Liber: Malmö.

Simons, R. (1995) *Levers of control: How managers use innovative control systems to drive strategic renewal*. Boston, MA: Harvard Business Press.

Wessén, E. (1960) *Våra ord: Deras uttal och ursprung*. Stockholm: Norstedts.

6 Sustainability management systems and processes

Gunnar Rimmel

Abstract

This chapter provides an overview of the most important sustainability management systems and their processes. In recent years, there has been a great growth in international standards regarding quality, environment, occupational health, safety and sustainability. These international standards are issued by an international standardization body, which is represented by national standardization institutions working on industrial and commercial standardization. This increase in standardization is largely due to the globalization of trade and economic integration in the European Union. The chapter begins with the emergence and work of the International Standardization Organization (ISO) regarding certification processes and standards. The ISO 9000 quality management system is presented. An overview of environmental management systems illustrates ISO 14000 and its scope. Next follows a presentation of ISO 45001, which is a series of standards that form the basis of a management system for work environment issues. A presentation of ISO 26000 shows how this sustainability guideline covers the broad spectrum of organizations' activities that exist. The chapter concludes with a reflection on the challenges that organizations face when introducing and using sustainability management systems and their processes.

Learning outcomes

After reading this chapter, you are expected to be able to:

- Understand the origin, development and use of sustainability management systems and their processes.
- Describe the most important sustainability management systems and their processes.
- Reflect on the usability and boundaries between different sustainability management systems.

6.1 Introduction

In recent years, there has been a great growth in international standards regarding quality, environment, occupational health, safety and sustainability. These international standards are issued by an international standardization body and represented by national standardization institutions working on industrial and commercial standardization. This increase in standardization is, to a large extent, due to the globalization of trade and economic integration in the European Union (Castka & Balzarova 2018).

Standardization can be described as a mechanism for coordination and is an instrument of regulation. Standardization comes in various forms, such as public regulations, market standards, certification standards or management systems. Standardization can generally be defined as an activity aimed at organizing practical uses and procedures, which are repeatedly occurring in industry, technology, science and economics. Standardization was first initiated in the early 1900s as a means of limiting the economically disadvantageous variety of components, parts and accessories to favour their interchangeability, which, in turn, would facilitate mass production, repair and maintenance of products and services. Standardization can thus stimulate international trade by eliminating excessive variations due to coordination. Coordination through standardization can therefore be a basis for reducing information-related transaction costs. In a global economy, the exchange of products and services would be very difficult without standardization (Nunhes, Ferreira Motta & de Oliveira, 2016).

At present, there are a large number of international and national standards available that aim at organizing and systematizing processes in business management systems in relation to a variety of functions and operations. In light of the many definitions, concepts and guidelines for the sustainability of organizations, the International Standardization Organization (ISO) wanted to use standardization of these comprehensive concepts. ISO was founded in London in 1946 and is a non–governmental body that works with industrial and commercial standardization. With 20,000 international standards, ISO is the world's largest developer of voluntary international standards and is represented by 162 national standardization institutions. In this way, ISO has the necessary structures and processes to reach an international consensus when it comes to attempting to standardize such a complex, controversial and discussed topic as sustainability. ISO has developed three successful standards in related areas, namely, Quality Management Systems (ISO 9000), Environmental Management Systems (ISO 14000) and Sustainability Management Systems (ISO 26000) (Tuczek, Castka & Wakolbinger, 2018).

Nowadays, most companies operate globally and their markets are characterized by intense competition. In order to survive this intense competition, it is necessary to meet at least the minimum requirements for customers and existing legislation. Certified management systems have become popular among companies around the world to ensure that procedures and processes are followed to achieve the goals of certification. A management system can be described as a set of procedures that must be followed to achieve their goals, or as a process of how matters need to be implemented. A certification of specific management systems approves the results of the requirements and objectives set in a specific normative standard (Nunhes, Motta Barbosa & de Oliveira, 2016).

In this context, the most widespread and well-known certification management systems of companies around the world today are quality management systems based on ISO 9000, environmental management systems based on ISO 14000 and systems for occupational health and safety management systems based on ISO 45001. The main focus of ISO 9000 is customer satisfaction. As far as the environmental perspective is concerned, many companies all over the world have started to follow ISO 14001 as a management system to manage their environmental issues. ISO 45001 certification has followed the global spread of ISO 9000 and ISO 14000. ISO 45001 has superseded OHSAS 18001, which was not developed by ISO but by the British standards organization, British Standards Institute (BSI). OHSAS had become the most internationally used standard for occupational health and safety management systems, and ISO 45001 took over this position. Another standard developed by ISO is ISO 26000 which addresses social responsibility (sustainability). ISO 26000 is a logical development of ISO to provide standardization on sustainability. Unlike ISO 9000, ISO 14000 and ISO 45001 standards, ISO 26000 is not a certifiable standard with controllable requirements and goals, but is an international ISO standard that is more of a guideline for user guidance (Zinenko, Rovira & Montiel, 2015).

In recent years, the various ISO management systems have been updated and more customized, so that they have a common base supporting the structure of ISO 9000, ISO 14000, ISO 45001 and ISO 26000. ISO has discovered that users of their standards often implemented the various management systems on quality, environment, occupational health and safety and sustainability in parallel. Therefore, ISO implemented its ISO standards to make it easier to integrate these with each other. This would make it a more efficient management system that reduces time and bureaucracy as well as the use of human, technical and financial resources.

6.2 ISO 9000 – Quality management

The ISO 9000 family of standards is the most popular reference model for establishing quality management systems in organizations. It is based on the BS 5750 series, developed in 1979 by the BSI in the United Kingdom. The BS 5750 series was successful in its use. In 1987, ISO 9001 was launched, which resulted in the quality management system spreading globally. However, the global success of the ISO 9000 family of standards was the result of the revision carried out in 1994 (ISO, 2015). The ISO 9000 family of standards does not try to measure the quality of companies' products or services and nor does it aim to achieve a

Table 6.1 ISO 9000 family of standards, focus and content

Standard	Focus	Content
ISO 9000	Quality management	Principles and terminology
ISO 9001	Quality management	Requirements
ISO 9004	Quality management	Guidance to achieve sustained success
ISO 19011	Auditing management	Guidelines to auditing management systems

specific goal or result. Instead, it consists of four standards that determine the need to systematize and formalize company information with the goal of producing products or services that meet customer requirements (see Table 6.1). In other words, it is a quality management tool that is based on systematization and formalization of data in order to achieve uniformity in the product and to comply with specifications set by the customer.

The ISO 9000 family of standards is intended to improve the quality of products and services, and is thus directly related to increased economic sustainability performance and the achievement of financial sustainability. The ISO 9000 family covers specific aspects such as basic vocabulary, performance improvements, documentation, training and financial aspects and auditing (Marimon Viadiu, Casadesús Fa & Saizarbitoria, 2006). It has a process orientation. Processes consist of one or more linked activities that require resources and must be managed to achieve a predetermined output. Output from one process can directly become the input to the next process. The end product is thus a consequence of a network or system of processes (Heras-Saizarbitoria & Boiral, 2013).

ISO 9000 provides a set of standardized requirements for a quality management system, regardless of what the user organization does, its size or whether it is in the private or public sector. It is the only standard in this family of standards from which organizations can become certified, that is, certification is not a mandatory requirement (ISO, 2016).

ISO 9001 contains requirements specifications to be used to create a quality management system that gives confidence in the organization's ability to provide products that meet customer needs and expectations.

ISO 9004 provides guidance on a wider range of quality management systems than ISO 9001, especially for managing an organization's long-term success. ISO 9004 is recommended as a guide for organizations whose top executives want to extend benefits according to ISO 9001, with the aim of systematically and continuously improving the organization's overall performance.

ISO 19011 contains guidelines for auditing quality management systems and environmental management systems. ISO 19011 provides guidance on audit programmes, conducting internal or external audits and information on auditor competence for both the ISO 9000 family and the ISO 14000 family. Effective audit ensures that an implemented quality management system meets the requirements of ISO 9001.

6.3 ISO 14000 – Environmental management

The first standard in the ISO 14000 family was launched in 1996 as a reference model for implementing environmental management systems in companies. These systems can be defined as part of a company's global management that includes the organizational structure, planning activities, areas of responsibility, routines, procedures, processes and resources required to develop, apply, review and maintain the company's environmental policy. The structure and philosophy of ISO 14000 is very similar to ISO 9000. The ISO 14000 standards are based on the BS 7750 series, developed in 1992 by the BSI in the United Kingdom. The BS 7750 series became the template for the ISO 14000 family (Rezaee & Elam, 2000).

The ISO 14000 family comprises of a number of standards, from environmental management systems to environmental labelling, communication and greenhouse gases (see Table 6.2). The overall purpose of all these standards is to create environmental management systems for organizations that want to conduct systematic and structured environmental work. The management system should be a tool for creating structure and order in the organization's environmental work to measure set environmental goals and on the basis of the current status quo–driven systematic development work. The ISO 14000 family is international and for all sorts of organizations, regardless of size or industry.

In general, the ISO 14000 family is not intended as a standard designed solely to measure the environmental impact of organizations that implement it. Rather, it should be seen as a set of standards that defines how to systematize and formalize processes of environmental impact in organizations. The ISO 14000 family can be regarded as a toolbox where special tools are used depending on the needs of the business.

ISO 14001 plays a key role in the ISO 14000 family as it contains a working model for mapping and reducing environmental impact with the help of an environmental management system. The standard is based on a process that includes environmental policy, planning, implementation, monitoring and improvement (Poksinska, Dahlgaard & Eklund, 2003). In 1996, the first version of ISO 14001 was launched, which was revised in 2004. Since 2017, the latest revision process is ongoing, which is trying to make it easier to use the standard with other ISO standards, such as the ISO 9001 quality standard.

The other ISO 14000 family standards can then be used for in-depth studies in a specific area such as ecolabelling (ISO 14020), life cycle analysis (ISO 14040), environmentally adapted product development (ISO 14062) or greenhouse gases (ISO 14064). Ecolabelling concerns third-party-controlled ecolabelling, such as Good Environmental Choice or the Swan. A life cycle analysis should describe a product's environmental impact, from raw material extraction to waste management. The greenhouse gas standard is about measurement, reporting and verification of emissions.

Table 6.2 ISO 14000 family of standards, focus and content

Standard	Focus	Content
ISO 14001	Environmental management system	Requirements with guidance for use
ISO 14004	Environmental management system	General guidelines on implementation
ISO 14005	Environmental management systems	Guidelines for a flexible approach to phased implementation
ISO 14006	Environmental management systems	Guidelines for incorporating eco-design
ISO 14015	Environmental management	Environmental assessment of sites and organizations (EASO)
ISO 14020	Environmental labels and declarations	General principles
ISO 14021	Environmental labels and declarations	Self-declared environmental claims (Type II environmental labelling)
ISO 14022	Environmental labels and declarations	Self-declaration-environmental claims – Terms and definitions
ISO 14024	Environmental labels and declarations	Type I environmental labelling – Principles and procedures
ISO 14025	Environmental labels and declarations	Type III environmental declarations – Principles and procedures
ISO 14031	Environmental management	Environmental performance evaluation – Guidelines
ISO 14040	Environmental management	Life cycle assessment – Principles and framework
ISO 14041	Environmental management	Life cycle assessment –Goal and scope definition and inventory analysis
ISO 14050	Environmental management	Vocabulary
ISO 14062	Environmental management	Integrating environmental aspects into product design and development
ISO 14063	Environmental management	Environmental communication – Guidelines and examples
ISO 14064	Greenhouse gases	Specification with guidance at the organization level of quantification and reporting of greenhouse gas emissions and removals

6.4 ISO 45001 – Occupational health and safety

ISO 45001 – Occupational Health and Safety – was launched in 2018, replacing OHSAS 18001. OHSAS 18001 was a series of standards that formed the basis of a management system for work environment and safety. OHSAS 18001 was developed by the British standardization organization BSI and was launched in 1999. It was adopted by a number of countries, as national standards for work environment and safety. But OHSAS 18001 is not an ISO standard. It had been accepted in more than 80 countries.

OHSAS 18001 contained a list of requirements and guidance for setting up a structure for how organizations build a management system that works with their work environment and safety issues. It specified the minimum requirements for best practice in occupational health and safety management. The standard also included monitoring, evaluating and reporting of the work environment and safety work. Like ISO 9001 and ISO 14001, OHSAS 18001 was the basis for certification. When certifying OHSAS 18001, an accredited certification body needed to be selected to guarantee impartiality, long-term perspective and international acceptance.

In 2013, ISO appointed a committee to produce an ISO standard based on OHSAS 18001. The new ISO standard is called ISO 45001. From 2015 to 2017, the committee failed to get an approval of the initial draft of ISO 45001 as not enough votes were received from the ISO members. ISO 45001 was revised and refined in a second draft. Subsequently, the ISO 45001 standard was successfully approved by a vote of the Final Draft International Standard (FDIS). Thus, the final ISO 45001 standard was published in March 2018. BSI kept in touch with ISO throughout the process, and upon announcing that ISO 45001 was successfully approved, BSI informed its members that OHSAS 18001 was revoked when publishing ISO 45001. All organizations currently are certified according to OHSAS 18001, having a three-year period for upgrading to ISO 45001. Thus, ISO 45001 has become the world's first international standard for occupational health and safety (ISO, 2018).

ISO 45001 – Occupational Health and Safety – is a minimum standard for protecting employees worldwide. It has the same structure and identical terms and definitions as ISO 9001 and ISO 14001. This was done to facilitate integration into the established management systems. In addition, ISO 45001 has been designed to closely follow ISO 14001, as it is recognized that many organizations combine their occupational health and safety issues internally with environmental management functions. This further simplifies the integration of ISO 45001 with ISO 14001 (ISO, 2018).

6.5 ISO 26000 – Social responsibility

ISO 26000 – Social Responsibility – covers a wide range of organizations' activities, ranging from economic, social, governance and ethical issues to environmental issues. ISO 26000 contains a global social responsibility guidance document that helps organizations around the world to meet their sustainability goals. The first version of ISO 26000 was published on November 1, 2010. The ISO 26000 standard has been developed by experts in a large multi-stakeholder process that took over six years. Social responsibility for organizations is conceptually associated with the development of sustainability in ISO 26000, since social responsibility requires the development of sustainability. ISO 26000 goes beyond profit maximization by presenting a standard for organizations to contribute to sustainable development and the welfare of society (ISO, 2010).

The ISO 26000 standard contains the following seven principles of corporate social responsibility that are mandatory for organizations to follow if they are to apply ISO 26000:

- accountability
- transparency
- ethical behaviour
- respect for stakeholders
- respect for law
- compliance with international standards of conduct
- respect for human rights.

ISO 26000 takes into account all aspects of triple bottom line (TBL (see Chapter 7. ISO 26000 encourages companies to recognize human rights as a critical aspect of social responsibility by ensuring that the countries in which they work respect citizens' political, civil, social and cultural rights. ISO 26000 accepts that the primary goal of organizations is to continue to generate profits, but in a socially responsible way that ensures that the desired return on investment is achieved (Pojasek, 2011).

ISO 26000 also contains seven core subjects that organizations should focus on. In each case, it is described in detail how the different areas of action should be understood and what measures can be expected from the organizations (see Table 6.3).

ISO 26000 describes the importance for organizations to engage in dialogue with their stakeholders from a number of perspectives. In an introductory chapter, the role of stakeholders is discussed in connection with the seven principles of social responsibility. ISO 26000 describes the basic methods for identifying and involving stakeholders in the implementation of social responsibility by organizations. This reflects that organizations and their stakeholders around the world are becoming increasingly aware that the purpose of social responsibility is to contribute to sustainable development. In the long run, business in all organizations is dependent on the health of the world's ecosystems (Hahn, 2013). As an international standard, ISO 26000 emphasizes the importance of results and improvements on the performance of social responsibility.

6.6 Criticism and challenges

Sustainability management systems and the processes associated with such systems entail some positive as well as some negative aspects within organizations that have implemented them. Standardization and management systems such as ISO 9000, ISO 14000, ISO 45001 or ISO 26000 can support the operationalization of sustainability (Nunhes, Ferreira Motta & de Oliveira,

Table 6.3 ISO 26000 focus and content

Core subject	Content
Organizational governance	Suggests tools for integrating social responsibility in to core organizational decisions
Human rights	Encourage users to identify and respond to members of vulnerable groups within their sphere of influence
Labour practices	Everyone should be able to earn a living wage through freely chosen work (not forced labour or slavery)
Environment	Prevent pollution; reduce emissions of pollutants in to the air, water and soil as much as possible
Fair operating practices	Practise honesty, respect property rights, treat suppliers and customers/consumers fairly, examine your value chain/supply chain to fulfil their social responsibilities
Consumer issues	Fair advertising, distribution and contracting practices, harmless and non-misleading information, protecting consumers' health and safety, sustainable consumption, customer service, complaint handling, protection and confidentiality of customer data, secure community services, consumer education and awareness
Community involvement and development	Society's commitment to education and culture, job creation and professional qualifications, developing technology and providing access to it, generating income to society, investing for the common good

2016). The ISO standards provide a practical framework for interpreting principles. This makes it possible to translate abstract concepts of sustainability into manageable tools. Standardization helps eliminate conceptual confusion in the use of sustainability in practice by promoting consistent application of methods and processes in the organization's context and practice. By standardization, it is possible for all organizations to adopt the same codified methods and processes, thus promoting comparison and a wider use of sustainability. Consistent use of the same standards can also help stakeholders understand how organizations apply sustainability in practice. Like accounting standards, sustainability management systems can be adapted to changing practical conditions and can be continuously improved.

On the negative side, there is the possibility that standardized sustainability management systems and processes are conceptually inadequate. Although standards have traditionally been developed to deal with technical problems, there are various methodological problems in defining and codifying complex social and ethical problems. In addition, there are several standards that overlap in some areas, which can lead to confusion among users when choosing which terminology to follow (Toppinen, Virtanen, Mayer & Tuppura, 2015). Implementation of sustainability management systems results in extra costs. The process of implementing sustainability management systems and following special ISO standards entails significant costs for obtaining external certifications. This can be especially problematic for Small and medium-sized enterprises (SMEs) that do not have the same financial resources as large international companies. Significant implementation costs can lead to many organizations failing to implement the standards despite the potential positive effects that such implementation could bring. Sustainability management systems comply with ISO standards on a voluntary basis. Therefore, these sustainability management systems may lack legitimacy as there are no strong penal mechanisms if organizations deviate from the standard (Zinenko, Rovira & Montiel, 2015). Although ISO standards often contain provisions on specific processes, they do not provide mechanisms to help stakeholders evaluate how well the standards have been implemented in the organization.

6.7 Summary

The introduction to this chapter describes that there has been a great growth in international standards for management systems regarding quality, environment, occupational health, safety and sustainability. Standardization can generally be defined as an activity aimed at organizing practical use and procedures, which are repeatedly performed in industry, technology, science and economics. At present, there are a large number of international and national standards aimed at organizing and systematizing, among other things, processes in business management systems in relation to a variety of functions and operations. The ISO uses the standardization of sustainability for industrial and commercial standardization. ISO has developed the most widespread and well-known certifiable management system of companies around the world. Today, quality management systems are based on ISO 9000, environmental management systems are based on ISO 14000 and systems for occupational health and safety management systems are based on ISO 45001. ISO 26000 covers a wide range of organizational activities including economic, social, governance, ethical and environmental issues. ISO 26000 contains a global social responsibility guidance document that helps organizations around the world meet their sustainability goals. ISO has discovered that users of their standards often implement the various management systems on quality, environment, occupational health and safety and sustainability in parallel. Therefore, ISO adaptation of ISO standards is carried out to make it easier to integrate these with each other. In doing so, they would become a more efficient management system that reduces time and bureaucracy and also reduces the use of human, technical and financial resources.

Study questions

1   In what way have international standards bodies adopted sustainability?
2   What is the role of the International Standardization Organization (ISO)?
3   How does ISO work?
4   What does standardization mean?

5   Why did ISO update and adapt its different management system standards?
6   What is the ISO 9000 family?
7   What specific aspects does ISO 9000 cover?
8   What is the ISO 14000 family?
9   How many standards does ISO 14000 include?
10 What is the overall purpose of ISO 14000?
11 What is ISO 45001?
12 How are OHSAS 18001 and ISO 45001 interconnected?
13 What is ISO 26000?
14 What are the seven core subjects of ISO 26000?

References

Castka, P. & Balzarova, M. A. (2018). An exploration of interventions in ISO 9001 and ISO 14001 certification context–A multiple case study approach, *Journal of Cleaner Production*, Vol. 174, pp. 1642–1652.

Hahn, R. (2013). ISO 26000 and the standardization of strategic management processes for sustainability and corporate social responsibility, *Business Strategy and the Environment*, Vol. 22, pp. 442–455.

Heras-Saizarbitoria, I. & Boiral, O. (2013). ISO 9001 and ISO 14001: Towards a research agenda on management system standards, *International Journal of Management Reviews*, Vol. 15 (1), pp. 47–65.

ISO (2010). *International standard ISO 26000*, Reference number ISO 26000:2010(E).

ISO (2015). *ISO 9001–Debunking the myths*. [Electronic]. www.iso.org/ files/live/ sites/isoorg/files/archive/pdf/en/iso_9001_debunking_the_myths.pdf.

ISO (2016). *Selection and use of the ISO 9000 family of standards*. [Electronic]. https:// committee.iso.org/tc176sc2.

ISO (2018). *ISO 45001 Occupational health and safety*. [Electronic]. www.iso.org/files/ live/sites/isoorg/files/store/en/PUB100427.pdf.

Marimon Viadiu, F., Casadesús Fa, M. & Saizarbitoria, I. H. (2006). ISO 9000 and ISO 14000 standards: An international diffusion model, *International Journal of Operations & Production Management*, Vol. 26 (2), pp. 141–165.

Nunhes, T. V., Ferreira Motta, L. C. & de Oliveira, O. J. (2016). Evolution of integrated management systems research on the *Journal of Cleaner Production*: Identification of contributions and gaps in the literature, *Journal of Cleaner Production*, Vol. 139, pp. 1234–1244.

Nunhes, T. V., Motta Barbosa, L. C. & de Oliveira, O. J. (2016). Identification and analysis of the elements and functions integrable in integrated management systems, *Journal of Cleaner Production*, Vol. 142, pp. 3225–3235.

Pojasek, R. B. (2011). ISO 26000 guidance on social responsibility, *Environmental Quality Management*, Vol. 20 (3), pp. 85–93.

Poksinska, B., Dahlgaard, J. J. & Eklund, J. A. E. (2003). Implementing ISO 14000 in Sweden: Motives, benefits and comparisons with ISO 9000, *International Journal of Quality & Reliability Management*, Vol. 20 (5), pp. 585–606.

Rezaee, Z. & Elam, R. (2000). Emerging ISO 14000 environmental standards: A step-by-step implementation guide, *Managerial Auditing Journal*, Vol. 15 (1/2), pp. 60–67.

Toppinen, A., Virtanen, A., Mayer, A. & Tuppura, A. (2015). Standardizing social responsibility via ISO 26000: Empirical insights from the forest industry, *Sustainable Development*, Vol. 23, pp. 153–166.

Tuczek, F., Castka, P. & Wakolbinger, T. (2018). A review of management theories in the context of quality, environmental and social responsibility voluntary standards, *Journal of Cleaner Production*, Vol. 176, pp. 399–416.

Zinenko, A., Rovira, M. R. & Montiel, I. (2015). The fit of the social responsibility standard ISO 26000 within other CSR instruments: Redundant or complementary?, *Sustainability Accounting, Management and Policy Journal*, Vol. 6 (4), pp. 498–526.

Part III

Reporting sustainability (From internal to external perspective)

7 Triple bottom line

Berit Hartmann

Abstract

This chapter introduces the triple bottom line (TBL) approach, one the most influential approaches to reporting and monitoring of sustainability performance worldwide. This tool aims to broaden the focus of managers and investors to a more holistic perspective on organizational performance. Instead of limiting the performance assessment to a financial bottom line, the TBL introduces three bottom lines: profit, people and planet. These different types of results can be used for both managing organizations and reporting performance. In addition, the basic principles of this useful tool build the foundation for many different reporting frameworks and financial management tools. The chapter introduces the reader to the development of the approach and the content of the TBL as well as various possibilities of calculation. The chapter concludes with a reflection on the problems that organizations face when introducing and using the TBL.

Learning outcomes

After reading this chapter, you should be able to:

- Understand the origin, development and use of the triple bottom line.
- Describe the different parts of the triple bottom line, their relationship to each other and their relationship to business transactions.
- Reflect on the usefulness and limits of this approach.

7.1 Introduction

Is capitalism sustainable? John Elkington – founder of a British consultancy firm called SustainAbility – posed this question before introducing in his book different social trends in our society (Elkington, 1997, p. 17). These trends, he claims, transformed a scattered movement of protest groups into "the most powerful social movement of the second half of the 20th century." In the author's eyes, the social movement will shape the markets and industries of our world today and in the future, with businesses as the key driver of transformation. Already in 1994, Elkington coined the concept of triple bottom line (TBL), sometimes also referred to as the 3P (profit, people and planet). This chapter introduces the famous idea that is widely used and integrated in many other models of today's sustainable management tools.

The TBL is an attempt to focus on comprehensive investment results (Slaper & Hall, 2011). The TBL perspective with its underlying idea of presenting a holistic view on organizational performance and on interrelations with the environment is widely spread and builds the basis for many reporting frameworks and management tools. According to Tullberg (2012, p. 314), a KPMG study found that 70 percent of the world's top 250 companies used some form of TBL accounting in 2005 (an increase of 15 percent over three years).

John Elkington coined the concept of TBL or 3P in the 1990s in order to extend the predominant focus of organizations and capital providers on the financial bottom line (operating profit or net profit) towards a more holistic perspective of organizational performance. A comprehensive investment assessment, in this approach, therefore includes economic (*profit*), social (*people*) and environmental (*planet*) measurements (Figure 7.1).

John Elkington was not the first who tried to incorporate wider social and environmental concerns into business practice; however, the TBL framework was and still is one of the most used frameworks all over the world, building the basis for the Global Reporting Initiative (GRI) framework (see Chapter 8) and the Dow Jones Sustainability Indices (Elkington, 2013), among others.

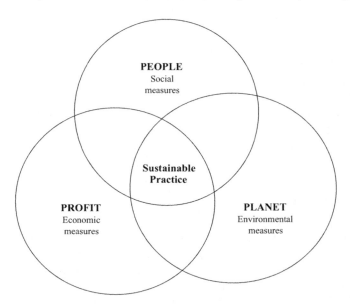

Figure 7.1 TBL Venn diagram.

The reason why TBL is so successful seems to lie in its managerial appeal: it presents an operational and manageable way of defining sustainability for business practice or "business brains" (Elkington, 2004). It is also connected with anecdotal evidence of improved long-term performance (Slaper & Hall, 2011). While this depicts the beauty of the approach, it also defines its limits, which will be discussed towards the end of this chapter. Without a focused definition, sustainability or sustainable development remains a buzzword, very important but hard to handle, especially in business practices. Therefore, the TBL provides a language that makes the holistic vision of social and environmental activists understandable and more manageable for organizations.

Elkington (2004) elaborates on seven trends in society that put pressure on organizations to take sustainability seriously, creating a new area of excellence and opportunities for business advantage:

* markets,
* societal values,
* transparency,
* life-cycle technology,
* partnerships,
* time and
* corporate governance.

Markets become more competitive because of globalization and technological developments. A more holistic approach to business and reporting opens new ways of thinking, enabling businesses to detect new market conditions and advantages. Many businesses today, for example, start reflecting over what it is they actually sell: the products and the services, or the emotions and experiences attached to them. Consider the purchase of a car. What is it that makes people choose a certain car? Some part of the decision probably will be size, price and technical details, that is, the actual product. Much of the decision, however, will also be based on how you feel about the car and how you experience the car when driving. These aspects are related, of course, but when selling a product, such elements need particular attention. An understanding of the social and environmental interrelations enables managers to broaden their perspective, to challenge the fundamental grounds of their business models and to market their products more effectively. Norway, for example, has the largest electric car fleet per capita in the world. One of the key reasons for this achievement is the fact that the Norwegian state decided to subsidize these cars, exempting them from the usual (quite substantial) purchase tax and VAT. The subsidization represents a strong financial incentive to by electric cars. However, the financial incentive is only one element. Most Norwegians have a strong emotional connection to nature and identify themselves as sporty and fit, through activities in nature. Using these emotional elements in their branding and product design, car sellers thrive best when understanding the interrelation between economic and societal values.

Societal values are culturally embedded, but they can change over time. In Western societies, we can see a clear trend towards what we might call sustainable enlightenment. Social and environment consequences of our personal and corporate actions become more and more important in the societal discussions today. This increases the expectations and the pressure on organizations to keep up and work with these shifts.

Transparency relates to the new requirements on sustainability reporting in many countries. Sweden is one of the countries that implemented explicit regulations on the reporting requirements of private organizations. The reporting initiatives aim to commit organizations to more transparency, but also to enable these organizations to create a more structured approach to their sustainability work inside the organization.

The life-cycle technology trend refers to the significantly broadened responsibility assigned to producing companies today. Producing companies are not only made responsible for their own actions but also for the activities along their total supply chain, including products in transit, in use and afterlife. The increased responsibility can create severe conflicts and brand damage for companies, such as accusations of child labour, exploitation of workers in Bangladesh or toxic production parts that endanger the health of thousands of workers.

Partnerships are a further trend described by Elkington. Due to tightening markets and opportunities, Elkington claims that organizations increasingly are forced to engage in partnerships they earlier would not have found acceptable or even doable. The new relations enable organizations to seek business advantages that might not have been interesting before.

Time has an aspect in this because financial markets and digitalization create a strong focus on short-term developments, while business survival builds at least as much on long-term planning as on short-term results.

Finally, *corporate governance* and increased focus on corporate governance are described as a societal trend, with important consequences for holistic management. Sustainability and sustainable development cannot be achieved by exclusively focusing on products and processes. The organizational boards have to become aware of the new challenges and need to build the vision of TBL into the "corporate DNA" from the outset. In the introduction to their book *The Triple Bottom Line*, Savitz and Weber (2014, p. 2) summarize the idea as follows:

> Sustainable organizations and societies generate and live off interest rather than depleting their capital. Capital, in this context, includes natural resources, such as water, air, sources of energy, and foodstuffs. It also includes human and social assets – from worker commitment to community support – as well as economic resources, such as license to operate, a receptive marketplace, and legal and economic infrastructure. A company can spend down its capital for a while, but generally not for long. A firm that honors the principles of sustainability, by contrast, is built to last.

Savitz and Weber (2014) claim that businesses that think and act sustainable will be able to survive in the long run, whereas unsustainable businesses will not because they will lose resources and support. Instead of considering social and ecological impacts as cost, TBL enables decision-makers *to see* the benefits of social and environmental engagements. Visibility here is the key to engaging in a more holistic management perspective. Companies like PUMA and Ikea have implemented the TBL successfully, giving an example on how organizations can strive for a more sustainable practice and at the same time mobilize this activity in their marketing programme.

7.2 The use and users of the TBL

The TBL is a flexible tool that aims to enable companies to plan, track and report their performance in a holistic manner. There is no universal standard on the components and calculation of the TBL. Instead, companies need to adapt the tool to their needs for both internal and external reporting. Internally, the TBL presents a tool for a systemized collection and follow-up of information. Managers use the approach to plan, decide and assess their performance based on the three dimensions (see Chapters 3–5 for detailed insights into internal sustainability accounting). Externally, sustainability reporting often builds on reporting frameworks which have their roots in the TBL perspective, for example, the GRI framework (Chapter 8) or the integrated reporting (IR) framework (Chapter 9). Both the GRI and IR frameworks build on a TBL perspective but give more detailed guidelines on their implementation in order to enable comparability of the information. Comparability of the information is important both in relation to the inner-company comparison to assess the development and between companies in order to allocate financial funds (by investors and other capital providers).

In some jurisdictions, external sustainability reporting is voluntary, and companies can choose which information to present based on the TBL. However, many jurisdictions today require public and private companies to report on their societal and environmental impact. In Sweden, for example, public and private organizations are legally required to present sustainability reports. Already since 2008, state-owned organizations have to prepare sustainability reports in accordance with the GRI framework. Since 2017, private organizations have to publish sustainably reports, subject to their size (small companies are exempted from the reporting requirement). The organizations are required to report about their environment and social impact, their employee treatment, respect for human rights and anti-corruption programmes.

In this chapter, you learn about the different ways in which companies can use and tailor the TBL according to their needs. It is important to note that some of the flexibility of the approach is taken away when guiding frameworks like GRI or IR are applied (see the respective chapters for more information).

The users of TBL reporting are all kinds of stakeholders including managers, financial markets, suppliers, customers, employees and governments. The information interests of these stakeholders differ substantially. However, the underlying idea of TBL reporting is that it separates and explicates information that cannot be summarized into one financial bottom line. From a legitimacy perspective, external sustainability reporting is one way to motivate companies to improve their suitability work. Companies strive to make a good impression in external reporting which motivates them to improve their sustainable development in order to being able to report something positive (see also Chapter 3). However, it is not only external pressures and expectations that are important. Many companies already collect a lot of information on social and environmental factors, but not in a systemized fashion. The TBL therefore also can help companies to focus, structure and monitor their sustainable development and thereby increase the efficiency of sustainable development efforts.

7.3 The three dimensions: calculation and narratives

TBL reporting differs from traditional reporting because it includes three dimensions: the economic (profit), the social (people) and the environmental (planet) dimension. A TBL report usually consists of different categories of indicators within the three dimensions that are reported in different measures and narratives in order to communicate the social and environmental footprint to the stakeholders.

The economic dimension represents the company's economic bottom line and monetary flow. This dimension puts focus on monetary values but includes financial and non-financial indicators. Examples of financial measures are sales, profits, return on investment, cash flows and taxes paid. Examples of non-financial measures are supplier relations, jobs created, average incomes and revenues by sector.

The social dimension represents the company's interrelation with its social environment and puts focus on how the company uses and impacts human resources. Companies may define different categories like labour practices, human rights, society and product responsibility. Indicators within these categories include education activities, health and safety records, work security measures, community impact, corruption-avoidance mechanisms, among others.

The environmental dimension represents the company's interrelation with and impact on the ecological environment and puts focus on how the company uses and impacts the natural resources on the planet. Examples of indicators in this dimension are carbon dioxide emission, water and energy use, amount of waste generated, biodiversity impact and recycled material use.

The general dimensions of the TBL are intuitive. Implementing TBL reporting, however, is more difficult and requires substantial resources. Companies that decide for sustainability reporting face several difficulties: the relevant indicators must be defined, the collection of information must be systemized and adjusted, software and IT landscape might need to be adjusted, employees need to be trained and so forth. More important, to enable and foster sustainable development, the TBL needs to be brought into the operations in a manageable form. Since sustainability reporting and sustainability assessment usually combine narrative and metrical information, the content and structure of the information is a key concern to the usefulness of the reports.

According to Slaper and Hall (2011, p. 4), "The trick isn't defining TBL. The trick is measuring it." The problem of measurement arises because the individual indicators do not share a unit of measurement. In reporting, we are used to monetary values. The profit dimension of bottom line is dominant in our world because it gives a clear and comparable measure to the different aspects of organizational activity. However, many aspects in organizational activity and in the interrelation between an organization and its environment cannot be measured in monetary terms. Proponents of the undefined nature of the three dimensions therefore argue that the flexibility enables companies to put focus on the aspects that are relevant in their particular context, and that reports can be better customized to the needs of the stakeholders. Critics of the approach, on the other hand, argue that the reported information about sustainable development loses its use without standardized and comparable indicators. Some claim that a TBL is only really useful if all three bottom lines are brought together into one total net present value calculation. Since there are no strict guidelines or regulations on how to implement sustainability reporting in this respect, companies that implement a TBL therefore have to ask themselves how to define the relevant indicators of their performance and how to create meaningful and comprehensive measures for these indicators.

With respect to measurement of the TBL, sustainability organizations and governments have several quantitative tools to assess and report their sustainability. These tools include benchmarks, indices and metrics. Benchmarks set an indicator in relation to a sustainability parameter as a point of reference to assess developments; indices draw together information from different sources to create one combined indicator of sustainability performance; metrics present individual calculations of indicators such as tons of CO_2 emission per annual turnover or wages paid above minimum wage.

Slaper and Hall (2011) present three options to measure a TBL. Companies might opt to monetize all their dimensions, that is, defining *monetary values as a common unit of measurement*. Proponents of this approach advocate the comparability of a common unit and the possibility to set the three dimensions into relation to calculate a total net present value. However, many ecological and social values are difficult to monetize (technically and/or ethically). What is the correct monetary value for a park in the middle of the city? From a traditional accounting perspective, the park will not create income but only cost — costs of preparing the land, building the site and then cleaning and possibly protecting the site. Taking into account a TBL perspective, however, opens the view for a positive side. For example, insurance companies provide records on the decrease in health care cost of individuals that frequently exercise in fresh air. A park increases opportunities for such activities, and therefore decreased health care costs can be calculated. Another example is the pollution reduction as a benefit of additional trees in the area. Monetary units can be very convincing. However, there are limits in the values that can be represented in monetary terms. It would, for example, be difficult to express the increase in life quality or the improved biodiversity because of additional living space.

Another option is to calculate the *TBL through an index*. An index puts specific indicators from a variety of sources in relation to a normalizing base which solves the problem of diverse units of measurement. The index, thus, becomes a combined indicator of sustainability performance. Although indices can be customized for individual projects or companies, large-scale indices are more common. These indices are scientifically developed and are typically used for the assessment of state or company performance. The S&P Dow Jones Indices (DJSI), for example, evaluates the economic, environmental and social performance of the largest 2,500 companies listed on the Dow Jones Global Total Stock Market Index. Another example is the Environmental Performance Index (EPI) which quantifies the environmental performance of states by bringing together categories like air quality, water and sanitation, biodiversity and habitat, as well as climate and energy.[1] Proponents of this approach highlight that indices improve comparability across companies or projects and that information becomes more useful for decision-making if it is summarized. However, the existing indices have also been criticized because of their aggregation of indices and a lack of weighting among the three dimensions and the different indicators (Böhringer & Jochem, 2006).

A third option is to report the individual indicators with *no common unit of measurement*. Proponents of this approach point out the benefits of detail and of flexibility in tailoring to the individual company or project which makes the information more relevant for local stakeholders. A drawback from this approach is the multitude and variety of information included that can make assessment of the development and performance difficult.

Notwithstanding the problem of measurability, the TBL is one way to explicate social and environmental aspects that bring non-financial values to the foreground. Peter Drucker's famous statement "If you can't measure it, you can't manage it" still resonates well with managerial thought, and the issue of designing relevant and useful indicators therefore is key to the successful implementation of TBL reporting. The usefulness of the reports to assess sustainable development relates to a company's ability to make their reports comparable, with prior company performance and in relation to other companies. To aid the measurability and comparability, companies usually opt to implement the TBL using guidelines from the GRI framework (Chapter 8) or the IR framework (Chapter 9). While the TBL can largely be understood as an underlying ideology, these frameworks give more guidance on how the reports should be prepared.

7.4 Challenges in using the TBL for reporting and control

The TBL is a very successful approach that built the basis for different management accounting tools and several sustainability reporting frameworks. Together with these tools and frameworks, TBL shares some problems in implementing, using and reporting the sustainable performance. Chapter 14 in this book presents a wider discussion of the limits of sustainability reporting and management today. This section shortly highlights the critique explicitly connected to the TBL approach.

Proponents of the TBL claim that the tool is so useful because it links to our preexisting understanding of a bottom line. Managers and capital providers are used to making decisions about investment or performance based on a bottom line. Extending the economic bottom line with two additional bottom lines therefore seems familiar. A drawback of this approach, however, is the expectation this link raises. As discussed earlier, the TBL tries to bring environmental and social factors into a familiar framework. In practice, this easily leads to the expectation that the different social and environmental aspects should be summarized in one bottom line – like the economic bottom line – despite their different units of measurement (or not being measurable at all). Some important information, therefore, is likely to be excluded because no indicators cover them properly. This is acknowledged even by the proponents of the TBL who would argue that it is better to include some ecological and social factors in decision-making than none. While this certainly is true, there is still a long way to go in relation to improving the indicators and to including relevant social and environmental issues in the performance indicators.

7.5 Summary

This chapter presented the TBL, a tool that was introduced by John Elkington in the 1990s to move the predominant focus of organizations, capital providers and governments from a mere economic bottom line towards a more holistic perspective that includes social and environmental aspects of performance. When limiting the view to economic indicators, decision-makers might undervalue the benefits of many long-term investments and actions. The TBL therefore aims to highlight the benefits and costs in a more holistic manner.

The TBL approach can be used for planning, decision-making, assessment and reporting of sustainable development and sustainability performance. Within management accounting, the TBL has been the basis for many management accounting tools. From a reporting perspective, the TBL thought underlies reporting frameworks such as the GRI or the IR.

While being very successful, the TBL approach also has its limits. It is complex to define relevant and measurable indicators. Like all sustainability reporting and assessment, the TBL approach also can only take in parts the social and economic effects and interrelation. Practitioners and researchers alike are therefore constantly striving to improve the ways in which we can include the holistic view into decision- making.

7.6 Study questions

1 What are the different dimensions of TBL?
2 Why do you need different dimensions?
3 How does a TBL perspective differ from a classic financial perspective?
4 Who can use TBL reporting?
5 How can TBL be used by different stakeholder groups?
6 What are the different possibilities for calculating TBL?
7 What are the pros and cons of different ways of measuring TBL?
8 What are the challenges when implementing TBL?
9 Why is it at the same time beneficial and problematic to approach sustainability through a focus on bottom lines?
10 Give a concrete example of a value that cannot (or very difficult) be calculated with a metric

Note

1 Böhringer and Jochem (2006) provide an extensive overview and assessment of different sustainability indices.

References

Böhringer, C., & Jochem, P. (2006) Measuring the immeasurable: A survey of sub-stainability indices, *ZEW Discussion Papers*, No. 06–73.

Elkington, J. (1997). *Cannibals with forks: The triple bottom line of 21st century*. Oxford: Captsone Publishing Limited.

Elkington, J. (2004). Enter the tripple bottom line. In A. Henriques & J. Richardson (Eds.), *The tripple bottom line: Does it all add up?* (pp. 1–16). London: Earthscan.

Elkington, J. (2013). Triple bottom line. In E. H. Kessler (Ed.), *Encyclopedia of management theory* pp. 902–4. Thousand Oaks: SAGE publications, Inc.

Savitz, A., & Weber, K. (2014). *The triple bottom line: How today's best-run companies are achieving economic, social and environmental success-and how you can too*. San Francisco: Jossey-Bass.

Slaper, T. F., & Hall, T. J. (2011). The triple bottom line: What is it and how does it work? *Indiana Business Review*, Vol. 86 (1), p. 4.

Tullberg, J. (2012). Triple bottom line—a vaulting ambition? *Business Ethics: A European Review*, Vol. 21 (3), pp. 310–324.

8 Global reporting initiative

Gunnar Rimmel

Abstract

This chapter provides an overview of the Global Reporting Initiative (GRI), which has become the most widely used framework for sustainability reporting in the world. The chapter describes the development of the GRI over the past 20 years, and how the evolution from standards guidelines has been adopted. The reader is introduced to the development of the different versions of guidelines from G3 / G3.1 to G4 to the GRI Sustainability Reporting Standards introduced in 2016. The most important features of the structure of the standards are briefly described to give an overview of how detailed comparability of sustainability information can be achieved. Furthermore, we briefly present how GRI collaborates with various organizations to strengthen sustainability reporting. Finally, criticism of GRI and the challenges it faces are discussed.

Learning outcomes:

After reading this chapter, you are expected to be able to:

- Explain the origin and importance of GRI for sustainability reporting.
- Explain differences between the different generations of GRI guidelines.
- Explain basic concepts related to GRI guidelines.

8.1 Introduction

In recent decades, the ideas of transparency and responsibility in environmental and sustainability performance have been based on the discourse on companies' social responsibility. Voluntary sustainability reporting has emerged as part of this trend and has quickly spread among large global companies. Already in the early 1990s, several companies began publishing reports separate from sustainability reports.

Since the 1990s, sustainability reporting has grown and changed significantly. Initially, only a few multinational companies voluntarily reported environmental and responsibility information about their company, but now the number of reporting companies has grown exponentially. At the same time, reported sustainability information has evolved from unstructured single pieces of information to much more comprehensive sustainability reports with clear business relevance. It has become increasingly important for companies to communicate the sustainability values that underpin their operations. One problem for companies in the globalized world is that the cost pressure has led to move production of goods to other parts of the world that can produce the products cheaper. At the same time, increasing demands are being placed on companies regarding their responsibility for the environment and for ethical and social conditions. Today, there is increased pressure on companies, both from financial markets and from various stakeholders (such as customers, employees and suppliers – see Chapter 2.3), to prepare a sustainability report. This has increased the pressure on companies to report and disclose their work on sustainability issues. A sustainability report seeks to focus on presenting the company's environmental, ethical and social conditions that are linked to the company's economic development. There has been a very large increase in the number of companies and organizations that have voluntarily started with sustainability reporting. While sustainability reporting has increased in importance for companies, this is also a reflection of the increased importance of sustainability issues in society. In part, global climate change has become an important driver for changing society in the direction of increased sustainability, while at the same time society also imposes changed sustainability requirements on companies.

The increase in importance of sustainability reports has led to the development of different guidelines that support companies in their quest to fulfil sustainable manufacturing and reporting. Among these guidelines, the most prominent is the *Global Reporting Initiative*, which is most commonly abbreviated *GRI* (Brown, de Jong & Lessidrenska 2009). GRI's purpose with the guidelines is to create a uniform way of presenting sustainability reporting in order to improve comparability between companies. Over the past 20 years, the GRI has quickly become a leader among voluntary global sustainability reporting frameworks. According to GRI's website (www. globalreporting.com), 74 percent of the largest global companies have used GRI's guidelines in their sustainability reporting. GRI's endeavour is to improve the usability and quality of information that companies report on sustainability. The organization's work with GRI has been favourably responded to in the global corporate world and among the users of sustainability information. The guidelines have proven to be a good tool for companies to communicate with their stakeholders about other than just financial information. GRI strives to become a regulatory sustainability framework that is able to provide the same level of comparability, review and general acceptance as financial reporting.

8.2 Global reporting initiative – development from guidelines to standards

The idea for establishing the GRI came up in the late 1990s. The non-profit organization CERES (Coalition for Environmentally Responsible Econo-mies), a coalition of investors, public pension managers, NGOs, foundations, organizations and unions, wanted to improve environmental performance and accountability among American companies. By demanding more and more information from companies on environmental performance and social responsibility through investment and shareholder activism, the volume of sustainability information grew exponentially. The idea of standardization, simplification and globalization of this large volume of sustainability infor-mation began to emerge in various organizations. However, it was CERES who, together with the Tellus Institute, took the initiative to create an organ-ization that focuses on developing a framework for sustainability reporting, which can be used by interested companies and organizations.

In 1997 in Boston, USA, GRI was jointly established by CERES and the Tellus Institute and supported by the United Nations Environment Pro-gramme (UNEP). The goal of GRI was to create a common sustainability reporting framework, which can link and unite different reporting stand-ards and guidelines for creating a global framework. The collaboration with UNEP was an important puzzle piece in this endeavour, as it ensured that GRI was established as a global platform. This became the starting point for the development of the GRI guidelines, illustrated in Figure 8.1.

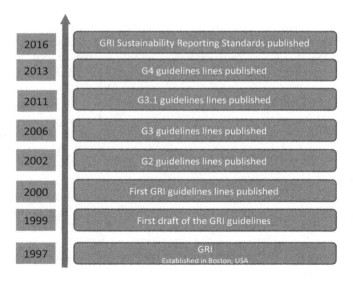

2016	GRI Sustainability Reporting Standards published
2013	G4 guidelines lines published
2011	G3.1 guidelines lines published
2006	G3 guidelines lines published
2002	G2 guidelines lines published
2000	First GRI guidelines lines published
1999	First draft of the GRI guidelines
1997	GRI Established in Boston, USA

Figure 8.1 Development of the GRI guidelines.

The first draft of the GRI guidelines was presented in March 1999 to a group of organizations and companies interested in sustainability reporting. Twenty-one companies, representing different countries and several industries, tested and submitted comments on the draft. GRI strives for the sustainability framework to reach the same level as the financial reporting regarding comparability, transparency and general acceptance (Willis 2003). During the consultation process, experts on human rights, bookkeeping, government agencies, companies and work organizations provided valuable comments on the draft GRI guidelines. To ensure its continued development, GRI had partnered with some 30 companies in a structured feedback process, which would result in recommendations for future updates to GRI guidelines.

The consultation process led to the publication of the first GRI guidelines on sustainability reporting in June 2000. GRI presented the guidelines to stakeholders in South America, North America, Australia, Europe, South Asia and Japan. As a result, 50 multinational companies and organizations began to use the GRI guidelines and released their sustainability reports according to these GRI standards. A year later, the number of organizations that used GRI guidelines had increased to 80, and GRI gained great interest globally. In 2001, the GRI guidelines were developed to include more key figures and parameters. Continued development to improve the first guidelines resulted in the second generation (G2) GRI guidelines.

In September 2002, during the *World Summit for Sustainable Development* in Johannesburg, GRI launched the G2 guidelines. At the same time, GRI and the new guidelines were recognized by several countries and international organizations. The EU emphasized the importance of GRI's work on sustainability reporting and the possible application of G2 guidelines for measuring, reporting and controlling corporate social responsibility in the European Union. In 2002, GRI's organization and governance was changed and transformed into an independent non-profit organization and moved from Boston to Amsterdam in the Netherlands. At the same time, the Stakeholder Council (SC) was formed. The SC became the GRI's formal forum for debating and considering important strategic and political issues surrounding GRI's development. In early 2003, GRI launched a programme of stakeholder membership for organizers to maintain GRI as an open, democratic and global network. Stakeholder members were given the opportunity to influence the continued development of the GRI guidelines.

Several multinational companies in various industries around the world began to choose GRI's G2 guidelines as their sustainability reporting tool. During the years 2003–2005, GRI managed to increase attention in sustainability reporting in accordance with the G2 guidelines. The number of companies and organizations that used GRI's G2 guidelines continuously grew in number. At the end of 2005, more than 750 organizations prepared their sustainability reports based on these guidelines. The development process for the next generation of GRI guidelines continued and began to involve hundreds of organizations and individuals. The large number of organizations that used the G2 guidelines covered several different industries. Acceptance of GRI's G2 guidelines in business became the catalyst for the creation of the *Sector Supplements* for specific industries. These sector supplements were developed to reflect the unique social and environmental problems in various industries. The first sector supplements were released in 2003 for the telecommunications industry. There were additional sector supplements in the areas of financial services, mining and metal industry, as well as logistics and transport.

The success of GRI's G2 guidelines and its increased application by companies and organizations around the world resulted in GRI continuing its work on development and improvement. This work led to new improved and amended guidelines G3 / G3.1 and G4, which have now been changed from guidelines to standards. Guidelines G3 / G3.1 and G4, as well as the transition to GRI standards, are presented in more detail in the next section. They are all based on each other, and G3 lives on as a basic framework even in G4 and GRI standards.

8.3 GRI guidelines G3 / G3.1

In order to further improve the transparency of companies and organizations' quest for increased sustainability, the third-generation (G3) GRI guidelines was developed, which were launched in 2006. GRI's G3 guidelines drew clear inspiration from the basic ideas of the triple bottom line (which was explained in Chapter 7) on providing sustainability information that includes economic, social and environmental measurements. The guidelines did not impose statutory requirements on companies or organizations using GRI's G3 guidelines. The G3 guidelines were voluntary, and the content, indicators and measurements were regarded more as recommendations. A major change compared to the G2 guidelines was that the G3 guidelines encouraged companies and organizations using G3 guidelines to specify the level of GRI application, C – A, for the issued sustainability report.

GRI's G3 guidelines consist of two parts (GRI, 2000–2006). The first part of the G3 guidelines addresses principles and guidance that are important in defining the content, quality and boundaries of reports. The second part of the G3 guidelines consists of a set of standard disclosures. The standardized information on strategy information and the organization's profile is also divided into three categories: economic, environmental and social information.

8.3.1 GRI G3 guidelines Part 1 – defining reports content, quality and boundaries

The first part of GRI's G3 guidelines focuses on the content of sustainability reporting. It describes how the content should be defined to ensure that the information in the reports has boundaries and is of satisfactory quality. According to the G3 guidelines, the content of sustainability reports is based on the following four principles: *materiality, stakeholder inclusiveness, sustainability context* and *completeness*.

Materiality is an important principle in connection with GRI's G3 guidelines, as companies and organizations have a wide range of topics and indicators that they could report. Significance for sustainability reporting is not just limited to those sustainability issues that have a significant financial impact on the organization. Significance requires that relevant topics and indicators be included as information in the report, whether they involve economic, environmental and social consequences of today's needs, or of future needs. In this way, all the material economic, environmental and social consequences would be included in the information, so that stakeholders can make decisions.

Stakeholder inclusiveness means that an organization that uses G3 guidelines needs to identify stakeholders and explain in the report how the organization has taken stakeholders' expectations and interests into account. Stakeholders' expectations and interests are an important reference point for many decisions when preparing a report, for example, the scope, boundary and application of indicators. But not all of the organization's stakeholders will use the sustainability report. Thus, the organization faces the challenge of balancing the various expectations of the stakeholders in the sustainability report.

Sustainability context encompasses that sustainability reports describe how the organization's development takes place in relation to growing knowledge about sustainability. This includes a discussion about the organization's performance in relation to the boundaries and requirements of environmental or social resources at sectoral, local, regional or global level.

Completeness primarily includes the scope, boundary and time period of the sustainability report. The concept of completeness can also be used to refer to information collection practices and whether the presentation of information is reasonable and appropriate. Completeness is related to report quality.

These four principles should be used in conjunction with GRI's standard disclosures, which is presented in Part 2, to determine whether the content of the sustainability reports is reliable.

8.3.2 GRI G3 guidelines Part 2 – standard disclosures

The second part of GRI's guidelines, the standard disclosures, has the function of simplifying the work of structuring the content of the sustainability report, helping to select which indicators are most suitable for measuring sustainability performance. The standard disclosure is divided into three categories: *strategy and the organization's profile, management approach* and *performance indicators*.

Strategy and the organization's profile deal with information that indicates the overall context for understanding organizational performance, such as strategy, profile and governance. Management approach includes information that describes how an organization takes up areas to create context to illustrate performance in a particular area. GRI's G3 performance indicators are divided into three different categories: economic, environmental and social. The social category contains four subcategories: labour practices and decent work, human rights, the organization's role in society and product responsibility. GRI's G3 performance indicators are also divided into core and supplementary indicators. The core indicators are the ones that are most relevant to companies and organizations and also most interesting to stakeholders. GRI recommends that companies report the core indicators in the first place, and these indicators must be essential. The additional indicators can be seen more as optional indicators as they are not as general, but more focused, on specific areas.

8.3.2.1 Economic indicators

The economic category of performance indicators includes the financial impact of the company or organization on its stakeholders, as well as the economic system in which it operates, at both local and national or global levels. The financial performance indicators illustrate the flow of capital between different stakeholders and show the main financial impact that the company or organization has on society. In order to understand an organization and its sustainability, financial results are a prerequisite. The financial information is usually already in the accounts.

8.3.2.2 Environmental indicators

The next category, environmental indicators, refers to the company's impact on nature and contains nine aspects: materials; energy; water; biodiversity; emissions, effluents and waste; products and services; compliance; transport and overall environment-related indicators. This applies to the impact that the company or organization has on the natural system throughout the life cycle, from the purchase of materials to production, which also involves emissions, wastewater and waste. The nine aspects contain 30 indicators that can be used to measure and assess environmental performance. The environmental indicators should describe how management works with resources such as materials, water and energy consumption.

8.3.2.3 Social indicators

The social category in the G3 guidelines contains indicators that provide information about the organization's impact on the social systems in which they operate. This category is divided into four subcategories.

Labour practices and decent work is the most comprehensive subcategory and is based on the UN Declaration on Human Rights and the ILO Tripartite Declaration on Fundamental Principles and Rights at Work. The companies must provide information on how management works with employment, the relationship between employees and management, occupational health and safety, training and education, as well as diversity and gender equality.

Human rights entail making demands on the organization to disclose the degree to which it takes human rights into account, for example, when selecting suppliers. This category also aims for companies to respect and provide information on how they work with non-discrimination, prohibition of child labour, indigenous rights, preventing forced labour, freedom of association and the right to collective bargaining.

Society is about the role of the organization and its impact on the society in which the company or organization operates. A description is required in the sustainability report, which explains how the risks that can arise through interactions with other social institutions are managed and communicated. This category is divided into aspects of community, corruption, politics, anti-competitive activities and compliance.

Product responsibility includes indicators that provide information on how the organization's products or services, directly or indirectly, affect its customers. Product responsibility consists of customers' health and safety, labelling of products and services, market communication, customer integrity and compliance.

8.3.2.4 Application levels of the G3 guidelines

GRI's G3 guidelines consist of three different application levels A, B and C. While A+ is the highest level, C is the lowest level of application. The different levels require different amounts of implementation and reporting of GRI's G3 guidelines. The idea of the different application levels is to give readers of a sustainability report information on the extent to which the GRI guidelines have been applied in the preparation of such a report.

The application levels of the three G3 guidelines require the following:

Level A requires reporting of each core indicator and also of each sector-specific indicator of GRI's G3 guidelines. However, companies must take into account the principle of materiality by either reporting the indicator information or explaining the reasons why indicators are not reported.

Level B requires reporting of at least 20 performance indicators. As a minimum, there must be one indicator provided within the economic, environmental and social categories of GRI's G3 guidelines, together with at least one indicator from the four subcategories of the social category: labour practices and decent work, human rights, society and product liability.

Level C requires reporting of at least ten performance indicators. As a minimum, one indicator should be from the economic, environmental and social categories of GRI's G3 guidelines.

GRI's application levels were intended to cover the various needs from beginners to experienced reports of sustainability information. If an external assurance of the sustainability report is carried out by auditors or companies that specialize in certifying sustainability reports (such as the classification society Norske Veritas), the sustainability report can receive a "plus" (+) in addition at each application level, such as A+, B+ or C+. GRI strongly recommended companies and organizations that used the G3 guidelines to use an independent assurer to ensure the sustainability information is quality-assured. While GRI's idea was to show how the sustainability report gradually increases the level of application, there was criticism that the level of application affects the quality stamp on the sustainability report. Therefore, GRI decided to remove the application levels from the G4 guidelines.

8.3.2.5 Update of G3 guidelines to G3.1

From the time when the GRI G3 guidelines were introduced in 2006, they have become GRI's cornerstone in the process of standardizing sustainability reporting. For a number of years, GRI focused on increasing the application of the G3 guidelines among companies and organizations. In March 2011, GRI published the G3.1 guidelines, which is an update and amendment of the third-generation GRI guidelines for sustainability reporting. GRI's G3.1 guidelines expanded the G3 guidelines by including an updated framework and new indicators for reporting on gender, society and human rights (GRI, 2012). The G3.1 guidelines also contain a technical protocol for applying the principles. The *technical protocol* addresses one of the key challenges facing businesses and organizations in preparing sustainability reports: determining what issues are important to stakeholders to assess the sustainability performance of organizations. The technical protocol makes it possible to produce relevant sustainability reports more easily. When the GRI published the G3.1 guidelines, it was decided that both versions of the G3 and G3.1 guidelines would be valid until the end of a two-year transition period for the next generation of guidelines, the G4 guidelines, which it had already planned to release in 2013. This is partly a recognition of the organizational transition costs from one generation of GRI guidelines to another.

8.4 GRI guidelines G4

In May 2013, the fourth generation of GRI guidelines, G4, was launched. When GRI launched the G3.1 guidelines in 2011, their extensive work on G4 began. For two years, GRI held extensive consultations and dialogues with hundreds of stakeholders and experts from all over the world. The work included various sectors, companies, work organizations, academics and the financial sector. GRI's purpose with the G4 guidelines was to help companies and organizations create sustainability reports that make a difference. For GRI, the G4 guidelines represent a major shift in reporting thinking. Instead of reporting as much as possible, emphasis was put on "less is more" thinking. The new thinking proposed that it is okay to report less, as long as what is essential to the organization is reported. The G4 guidelines should contribute to a robust and standardized practice in sustainability reporting. To achieve increased standardization in practice, there are clear references in the G4 guidelines to other global frameworks, codes and standards for sustainability. GRI's work includes harmonization with other important global frameworks, including the Organization for Economic Cooperation and Development (OECD) guidelines for multinational companies, the UN Global Compact Principles and the UN guidelines for business and human rights (GRI, 2013a).

The G4 guidelines are divided into two supplementary documents. Document 1, *Reporting Principles and Standard Disclosures*, consists of principles and standard disclosures for sustainability reporting. The first document gives companies and organizations applying the G4 guidelines flexibility in choosing what information they want to focus on and how efforts can be adapted to national reporting requirements or frameworks. Document 2, *Implementation Manual*, is a separate implementation manual to assist companies and organizations that apply the G4 guidelines to get through the reporting process.

The main differences between the G3 / 3.1 guidelines and the G4 guidelines are mainly in materiality and boundaries, stakeholder engagement and reporting options (GRI, 2013b).

Materiality and boundaries have received increased attention. The G4 guidelines emphasize that materiality should focus on "what is important" and "where it matters". Boundaries should help to define where each impact occurs, so that information is provided on whether the impact occurs internally or externally. Together, assessment of materiality and boundaries can help a company or organization that uses the G4 guidelines to identify and determine which sustainability areas are critical to the business and which have the greatest impact. In this way, sustainability efforts can be adapted to the areas that are most strategic to the business.

Stakeholder engagement is emphasized in the G4 guidelines, as it is important for companies and organizations to understand and engage their stakeholders. At the same time, it helps to determine the materiality and limits in the sustainability report. The G4 guidelines emphasize the role of stakeholders as a central element in the reporting process. A systematic process for stakeholder participation is to be established and presented in the sustainability report.

Reporting options have changed in the G4 guidelines. The criticism of the three application levels of the G3 / 3.1 guidelines (A, B and C) led to the GRI removing the three application levels in the G4 guidelines. Instead, the G4 guidelines introduced the classification of sustainability reports according to two alternative levels, *core (at least one indicator)* or *comprehensive (all indicators)*. These levels depend on the scope of the information provided in the sustainability report. For example, if a company or organization has identified 15 aspects that are essential to its operations, it must report at least one indicator for each identified aspect in order for the sustainability report to be consistent with the core alternative. For the comprehensive reporting alternative, information is required on all indicators contained in the G4 guidelines within the 15 identified aspects that meet the materiality criterion.

GRI continues to recommend external assurance of sustainability reports. However, external assurance is not necessary to fulfil the expression *in accordance with the G4 guidelines*. According to GRI, the G4 guidelines help make sustainability reports more focused, more credible and easier to navigate for users (GRI, 2013a).

8.4.1 Transition from G4 to GRI Standards

In October 2016, GRI launched a new generation of its previous guidelines, but instead of *guidelines*, this new generation is called *GRI standards*. GRI standards became effective in 2018 and replaced the G4 guidelines. GRI standards are issued by the Global Sustainability Standards Board (GSSB). The GSSB is an independent standardization body created by GRI. The GSSB is responsible for developing globally accepted standards for sustainability reporting. The GSSB has defined a formal Due Process Protocol to develop new and existing GRI standards. This was done to ensure that GSSB's work promotes the public interest and fits GRI's vision and mission. Here, GRI drew inspiration from accounting standards such as the International Accounting Standards Board (IASB). The GSSB's process protocols ensure a clear and transparent process, from project identification, project development, public exposure, to drafts, consideration of received feedback and finally the adoption of new standards or amendment to existing standards.

The GRI standards are based on the G4 guidelines. The G4 guidelines have neither been changed nor have new elements been added to the GRI standards to minimize the effects of sustainability reporting in the transition from the G4 guidelines to GRI standards. The content of the G4 guidelines has been edited for greater clarity and simpler language. Therefore, the G4 guidelines have been restructured into a modular structure, which means that the GRI standards are organized as a set of standard modules linked to other GRI standards. The GRI standards combine content from the G4 guidelines Document 1, *Principles and Standard Information*, and Document 2, *Implementation Manual*. The revised format of the GRI standards now makes clear differences between requirements, recommendations and guidance. Some information and aspects from the G4 guidelines have been merged or integrated into other sections to reduce duplication and improve the logical flow of the work on sustainability reporting. Key concepts and information from the G4 guidelines have been clarified to improve the understanding and application of the GRI standards. GRI developed a document *Mapping G4 to GRI Standards* to show which standard has been changed or restructured (GRI, 2016).

Following the launch of the GRI standards, they consist of three universal standards and 33 subject-specific standards that include economic, environmental and social reporting methods. For companies and organizations that had already been reporting in accordance with G4, the impact in the process of sustainability reporting was relatively small. GRI standards are an important step for GRI to establish its organization as a future standard setting benchmark for sustainability reporting, in the same way that, for example, IASB is for accounting standards.

8.5 GRI's harmonization role with the EU, other initiatives and frameworks

The GRI guidelines are often used in combination with other international initiatives, frameworks, codes or guidelines for sustainability. Since 1997, GRI has strong links with the United Nations Environment Program (UNEP). Over the years, GRI has developed global strategic partnerships with the OECD, the UN Environment Programme and the UN Global Compact. GRI guidelines and standards have synergies with guidelines from the International Finance Corporation, the International Organization for Standardization, the UN Conference on Trade and Development, Principles for Responsible Investment, Earth Charter Initiative and International Integrated Reporting Council (IIRC).

To help companies and organizations with the application of GRI standards in conjunction with other guidelines and standards, GRI has shown the clear links to these other guidelines and standards since the G4 guidelines. GRI strives to serve as a platform for multiple stakeholders focusing on sustainability reporting to explore how exchanges in collaboration with investors, regulators and companies can improve transparency, governance and performance in issues related to the environmental, social aspects and corporate governance that encourage sustainable investment.

GRI has also been active in the formation of the IIRC to create the Integrated Reporting Framework, that is, integrate sustainability reporting with financial reporting (see Chapter 9). To achieve increased sustainability reporting standardization in practice, regulatory requirements are changing in the European Union. The *EU Directive 2014/95/EU – Directive on disclosure of non-financial and diversity information by certain large companies* has mentioned GRI as one preferred standard for sustainability reporting. Together with CSR Europe and Accountancy Europe, GRI has produced a document describing the main elements of the laws of the 28 member states and provides insight into how non-financial reporting has developed in Europe.

In the future, GRI will continue its cooperation with various organizations throughout the world to promote sustainability reporting.

8.6 Criticisms and challenges with GRI

There are both positive and negative aspects of applying GRI standards. The growing application of GRI guidelines has been partly driven by its potential benefits. Because of its flexibility and global reach, GRI standards open up opportunities for benchmarking, comparing and communicating social and environmental efforts from different companies and organizations across different industries and sectors (Willis 2003). GRI standards can serve as a tool for managing the reputation of companies and organizations and driving competitive advantages. Sustainability reports using GRI standards provide a platform for dialogue between companies, organizations and various stakeholders. These sustainability reports promote information that can support a variety of purposes, such as ethical investment, political positioning or academic research. Another positive point of view is that GRI's standards can be used for both internal and external reporting and can facilitate companies and organizations to get an idea of what has actually been done and also to be able to make improvements.

One criticism that has been put forward as one of the most problematic aspects of GRI's reporting model is its focus on the organizations "internal" performance. Since GRI encourages reporting of internal performance, there is the risk that the reporting promotes information that lacks information about the effects of the organization in relation to its external environment. This means that the framework risks promoting reports that mislead the reader about corporate sustainability development (Gray & Bebbington 2007).

Something that can be perceived negative is that the guidelines leave a lot of room for their own interpretations and adjustments for the user (Milne & Gray 2007). This can be explained by the fact that GRI's standards have been for a long time only guidelines and recommendations. The fact that companies themselves choose which application level they want to report on makes the comparability between the companies more difficult. Another negative aspect is that there are no requirements that say that all information must be included to prepare a report according to GRI (Milne & Gray 2013). Also, companies or organizations that use GRI for their sustainability reports need not to justify why they do not include all parts of the guidelines (Moneva, Archel & Correa 2006).

With GRI's move from guidelines to standards, it has begun to move sustainability reporting towards more robust reporting that reduces companies' opportunities for their own interpretations. Furthermore, GRI also tries to balance internal and external reporting interests. The fact that GRI has so far been solely voluntary information may change in the future, as EU Directive 2014/95 / EU-Non-financial reporting is a first step in regulating sustainability reporting. In the future, this will certainly lead to further regulation in sustainability reporting. This will propel further future challenges, such as increased assurance and auditing requirements of sustainability reports.

8.7 Summary

Since the 1990s, sustainability reporting has grown and changed significantly. While at the beginning only a few multinational companies voluntarily began reporting environmental and responsibility information about the company, the number of reporting companies has grown exponentially. The increase in significance has led to different guidelines providing support for companies in their quest to meet the requirements for sustainable manufacturing and reporting.

Among these guidelines in sustainability reporting, the most prominent is the GRI. In 1997, GRI was established by CERES and the Tellus Institute in the United States and was supported by the UNEP. In March 1999, the first draft of the GRI guidelines was presented to a group of organizations and companies interested in sustainability reporting. In 2001, the GRI guidelines were developed to include more key figures and parameters. Continued development to improve the first GRI guidelines resulted in the second generation (G2) of GRI guidelines. The first sector supplements were released in 2003 for the telecommunications industry. There were then additional sector supplements in the areas of financial services, the mining and metal industry as well as logistics and transport. In order to further improve transparency in companies and organizations' quest for increased sustainability, the third-generation (G3) GRI guidelines were released in 2006. GRI's G3 guidelines consist of two parts. The first part deals with principles and guidance that are important for determining the content, quality and boundaries of accounting. The second part consists of a set of standardized information. GRI's G3 guidelines also consist of three different application levels A, B and C, with the possibility of adding a "plus" (+) when independently reviewing the sustainability report. In March 2011, GRI published the G3.1 guidelines, which are an update. In May 2013, the fourth generation of GRI guidelines, G4, was launched. The previous application levels A, B and C were removed. In October 2016, GRI launched a new generation of its previous guidelines, but instead of calling these guidelines, the new version is called GRI Standards. The GRI Standards are effective since 2018 and replaced the G4 guidelines. The GRI Standards are issued by the GSSB, which is an independent standardization body created by GRI. They are based on the G4 guidelines. The G4 guidelines have not changed, and no new amendments have been added. This has been done to minimize the effects on sustainability reporting during the transition. The GRI standards are often used in combination with other international initiatives, frameworks, codes and guidelines for sustainability. Since 1997, GRI has strong ties with the UNEP. Over the years, GRI has developed global strategic partnerships with international organizations. There are both positive and negative aspects of applying GRI standards. GRI has also been active in the formation of the IIRC. Through its flexibility and global reach, GRI's standards enable benchmarking, comparing and communicating social and environmental efforts from different companies and organizations across different sectors and industries. At the same time, GRI's flexibility is something that can be seen as negative as the standards give a lot of room for their own interpretations and adjustments for the user.

Study questions

1 Why has it become increasingly important for companies to communicate the sustainability values that underpin their business?

2 On what four principles the G3 guidelines base the content of GRI sustainability reports?

3 What feature does the second part of GRI's G3 standard information guidelines have?
4 What are the four subcategories in the social category of the G3 guidelines?
5 What do the three different levels of application mean in GRI's G3 guidelines?
6 What is the difference in updating the G3 guidelines to G3.1?
7 What was the purpose of GRI with the G4 guidelines?
8 What are the main differences between the G3 / 3.1 guidelines and the G4 guidelines?
9 What does the transition from G4 guidelines to GRI Standards mean for companies and organizations?
10 Explain the role of GRI in harmonizing sustainability reporting in the EU and with other initiatives and frameworks.
11 What criticism was made against GRI's work?
12 What are the future challenges for GRI?

References

Brown, H. S., de Jong, M. & Lessidrenska, T. (2009). The rise of global reporting initiative (GRI) as a case of institutional entrepreneurship, *Environmental Politics*, Vol. 18 (2), pp. 182–200.

Gray, R. & Bebbington, J. (2007). Corporate sustainability: Accountability or impossible dream? in G. Arkinson, S. Dietz & E. Neumayer (ed.), *Handbook of sustainable development*, pp. 376–394, Cheltenham: Edward Elgar.

GRI (2000–2006). GRI Sustainability Reporting Guidelines–G3, www. globalreporting.org/resourcelibrary/G3-Guidelines-Incl-Technical-Protocol.pdf

GRI (2012). GRI G3 and G3.1 update–Comparison sheet, www. globalreporting. org/resourcelibrary/G3.1-Comparison-Sheet.pdf

GRI (2013a). www.globalreporting.org/resourcelibrary/GRI-An-introduction-to-G4.pdf

GRI (2013b). Overview of changes in Standard Disclosures from G3.1 to G4 Guidelines, www.globalreporting.org/resourcelibrary/GR   I-G4-Overview-Tables-G3.1-vs-G4.pdf

GRI (2016). Mapping G4 to the GRI Standards–disclosures full overview, www. globalreporting.org/standards/media/1098/mapping-g4-to-the-gri-standards-disclosures-full-overview.pdf

Milne, M. J. & Gray, R. (2007). Future prospects for corporate sustainability reporting, in J. Unerman, J. Bebbington & B. O'Dwyer (ed.), *Sustainability accounting and accountability*, pp. 184–207. London and New York: Routledge.

Milne, M. J. & Gray, R. (2013). W(h)ither ecology? The triple bottom line, the global reporting initiative, and corporate sustainability reporting, *Journal of Business Ethics*, Vol. 118 (1), pp. 13–29.

Moneva, J. M., Archel, P. & Correa, C. (2006). GRI and the camouflaging of corporate unsustainability, *Accounting Forum*, Vol. 30 (2), pp. 121–137.

Willis, A. (2003). The role of the global reporting initiative's sustainability reporting guidelines in the social screening investments, *Journal of Business Ethics*, Vol. 43, pp. 233–237.

9   Integrated reporting

Gunnar Rimmel

Abstract
This chapter provides an overview of integrated reporting <IR>, which has become a new development in sustainability reporting. IR has quickly become a well-known framework in the world and has begun to change corporate reporting. The big change is to integrate sustainability information with financial information. The chapter describes the development of IR as an organization whose ideas originate from South Africa's work with corporate governance codes, the so-called King Report, for the last 15 years. Furthermore, the chapter briefly presents how the International Integrated Reporting Council works with various organizations to strengthen sustainability reporting. It explains how integrated reporting framework has been developed and has found acceptance in use among companies worldwide. Concisely, the most important features in terms of content and structure of integrated reporting are described to provide an overview of how the method integrates traditional financial information with sustainability information. Finally, criticism and challenges are discussed with IR.

Learning outcomes:

After reading this chapter, you are expected to be able to:

*   Describe the origin and importance of integrated reporting;
*   Explain differences between the different capitals that play a central role in integrated reporting;
*   Explain basic concepts related to integrated reporting frameworks.

9.1 Introduction

In principle, the traditional corporate reporting model dates back to the early 1960s, when it focused solely on financial reports. Complementary information to the financial information in form of descriptive non-financial information became more and more interesting in the ensuing decades. Focus on shareholders increased, and financial information was criticized for not delivering satisfactory information about the companies' environment. Financial reports were criticized for not providing a realistic picture of the company, or enabling sufficiently good forecasts to predict future performance developments or providing insight into the company's value chain. During the 1980s, corporate reporting had developed a step further. Financial reports included not only the balance sheet and income statement or the first cash flow statements, but also the letter to the shareholders, the management report, information about corporate governance and remuneration to employees and environmental reporting.

While the financial information of the companies was criticized, the supplementary non-financial information was positively viewed as it provided more insight into the company's external factors that may influence the company's future development and results. This focus was of great interest in informing the various stakeholders, but the supplementary non-financial information resulted in information that was not always important to the shareholders. The supplementary information with its descriptive non-financial information was often about informing stakeholders about corporate social responsibility or sustainability. The trend continued, and, as shown in Chapter 7, the term triple bottom line was introduced in 1997. This meant that economic, environmental and social development was presented in the company reports. As shown in Chapter 8, this was the starting point for the Global Reporting Initiative, which aims to standardize sustainability reporting (Eccles & Serafeim, 2011).

In parallel with this development of presenting information on financial, environmental and social responsibility in the company reports, integrated reporting bases began to emerge in South Africa. In 1994, in South Africa, the first *King Code of Corporate Governance Principles*, commonly known as *King I*, was launched, named after Mervyn E. King. Mervyn E. King has been a judge of the Supreme Court of South Africa and was commissioned by the Government of South Africa to chair the King Committee to develop a corporate governance code. The King Report was developed in South Africa, as the country had begun its path to democracy. It was considered by the South African government that the private sector also needed a new corporate governance system. The King Report consisted of recommendations of rules of conduct for listed companies, banks and government companies. *King* I focused on the interests of stakeholders in an attempt to improve economic, social, ethical and environmental practices (SAICA, 2010). The main source of inspiration for publishing *King I* was the Cadbury Report (1992), as there are similarities in the *King I* recommendations. The World Summit on Sustainable in Johannesburg inspired Mervyn King to update *King I*.

The King Committee set up a working group to analyse the wide range of reporting attempts in the complex area of non-financial reporting. This work led to the second South African corporate governance report *King II*, which was published in 2002. This new report was inspired by the Global

Reporting Initiative (see Chapter 8) and triple bottom line (see Chapter 7) reporting. *King II* aimed at integrating sustainability reporting with companies' financial reports. The *King II* report introduced *Integrated Sustainability Reporting* as a concept. The application of *King II* was on a voluntary basis.

In September 2009, the *King III* report was presented, which is considered to be the first national attempt to release a corporate governance code requiring integrated reporting (IoDSA, 2009). *King III* emphasizes the importance of companies reporting annually their impact on the economic environment in which they operate and promoting awareness of both negative and positive effects. In addition, companies are asked to report on how to increase the positive effects, and reduce the negative effects on the economic life of their society. The vision that governance, strategy and sustainability work together and should not be separated is one of the fundamental principles of *King III* (IoDSA, 2009). The Global Reporting Initiative is recognized by *King III* as the accepted international standard for reporting non-financial information. *King III* builds "apply or explain" which means that companies can choose to apply the recommendations or explain the deviations. In March 2010, the Johannesburg Stock Exchange changed its listing agreement, making it compulsory for all listed companies at the Johannesburg Stock Exchange to comply with *King III*, which requires all information on sustainability and the statutory financial information to be integrated into the *integrated report*.

Mervyn King's work in South Africa and *King III*'s approval of the Global Reporting Initiative as the accepted international standard for reporting non-financial information led to increased collaboration that laid the foundation for a new organization.

9.2 International integrated reporting council – IIRC

In August 2010, the International Federation of Accountants (IFAC), the Global Reporting Initiative (GRI) and HRH the Prince of Wales' Accounting for Sustainability Project (A4S) initiated the International Integrated Reporting Committee (IIRC). In 2012, the IIRC was changed to the *International Integrated Reporting Council*. The IIRC's mission is to establish integrated reporting as a common business practice in the public and private sectors. Its vision is to adapt capital allocation and corporate behaviour to broader goals for financial stability and sustainable development through integrated reporting. The organization IIRC consists of a large group of different representatives such as companies, investors, not-for-profit organizations, academics, regulatory authorities, accounting standards, sustainability groups and other stakeholders.

With his background from integrated reporting in South Africa, Mervyn King became a central figure in the IIRC organization. Since 2011, Mervyn King is IIRC's chairman. Together with Paul Druckman, who was IIRC's CEO until 2017, Mervyn King pushed IIRC's work and development forward. The IIRC is based in London and is run as a multi-stakeholder in-itiative that seeks to link together different networks interested in integrated reporting. The IIRC has found broad institutional support from the A4S, GRI, IFAC, the Carbon Disclosure Project, the World Business Council of Sustainable Development and the World Intellectual Capital Initiative to de-velop a framework for producing integrated reports. At the same time, the IIRC began to establish a number of <IR> networks that include business networks, academic networks, professional accounting agencies, banking networks, insurance networks, investor networks, pension fund networks, technology initiatives and public administration networks.

As Figure 9.1 illustrates, the IIRC has a pronounced four-phase strategy. In Phase 1 Feasibility, from January 2001 to December 2011, the conceptual fea-sibility and market support for integrated reporting were determined. Phase 2 Creation, from January 2012 to September 2014, developed the international integrated reporting framework, focused on creating global awareness of in-tegrated reporting and encouraged experiments. Phase 3 Breakthrough, from October 2014 to 2017/2018, will achieve an important shift towards early use of the integrated reporting framework. Phase 4 Global use, from 2018 onwards, continued efforts to achieve a comprehensive use of an integrated reporting framework and established integrated reporting as a global norm in corporate reporting.

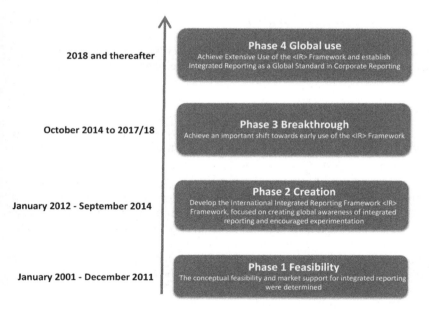

Figure 9.1 IIRC's four-phase strategy.

9.3 IIRC pilot programme

In 2011, the IIRC presented a discussion paper with the intention of initiating the practical work of creating an internationally accepted integrated reporting framework. The IIRC began Phase 2 with the start of the pilot programme. The participants in the pilot programme were about 100 companies and 30 institutional investors who shared their individual experiences with the introduction of integrated reporting. The companies that participated in the pilot phase covered 26 countries, ranging from banks, food producers, auditors, to energy and mining companies.

The participants in the pilot programme were responsible for testing and further developing the principles, content and application of integrated reporting. The first version of the IR framework was published in December 2013. The pilot programme continued until September 2014 so that the participants had time to test the integrated reporting framework for several reporting periods. Thus, the IIRC had the opportunity to evaluate the use and practice of integrated reporting. After the pilot programme ended, the *business network <IR> Business Network* and *investor network <IR> Investors Network* were formed. During the pilot programme, the EU has also begun to express interest in the work of the IIRC.

In the summer of 2015, IIRC restructured its organization and was given a new governance structure to increase the efficiency of its work. Nowadays, the IIRC has a board of 12 members and a council of 60 representatives from organizations interested in IIRC's work. Furthermore, IIRC created <IR> Framework Panel. The role of the framework panel is to recommend that the IIRC board propose any changes, modifications or updates to the IR framework. Thus, the IIRC has the opportunity to access resources and expertise, as well as networks with leading companies, investors and organizations to learn about experiences and insights to stimulate new developments.

9.4 IR framework

The IIRC published the IR Framework in 2013, which covers 35 pages (IIRC, 2013). As previously mentioned, there has been an increased interest in companies' value creation over time. How they create value can be explained by means of integrated reporting. In any case, this is the primary reasoning for the international IR framework. Integrated reporting promotes a more coherent and efficient corporate reporting strategy and aims at improving the quality of information available to investors to enable a more efficient and productive distribution of capital. The IR framework should support organizations that want to use integrated reporting. Through the IR framework's guidance, complex reports can be reported in a simpler way, reducing disconnected and static reporting (IIRC, 2011).

The IR framework developed by the IIRC is an important cornerstone for the development of integrated reporting, as it provides an internationally developed functioning foundation for creating a unified understanding of

Table 9.1 The key functions of the IR framework

Fundamental concepts	Guiding principles	Content elements
• Value creation for the organization and for others • The capitals • The value creation process	Seven principles that inform about the content and presentation of an integrated report: • Strategic focus and future orientation • Connectivity of information • Stakeholder relationships • Materiality • Conciseness • Reliability and completeness • Consistency and comparability	An integrated report should contain the following content elements: • Organizational overview and external environment • Governance • Business model • Risks and opportunities • Strategy and resource allocation • Performance • Outlook • Basis of preparation and presentation

integrated reporting that has not existed so far. The content of the framework focuses on the integrated report and defines its purpose, basic content and basic principles for creation (see Table 9.1).

In order to encourage the transition to integrated reporting, the IIRC has formulated the goals of the IR framework which clarify why companies should use integrated reporting.

The goals of the IR framework are:

- To support information needs of long-term investors by showing the consequences of broader and longer term.
- Reflect the interconnections between environmental, social, governance and economic factors in decisions that affect long-term results and position, which provides a clear link between sustainability and economic value.
- To provide organizations with a tool for systematic environmental and social factor reporting.
- Rebalance key ratios and leave the short-term perspective focused only on financial performance.

In the introductory summary of the IR framework, the IIRC makes it clear that the integrated report should have an integrated reporting system implemented in the company's information system that can handle integrated information, which, in turn, would reflect *integrated thinking* in integrated reports. The IIRC emphasizes its basic idea that integrated reporting for external users should ultimately represent internal reporting. This should lead to a management concept that considers the different dimensions and factors that affect the company's value (IIRC, 2013, p. 2). Thus, an integrated report is not just a reporting tool, but an expression of a certain corporate management concept. According to the IIRC, integrated reporting is a process that results in communication about value creation over time. Therefore, IIRC expresses its conviction that with the widespread use of integrated reporting in corporate practice, a more efficient allocation of capital will be achieved, and thus more financial stability and sustainability (IIRC, 2013, p. 2).

The IIRC did not consider that the IR framework should follow a rules-based approach, but instead be seen as a principle-based set of rules. Being principle-based means that the IR framework can give companies an appropriate answer on how to balance the great variety and the different circumstances that arise for different companies. For this reason, the framework does not determine any particular data types, data content, indicators or key figures that should be included in an integrated report. At the same time, the IR framework's guidance creates a sufficient degree of comparability so that relevant information is applied instead of information that is considered unnecessary. In other words, the IR framework aims to lead organizations on how to create value over time through a focus on flexibility and description rather than defining rules about measurements, data types, key figures or specific performance indicators.

Nevertheless, the IIRC tries to emphasize the normative nature of the IR framework. This can be seen when all passages in the IR framework are formulated as mandatory, when they are expressed as should (should). Furthermore, in the IR framework, the IIRC presses that every report should be called an integrated report which is based on the IR framework, and must therefore comply with all requirements specified in the IR framework or contain information on how and why the report differs from the IR framework. Similarly, the management should declare in the integrated report that it considers itself responsible for the content of the report. In the absence of such an explanation, the management of the integrated report shall state the role it played in the production of the integrated report.

9.5 The basic concept of the IR framework

According to the IIRC, the primary purpose of an integrated report is to explain to investors how an organization creates value over time. The purpose of an integrated report is to inform all stakeholders about an organization's ability to create value over time, including employees, customers, suppliers, business partners, local communities, legislators, regulators and decision-makers. An integrated report is intended to provide insight into the resources used by an organization. These resources are called capital in the IIRC's IR framework. At the same time, an integrated report will also explain how the organization interacts with the external environment, such as the outside world, and how different capital creates value in the short-, medium- and long-term.

Capital is a fundamental concept for IIRC's IR framework, which is based on the understanding that value is not created alone within an organization, but that value is affected by the external environment (including economic conditions, technical changes, societal problems or environmental challenges). The value is created through relationships with other stakeholders and is dependent on availability, affordability, quality and management of various resources.

Therefore, the IIRC believes that all organizations depend on different forms of capital for their success. The IR framework contains six different capitals that represent values that are increased, reduced or converted through the organization's operations. These six capital categories are categorized in the IR framework as financial capital, production capital, intellectual capital, human capital, social and relational capital and natural capital.

The IIRC defines the six capitals as follows:

1 *Financial capital* – funds obtained through financing (debt, equity or contribution) or generated through business or investment
2 *Manufactured capital* – physical objects (buildings, equipment, infrastructure) available for the production of goods or services
3 *Intellectual capital* – organizational, knowledge-based intangible assets, including rights (patents, copyrights, licenses, etc.) and organizational capital (silent knowledge, systems and procedures)
4 *Human capital* – people's competence, skills and experience, motivation and ability to innovate
5 *Social and relational capital* – institutions and relationships within and between communities, interest groups and other networks, and the opportunity to share information to improve individual and collective well-being (common norms and values, relationships with key stakeholders, intangible assets linked to brand and reputation)
6 *Natural capital* – all environmental resources and processes that provide goods or services that support the past, present or future prosperity of an organization (air, water, land, minerals, forests, biodiversity and environmental health)

An organization's ability to create value is important as it enables stakeholders to obtain a return on investment. The fact that the various capitals contribute to the value that the organization creates for stakeholders is reflected by a wide range of activities, interactions and relationships in the value-creating process. When the efforts of these different chapters are important for the organization's ability to create value, they should be included in the integrated report.

Although the concept of *value* is not defined in the IR framework, it can be noted that value need not be limited to financial results, as there is a broader concept in the IIRC's description of value creation process (see Figure 9.2) in the IR framework (Adams, 2013). Integrated reports are therefore not only designed to promote disclosure to only financial stakeholders, such as shareholders, but to all stakeholders, such as customers, suppliers, employees and regulators. Therefore, integrated reporting should show the *connectivity* between the various capital resources.

The value concept is directly related to the resources used. The different types of capital are seen as value resources that act as *inputs* to the business

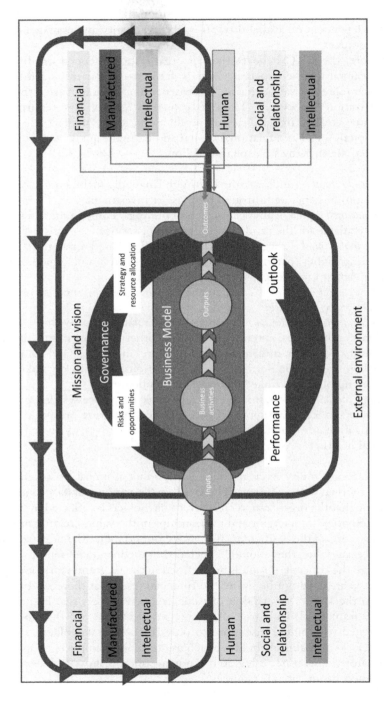

Figure 9.2 IIRC's value-creation process (courtesy of IIRC). International <IR> Framework, International Integrated Reporting Council, December 2013.

model and are increased, reduced or converted as part of the *business activities* into *outputs* that contribute to the company's results (*outcomes*). A key role for value creation is the company's business model, whose key structures and content as well as the associated strategic and operational resource allocations that create the opportunities and risks are therefore included in the IR framework. The business model and its connection to the various capitals and thus added value were illustrated by IIRC's value-creating process. Implementation of the company's mission and vision requires the management's understanding of the company's operations, which is reflected in the integrated report, and the strategic and operational decisions that have been made affecting the company's external environment.

9.6 Principles and content of the IR framework

Like any form of financial reporting, the use of integrated reporting and the production of an integrated report must also be based on principles to achieve the expected benefits. Therefore, the IIRC developed guiding principles that will form the basis for the preparation and presentation of an integrated report.

The following *seven principles* of the IR framework inform the content and presentation of an integrated report:

1   *Strategic focus and future orientation:* An integrated report should provide insight into the organization's strategy and how it relates to the organization's ability to create value in the short-, medium- and long-term and to its use and effects on the various six capitals.
2   *Connectivity of information:* An integrated report should show a comprehensive picture of the combination, connection and dependence between the factors that influence the organization's ability to create value over time.
3   *Stakeholder feedback:* An integrated report should provide insight into the nature and quality of an organization's relationships with key stakeholders, including how and to what extent the organization understands, takes into account and responds to their legitimate needs and interests.
4   *Materiality*; An integrated report should provide information on issues that significantly affect the organization's ability to create value in the short-, medium- and long-term.
5   *Conciseness:* An integrated report should be concise.
6   *Reliability and completeness:* An integrated report should cover all significant issues, both positive and negative, in a balanced way and without material errors.
7   *Compatibility and comparability*: The information in an integrated report should be presented on a basis that is consistent over time and in a way that enables comparison with other organizations insofar as it is essential to the organization's own ability to create value over time.

These guiding principles are applied individually and collectively to prepare and present an integrated report. Consequently, judgement is needed when applying them, especially when there is obviously tension between them (e.g., between summary and completeness).

In its Part II, the IR framework describes *eight content elements* that are important for an integrated report. The eight content elements should not be seen as a standard structure for an integrated report where information is displayed in a specific sequence or as isolated independent sections. Rather, information in an integrated report should be presented in a way that shows clear links between the various eight content elements, which are fundamentally linked to each other and should not be mutually exclusive. The content of an integrated report depends on the individual circumstances prevailing in different companies. Therefore, the IIRC specifies the eight content elements of the IR framework in the form of questions rather than checklists of specific tasks. When using the IR framework, companies must make assessments for each content element to determine what information and how the information should be reported.

According to the IIRC IR framework, an integrated report should contain and answer questions on the following eight content elements:

1   *Organizational overview and external environment* – What does the organization do and in what circumstances does it work?
2   *Governance* – How does the organizational governance structure support its ability to create value in the short-, medium- and long-term?
3   *Business model* – What is the organization's business model?
4   *Opportunities and risks* – What are the specific risks and opportunities that affect the organization's ability to create value in the short-, medium- and long-term, and how does the organization manage them?
5   *Strategy and resource allocation* – Where does the organization want to go and how does it intend to get there?
6   *Performance* – To what extent has the organization achieved its strategic objectives for the period and what are its results in terms of effects on capital?
7   *Future outlook* – What challenges and uncertainties an organization will likely encounter when following its strategy, and what are the potential consequences for its business model and future results?
8   *Basics of presentation* – How does the organization decide what is important to include in the integrated report and how are such issues quantified or evaluated?

These definitions contain a considerable scope of interpretation space. This currently leads to a great deal of flexibility, which in IIRC's continued work with future updates and changes will be fulfilled through the specification of the content. But the IR framework clearly shows that the IIRC considers that a distinction should be made between the integrated reporting as a process and the integrated report as a document. The first is the requirement to implement the second.

9.7 Criticism and challenges with integrated reporting

A discussion has arisen about whether the IIRC's work with the IR framework actually leads to more sustainability for companies. Criticism has been put forward by Milne and Gray (2013) that the IIRC's view of integrated reporting focused exclusively on investors and corporate investors and almost nothing on accountability or promoting sustainability. IIRC's start with integrated reporting was described as an experiment by companies that would instead have worked to produce better user-friendly information according to the triple-bottom agenda. According to Flower (2015), the auditors are determined to direct a new initiative that threatened their established position on accounting, as IIRC's original idea of integrated reporting was to increase reporting on sustainability.

Society faces many environmental and social challenges, and today's companies have far more demands than before. According to Thomson (2015), the IIRC must have its future main focus for integrated reporting on changes in corporate behaviour that motivates the adoption of a sustainable modernization of the company's activities. Another criticism that has been made relates to the capital market's continued focus on short-term profits instead of the companies' financial results. This can lead to the ability of companies to adopt various long-term changes in the value-creating process.

However, there are also many positive comments. Integrated reporting has the potential to overcome the limitations of traditional reporting, such as short-term, lack of link between financial and sustainability information (Atkins & Maroun, 2015). A study on the value relevance of integrated reports for capital market participants in South Africa clearly showed that investors consider integrated reports more value-relevant than traditional financial reports that increased even stronger after the requirement of integrated reporting was introduced in the listing agreement (Baboukardos & Rimmel, 2016).

Future challenges for the IIRC lie in minimizing the vast scope of the IR framework, as studies of reports from the pilot programme group showed very varied results (e.g. de Villiers et al., 2014; Rowbottom & Locke, 2016). At present, it is difficult to compare integrated reports with one another. Without more guidance on the content, indicators or a set of generic key figures, this will be difficult to achieve.

9.8 Summary

In principle, the traditional corporate reporting model dates back to the early 1960s, when it focused solely on financial reports. Complementary information to the financial information in the form of descriptive non-financial information became more and more interesting in the ensuing decades. In parallel with the development of presenting information on financial, environmental and social responsibility in the company reports, integrated reporting bases began to emerge in South Africa. In August 2010, IFAC, GRI and A4S founded the organization International Integrated Reporting

Committee, which, since 2012, is called the Integrated Reporting Council – IIRC. In 2011, the IIRC presented a discussion paper with the intention of initiating the practical work of creating an internationally accepted integrated reporting framework. The IIRC began a new phase of its work with the start of the pilot programme. The pilot programme consisted of approximately 100 companies and 30 institutional investors who shared their individual experiences with the introduction of integrated reporting. The IIRC published the IR framework in 2013. The IR framework is an important cornerstone for the development of integrated reporting, as it provides an internationally developed functioning foundation for creating a uniform understanding of integrated reporting. The IIRC believes that all organizations depend on different forms of capital for their success. The IR framework contains six different capitals that represent values that are increased, reduced or converted through the organization's operations. These six capital categories are categorized in the IR framework as financial capital, production capital, intellectual capital, human capital, social and relational capital and natural capital. Integrated reporting should show the connectivity between the various capital resources. The IR framework provides seven principles for the content and presentation of an integrated report. The IR framework describes eight content elements that are important for an integrated report. Integrated reporting has the potential to overcome the limitations of traditional reporting, such as short-term, lack of link between financial and sustainability information. But there has also been a discussion about whether the IIRC's work with the IR framework actually leads to more sustainability for companies. At present, it is difficult to compare integrated reports with one another. Without more guidance on the content, indicators or a set of generic key figures, this will be difficult to achieve.

Study questions

1 In what way does the work of the IIRC originate from the operations in South Africa?
2 Which organizations founded the International Integrated Reporting Committee?
3 What role does Mervyn King play in the development of IIRC's work?
4 What did the IIRC pilot programme mean?
5 How was work done with the IR framework?
6 What are the key functions of the IR framework?
7 What are the goals of the IR framework?
8 What is the basic concept of the IR framework?
9 What are the main differences between the different capitals of the IR framework?
10 What are the seven guiding principles in the IR framework?
11 What are the eight content elements of the IR framework?

12   How is the IR framework's value creation process explained?
13   What criticism was made against the work of the IIRC?
14   What are the future challenges for the IIRC?

References

Adams, C.A. (2013). "Sustainability reporting and performance management in Universities: Challenges and benefits", *Sustainability Accounting, Management and Policy Journal*, Vol. 4 (3), pp. 384–392.

Atkins, J. & Maroun, W. (2015). "Integrated reporting in South Africa in 2012", *Meditari Accountancy Research*, Vol. 23 (2), pp. 197–221.

Baboukardos, D. & Rimmel, G. (2016). "Relevance of accounting information under an integrated reporting approach: A research note", *Journal of Accounting and Public Policy*, Vol. 35 (4), pp. 437–452.

de Villiers, C. D., Rinaldi, L. & Unerman, J. (2014). "Integrated reporting: Insights, gaps and an agenda for future research", *Accounting, Auditing & Accountability Journal*, Vol. 27 (7), pp. 1042–1067.

Eccles, R. G. & Serafeim, G. (2011). *Accelerating the adoption of integrated reporting: CSR INDEX*. Rapperswil, Switzerland: InnoVatio Publishing Ltd.

Flower, J. (2015). "The international integrated reporting council: A story of failure", *Critical Perspectives on Accounting*, Vol. 27, pp. 1–17.

IIRC (2011). *Towards integrated reporting: Communicating value in the 21st century*, www.integratedreporting.org/wp- content/uploads/2011/09/IR-Discussion-Paper-2011_spreads.pdf.

IIRC (2013). *The international <IR> framework*, www.integratedreporting.org/wp-content/uploads/2015/03/13-12-08-THE-INTERNATIONAL-IR-FRAMEWORK-2-1.pdf.

Institute of Directors in Southern Africa (IODSA) (2009). *The King Code of Governance for South Africa (2009) and King Report on Governance for South Africa (2009) (King-III)*, Johannesburg: Lexis Nexus South Africa.

Milne, M. J. & Gray, R. (2013). "W(h)ither ecology? The triple bottom line, the global reporting initiative, and corporate sustainability reporting". *Journal of Business Ethics*, Vol. 118 (1), s. 13–29.

Rowbottom, N. & Locke, J. (2016). "The emergence of <IR>", *Accounting and Business Research*, Vol. 46, pp. 83–115.

SAICA (2010). *The King Report on Corporate Governance*, www.saica.co.za/Technical-Information/LegalandGovernance/King/tabid/626/language/en-ZA/Default.aspx#king1.

Thomson, I. (2015). "But does sustainability need capitalism or an integrated report': A commentary on 'The International Integrated Reporting Council: A story of failure'", *Critical Perspectives on Accounting*, Vol. 27, pp. 18–22.

International Integrated Reporting Council (IIRC) website:

www.integratedreporting.org

10 Accounting communication for sustainability

Svetlana Sabelfeld

Abstract

This chapter discusses sustainability accounting from communication perspective. The increasing length of annual reports and sustainability reports, its variation (integrated, combined, independent), the use of media (websites and social media) and society's growing use of public information are indicative of the growing importance of accounting communication for sustainability.

The chapter begins with the questions why, to whom and how information about environmental and social aspects of the business is communicated, both internally in companies and externally, from company to various stakeholders. The focus in Section 10.1 is on the motives (10.1.1), target groups (10.1.2) and channels (10.1.3) for sustainability reporting. Sections 10.2 and 10.3 discuss how sustainability information is communicated externally. Here we present communication strategies (10.2) and linguistic strategies (10.3) used by companies in sustainability reporting. The rest of the chapter provides an overview of research traditions in the area of accounting communication (10.4), as well as research methods (10.5) that can help researchers to study aspects of accounting communication of sustainability.

Learning outcomes:

After reading the chapter, the reader is expected to be able to:

- Describe motives that drive companies to report on sustainability.
- Explain differences between various channels for accounting communication of sustainability and link them to the users´ perspectives.
- Explain communication strategies for reporting sustainability aspects.
- Explain theoretical perspectives and research traditions in the field of accounting communication for sustainability.

10.1 Communicating sustainability – why, to whom and how?

The communicative function of accounting has long been recognized and discussed as one of the central ones along with the function of measurement. Accounting communication involves a wide range of activities, such as collecting and processing information and selecting media, language and rhetoric to convey a message to a specific type of audience about company's development and outcomes. Studying accounting communication allows us to understand and analyze channels and media that organizations use to communicate with stakeholders, as well as the stories, messages and images, constructed by organizations and projected towards the external audience.

By using the communication perspective, accounting researchers examine the content of communicated information in relation to different stakeholders. The premise is that sustainability reporting is seen as a language that managers use to communicate with their various stakeholders, to signal about value drivers and future potential of the company. By analyzing the corporate rhetoric and its surrounding context, we can better understand whether management takes care of its employees, whether it cares about the product and service quality and whether the company cares about its impact on the environment or not. Thus, important parts of the analysis are managers who produce sustainability information, the content of sustainability report, the recipient of the information and a specific context in which the information is produced and used.

Originally, the perspective of accounting communication has its roots in Aristotle's model of communication and rhetoric, which consists of three essential parts: "speaker", "message" and "listener". The interaction between the speaker and the listener is considered to be crucial in the communication process (Bedford & Baladouni, 1962; Merkl-Davies & Brennan, 2017; Sabel-feld, 2013). Depending on how sustainability information is communicated, the company's stakeholders may react differently. Consumers may choose or refuse to buy products and services, investors may retain or sell the company's shares, different stakeholders may write positive or negative feedback in social media, employees may leave or stay with the company. Thus, in response to stakeholders' various needs for information, companies are motivated to engage in sustainability reporting. Next sections describe motives that drive accounting communication for sustainability and address the questions to whom and how sustainability accounts are communicated.

10.1.1 Motives behind sustainability reporting

In Chapter 2, a number of theoretical perspectives explain why companies present sustainability reports. This section specifically links motivational factors to accounting communication for sustainability. A strong motivation for management is to increase trust from various stakeholders through communicating a "story" about how the company's internal sustainability works and creates value for society (and not just for investors). Increased trust can, in turn, lead to a better reputation in the capital market and, consequently, an increased corporate value. Another motive is legitimacy in society that the company creates through its external communication of sustainability.

Legitimacy means that the company's operations, products and services are accepted in society. Acceptance in society is a condition for company's survival in the long run, through the times of financial crises and downturns. This can be linked to the fourth motive, namely, to build closer relationships with the increasingly conscious stakeholders and meet their needs for information related to social, environmental and economic aspects of the business. Finally, the fourth motive is to gain a competitive advantage by becoming a role model for others in the area of sustainability reporting, or being, at least, as good as the competitors. These motives have a strong connection to each other. What matters from the societal perspective is whether the company takes sustainability issues seriously in its internal decision-making and operations and whether the information communicated externally reflects the internal corporate sustainability work.

10.1.2 Target group for sustainability communication

In contrast to financial information, sustainability information is communicated to a much wider group of stakeholders. Figure 2.1 in Chapter 2 (p. 19) illustrates stakeholder model from the long-term sustainability perspective.

The complexity of accounting communication for sustainability is that different types of recipients may have opposite interests and information needs regarding different aspects of sustainability. While investors and other capital market actors look for a positive relationship between corporate sustainability activities and shareholder value, maximization of financial value is not always a priority issue for local communities, consumers, NGOs, media and politicians. For example, the tourism industry can have a significant positive economic impact in local communities, but also a significant negative effect on the local natural environment, affecting the lives of local inhabitants and biodiversity. For a company, it is therefore important to find a balance between the needs of different stakeholders and to be in a continuous dialogue with them in order to survive in the communities in which they operate. However, here, there is a risk that companies and other organizations engage in hypocrisy behaviour when trying to address different stakeholders' needs through communication (Cho, Laine, Roberts, & Rodrigue, 2015).

To summarize, the logic of short-term profit maximization of some stakeholders can be in conflict with a long-term survival logic of other stakeholders. It makes accounting communication for sustainability complex, and sometimes controversial. As such, to find solutions to social problems sometimes requires freedom from the economic logic of profit maximization. What would the company prioritize and how these priorities are mirrored in the corporate accounts of sustainability are therefore vital issues from the societal, environmental and economic sustainability point of view.

10.1.3 Channels for reporting the communication of sustainability

Because there are different types of recipients for sustainability information, companies use different channels to communicate about their sustainability work. The channels used may also vary, depending on the company's size.

Overall, the stakeholders' expectation regarding which information is important is a moving target that needs to be revised over time (Morsing & Schultz, 2006). With the fast development of web-based technologies, stakeholder awareness has increased significantly in recent decades. It means that consumers, customers, suppliers and other stakeholders can share information anytime and anywhere, even if the company does not want to disclose it (Colleoni, Arvidsson, Hansen, & Marchesini, 2011). That is why, companies and other organizations try to avoid the situation when other stakeholders reveal sensitive information, and are prepared to disclose information by using a number of channels such as annual reports, integrated reports, separate sustainability reports, press releases, corporate websites and social media.

Annual report is one of the most common mediums where sustainability aspects are communicated as part of a management report or part of the annual report. As one of the first transnational regulatory initiatives, the European Union (EU) parliament introduced the EU Directive2014/95/EU as regards disclosure of non-financial and diversity information by certain large undertakings and groups (La Torre, Sabelfeld, Blomkvist, Tarquinio, & Dumay, 2018).

Sustainability report produced separately from the annual financial report is also a frequently used medium for communication with stakeholders. The advantage of a separate sustainability report (especially those designed according to GRI) is that there may be opportunities for comparisons between different reports, for example, over time or between companies within the same industry. The disadvantage, however, is that separate sustainability reports become too extensive in number of pages, and thus irrelevant to investors because they are disconnected from the financial information presented in annual reports. The EU directive, mentioned earlier, allows companies to disclose sustainability accounts in a separate sustainability report.

Integrated report is another format for sustainability communication proposed by the International Integrated Reporting Council in 2013 (see Chapter 9). As a communication channel, an integrated report provides the opportunity to present sustainability as an integral part of company's business model and value creation. The challenge, however, is that the integrated reporting framework and its main concepts can be interpreted in different ways and thus result in reports that are difficult to compare with each other.

Corporate websites have become an increasingly common place for communicating sustainability. On the web, the information can be grouped under different headings tailored to specific stakeholders, which is a great advantage if the information is to be communicated to a broad group of stakeholders.

Sustainability information can be part of the investor relations section of a company's website where reporting is directed at investors and other financial market actors. Alternatively, the sustainability information can be published under a separate Corporate Social Responsibility (CSR) section of the corporate website, addressing environmental, social and employee-related issues and supply chain policies, for example.

Social media is a communication channel where companies have the opportunity to engage in a dialogue with their stakeholders, such as consumers, environmental activists and other representatives of the society. Moreover, through social media, companies have the opportunity to listen to their stakeholders and identify unexpected concerns. By receiving feedback from the stakeholders, the company has the opportunity to analyze future risks and opportunities, which is an important part of the internal sustainability work. However, research shows that companies seldom use this opportunity. Previous study observing social media communication found that most companies were using social media with the purpose to promote themselves, providing a one-sided and too positive image of selves. Because of the fear of potential scepticism of stakeholders, companies tend to use websites as a traditional one-way communication media for corporate self-presentation (Insch, 2008).

However, from the stakeholders' perspective, the diffusion of social media, such as Twitter and Facebook, means that stakeholders are no longer passive recipients of the communication. Instead, they are increasingly involved in both the process of creation and evaluation of content of corporate reports (Dellarocas, 2003). This sparked great potential but also exposed companies to pressures and challenges that require a clearer strategy for what to present and how to present their commitment to sustainability (Dawkins 2004). The following two sections describe communication strategies that companies use in their sustainability reporting, as well as linguistic rhetorical strategies used in this communication.

10.2 Communication strategies in sustainability reporting

Morsing and Schultz (2006, p. 326) have developed a model for communication strategies used by companies in their accounting communication of sustainability. Table 10.1 illustrates three main strategies: *information strategy, response strategy and commitment strategy.*

Information strategy means that accounting communication of sustainability is only seen as a technical dissemination of information to recipients, a linear accounting communication (Sabelfeld 2016). Here, the company management decides which sustainability-related disclosures should be provided to stakeholders. The content is based on company's own definition of what sustainability is and what dimensions to include in sustainability report.

Table 10.1 Communication strategies for reporting sustainability

	Information Strategy	*Response Strategy*	*Involvement Strategy*
Type of communication	Public information, one-way communication	Two-way asymmetric Communication	Two-way symmetric communication
Sensemaking and sensegiving	Sensegiving	From sensemaking to sensegiving	Sensemaking and sensegiving as iterative progressive processes
Stakeholders	Request more information on corporate CSR efforts	Must be reassured that the company is ethical and socially responsible	Co-construct corporate CSR efforts
The role of the stakeholder	Stakeholder influence: support or oppose	Stakeholders respond to corporate actions	Stakeholders are involved, participate and suggest corporate actions
Identification of CSR focus	Decided by top management	Decided by top management. Investigated in feedback via opinion polls, stakeholder dialogue, networks and partnerships	Negotiated concurrently in interaction with stakeholders
Strategic communication task	Inform stakeholders about favourable corporate CSR decisions and actions	Demonstrate to stakeholders how the company integrates their concerns	Invite and establish a frequent, systematic and pro-active dialogue with stakeholders, i.e. opinion makers, corporate critics, the media, etc.
Corporate communication department's task	Design an appealing concept message	Identify relevant stakeholders	Build relationships
Third-party endorsement of CSR initiatives	Unnecessary	Integrated element of surveys, rankings and opinion polls	Stakeholders are themselves involved in corporate CSR messages

Source: Morsing and Schultz (2006, p. 326).

Response strategy is based on a two-way asymmetric communication model, which means that even if the communication goes to both directions, the stakeholders do not influence the company's decisions and actions. However, the company tries to influence the stakeholders' behaviour through the language used in communication. By involving stakeholders in the sustainability reporting process, they make the company's sustainability work feel more relevant and "fair" to the stakeholders. In essence, this approach is not a big step away from the one-sided communication strategy.

Involvement strategy requires corporations to take stakeholder dialogue seriously. Here, the companies can still try to persuade their stakeholders, but the persuasion comes from both the stakeholders and from the company (both ways). In other words, companies and stakeholders in their dialogues try to convince each other about the changes needed in the process. It is the symmetrical communication that can lead to changes, both on the company's and stakeholders' side, which Morsing and Schultz (2006) call a progressive iterative process of sensemaking and sensegiving. By using this communication strategy, companies aim to build relationships with their stakeholders. The ambition is thus not only limited to influencing their stakeholders, but companies also allow stakeholders to influence corporate decisions and actions in the search of new opportunities for change.

10.3 Linguistic strategies in sustainability reporting

Research has shown that many companies, especially those having a negative social and environmental impact, create too positive and distorted image of their business in sustainability reports, and may even entirely avoid communicating on sensitive aspects, shifting the focus to less sensitive aspects. Previous studies have identified a number of rhetorical strategies used in sustainability reports for this purpose, for example, when addressing environmental impact issues. Based on Thompson (1990) model, Ferguson, de Aguiar and Fearfull (2016, p. 283) introduced linguistic strategies, or rhetorical tactics, which companies can use in communication of their environmental impact (Table 10.2).

In contrast to the financial reports, sustainability reports are more descriptive and less regulated, which leaves room for linguistic manipulation, or impression management, a term often used by accounting researchers (Brennan & Merkl-Davies, 2013).

10.4 Theoretical framework for external accounting communication for sustainability

Researchers of accounting communication (Merkl-Davies & Brennan, 2017) have summarized the field of external accounting communication and identified theoretical perspectives used in the field. The theoretical framework presented in Table 10.3 is relevant for the context of sustainability reporting. The framework's different theoretical angles can be used in the analysis of

Table 10.2 Linguistic rhetorical strategies in communication of sustainability

Goal	Linguistic strategy	Description
Legitimation	Rationalization	Justify or rationalize social relations
	Universalization	Argues that institutional relations that serve a few groups are benefitting everyone
	Narrativization	Current social relations are located within traditions and stories from the past
Dissimulation	Displacement	Use of a term that normally refers to something else
	Euphemization	
	Trope	Shift in descriptive language that gives social relations a positive "spin"
		Includes synecdoche, metonymy and metaphor
Unification	Standardization	Standardization of language and symbols to create a union of individuals or groups
	Symbolization of unity	Adoption of a shared set of symbols to create a collective identity among groups
Fragmentation	Differentiation	Emphasis on differences between groups
	Expurgation of the other	Creating a common enemy – to unite people in opposition
Reification	Naturalization	Presenting situations as natural and as the outcome of a natural historical process
	Externalization	Portraying situations without their historical background
	Nominalization	Actors and action within a sentence are turned into nouns

Source: Ferguson et al. (2016, p. 283).

corporate accounting communication for sustainability, depending on the focus of research question.

According to Merkl-Davies and Brennan (2017, p. 436), the term "external accounting communication" is more useful than "corporate reporting", if one wants to refer to communication of accounts to external stakeholders. The term "reporting" originates from Latin, "the words re- (back) and portare (to carry, to bring), i.e., to carry/bring back" (Merkl-Davies & Brennan, 2017, p. 436), which literally means that corporate reporting focuses on the information about past events rather than on the communication process.

The field of accounting communication for sustainability is part of accounting research field, focusing on the communication between companies and various stakeholders. According to Merkl-Davies and Brennan (2017, pp. 436–437), accounting communication can be studied as a specific context in which the communication phenomenon takes place. Here, communication can be studied through various narrative documents produced by organizations (Merkl-Davies & Brennan, 2017). Accounting communication can also be seen as a social practice. Within this perspective, corporate communications is studied in specific cultural and institutional context surrounding organization (Craig, 2006). Accounting communication can also be studied as a medium, where researchers focus on various communication channels, tools and formats.

There are two major theoretical perspectives in accounting communication research. The first is functionalist-behavioural transmission perspective of where accounting communication is seen as one-way transmission of information to its recipients. Within this perspective, communication is framed as technology providing a range of cognitive, emotional and behavioural effects (Merkl-Davies & Brennan, 2017). The other is symbolic-interpretive narrative perspective, defining accounting communication as a two-way social interaction that produces and reproduces shared meanings and social reality. This perspective is based on interpretive and critical social science research traditions (Fiske, 2010), emphasizing cultural and political aspects of communication, in which negotiation of meanings and construction of reality take occur (Craig, 2007). While the functionalist perspective focuses on analyzing words, pictures and facial expressions of the individuals constituting communication, the interpretive perspective views accounting communication as a social phenomenon, which means that all behaviours, including silence, create meaning and thus constitute communication. Thus, the receiver can interpret the meaning of silence when expecting corporate accounts about particular problems or events.

Table 10.3 illustrates a typology developed by Merkl-Davies and Brennan (2017, pp. 435–436), outlining research traditions in the two aforementioned theoretical perspectives, including examples of specific theories and studies of accounting communication.

10.5 Research methods for accounting communication of sustainability

As shown in Table 10.3, research in accounting communication may have different focus, depending on research tradition and perspective. The functionalist perspective views accounting communication as one-way transmission of information. Scientists sharing this view, conduct, for example, *mathematical* experimental studies of how companies' information affects financial analysts' assessment of the corporate value (Barton & Mercer 2005; Stocken, 2000). Within this perspective, researchers can also study *socio-psychological* and *system-oriented* aspects of "communicators" (corporate leaders) and the ways they explain good and bad news. This can be done using a longitudinal statistical cross-sectional analysis and comparative content analysis of company reports to elucidate the phenomenon of impression management (Aerts, 2001; Hooghiemstra, 2010) and its retrospective sensemaking in narrative sections of annual reports (Aerts, 2005; Merkl-Davies, Brennan, & McLeay, 2011). The studies in the functionalist perspective are usually based on a large number of observations that require statistical processing of data.

Table 10.3 Theoretical perspectives and research traditions in accounting communication

Research Tradition	Focus in analysis	Theories and references
A. The functionalist perspective of accounting communication (information, one-way communication)		
1 Mathematical tradition	Message transmission	• Mathematical theory of communication (Shannon and Weaver, 1949), focus on message
2 Socio-psychological tradition	Information processing, focus on communicator	• Attribution theory (Aerts, 2005; Hooghiemstra, 2010) • Accountability theory, (Merkl-Davies, Brennan, & McLeay, 2011) • Belief-adjustment model (Hogarth & Einhorn, 1992)
3 Cybernetic/system-oriented tradition	Connection, system, interdependence, focus on communicator	• Organizational information theory (Aerts, 2005; Merkl-Davies et al., 2011; Weick, 1979) • Control theory
B. Symbolic-interpretative narrative perspective of accounting communication (interactive, dialogic accounting communication)		
4 Semiotic tradition	Sign, signals, focus on message	• Theory of the linguistic sign (Davison, 2004; Saussure, 1916; Tinker, 1991)
5 Rhetorical tradition	Argument, persuasion	• Rhetorical theory – Aristotle, focus on organization, relationship (Brennan & Merkl-Davies, 2014; Green, 2001; Higgins & Walker, 2010) • Ideology-sustaining rhetoric, focus on organization (Craig & Amernic, 2004a) • Framing theory, focus on communicator (Amernic, Craig, & Tourish, 2007; Entman, 2007) • Theory of dialogism, focus on relationships (Bakhtin, 1981; Brennan, Merkl-Davies, & Beelitz, 2013) • Theory of objective rhetorical situation, focus on relationship (Bitzer, 1968) • Theory of subjective rhetorical situation, focus on communicator (Vatz, 1973)

(Continued)

Research Tradition	Focus in analysis	Theories and references
6 Phenomenological tradition	Interpretation, meaning	• Theory of the symbolic meaning of communication – cultural hermeneutics, focus on society (Prasad & Mir, 2002) • Theory of distanciation, focus on message (Milne, Tregidga, & Walton, 2009; Ricoeur, 1976) • Speech act theory, focus on message (Ng & Cock, 2002; Ricoeur, 1978) • Reader-response theory, focus on message (Fish, 1980)
7 Socio-cultural tradition	Values, norms, beliefs	• Media agenda-theory, focus on media (Brown & Deegan, 1998; Kent & Zunker, 2013) • Speech–act theory, focus on message (Palmer, King, & Kelleher, 2004) • Impression management theory, focus on communicator (Cho & Roberts, 2010; Goffman, 1978) • Conversational analysis, focus on conversation (Brennan & Conroy, 2013)
8 Critical tradition	Power, dominance, conflict Focus on society	• Marxism (Preston, Wright, & Young, 1996) • Habermas/Frankfurt School (Craig & Amernic, 2004b; Yuthas, Rogers, & Dillard, 2002) • Critical rhetoric (Moerman & van der Laan, 2007) • Post-colonialism (Kamla, 2007) • Foucault (Hartt, Mills, Mills, & Durepos, 2012) • Critical discourse analysis (Beelitz & Merkl-Davies, 2012; Merkl-Davies & Koller, 2012; Tregidga, Milne, & Kearins, 2014)

Source: Merkl-Davies and Brennan (2017, pp. 435–436).

Within the symbolic-interpretive narrative perspective, researchers view accounting communication as an interaction or dialogue between the actors involved in the communication. According to Table 10.3, it consists of five different traditions – semiotic, rhetorical, phenomenological, socio-cultural and critical tradition. Common denominator for these traditions is that they focus on the language in communication, that is, messages, discourses, arguments and the way meaning is shaped by actors, their power relations, norms and cultures. To assess these aspects, this research perspective requires qualitative methods. Davison (2004) and Crowther, Carter and Cooper (2006) are two studies that represent the *semiotic tradition*, where linguistic and semiotic aspects of companies' annual reports are studied using qualitative analysis of text, images, figures and other visualization techniques used in accounting communication. Studies that focus on management rhetoric and persuasion strategies belong to the *rhetorical tradition* and use rhetorical analysis of reports or verbal communication between company management and stakeholders (see, e.g., Brennan, et al., 2013; Higgins & Walker, 2010).

Furthermore, within the *phenomenological tradition,* researchers focus on the meaning that is created in the communication, which can be studied using discourse analysis of text (see Milne, Tregidga, & Walton, 2009; Prasad & Mir, 2002). In contrast, studies that analyze *socio-cultural* aspects of communication build their results on a larger number of observations by using both quantitative and qualitative approaches to content analysis (see, e.g., Cho & Roberts, 2010; Palmer, King, & Kelleher, 2004). Finally, the *critical tradition* is represented by researchers using critical rhetorical analysis (Craig & Amernic, 2004a), critical discourse analysis (Merkl-Davies & Koller, 2012) and qualitative longitudinal analysis of corporate communication and information (Williams & Adams, 2013; Yuthas, Rogers, & Dillard, 2002).

10.6 Summary and reflection

From the discussion of motives, audiences, channels and approaches to accounting communication of sustainability, it can be summarized that sustainability information can be communicated strategically with the aim of influencing stakeholder decisions and actions. If sustainability is integrated in company's business model and operations, the company becomes more open in its communication of sustainability to the stakeholders, because the company gains long-term benefits from being legitimate and trusted in the society. The problem arises when companies do not behave sustainably and start painting a picture of "a sustainable organisation" by using various communication strategies. Studying organizational accounts and narratives of sustainability work by using theoretical perspectives and methods mentioned in this chapter, enables researchers to relate the text, numbers and pictures to the needs of stakeholders and also to companies' commitment and actions, which is important in the assessment of the credibility of accounting communication for sustainability.

Control questions (1–10)

1 Explain motives that drive companies to report on sustainability.
2 Describe different types of stakeholder groups and users of sustainability information.

3 What are the differences between various channels for accounting communication? Link the discussion to the user perspective.
4 What communication strategies do companies use when communicating about their social and environmental impact?
5 Explain differences between information strategy, response strategy and engagement strategy.
6 What linguistic strategies do companies use when communicating about their social and environmental impact? Discuss the linguistic strategies from a critical perspective.
7 Explain two major research perspective in the field of accounting communication.
8 Explain differences between different research traditions for accounting communication.
9 What types of research questions can each above mentioned research tradition address?
10 What research methods can be used within the two major theoretical perspectives on accounting communication for sustainability?

References

Aerts, W. (2001). Inertia in the attributional content of annual accounting narratives. *European Accounting Review, 10,* 3–32.

Aerts, W. (2005). Picking up the pieces: Impression management in the retrospective attributional framing of accounting outcomes. *Accounting, Organizations and Society,* Vol. 30, pp. 493–517.

Amernic, J., Craig, R., & Tourish, D. (2007). The transformational leader as pedagogue, physician, architect, commander, and saint: Five root metaphors in Jack Welch's letters to stockholders of General Electric. *Human Relations,* Vol. 60, pp. 1839–1872.

Bakhtin, M. (1981). Discourse in the novel, In M. Holquist (ed.), *The dialogic imagination* (pp. 259–422). Austin: University of Texas Press.

Barton, J., & Mercer, M. (2005). To blame or not to blame: Analysts' reactions to external explanations for poor financial performance. *Journal of Accounting and Economics,* Vol. 39 (3), pp. 509–533.

Bedford, N. M., & Baladouni, V. (1962). A communication theory approach to accountancy. *The Accounting Review,* Vol. 37, p. 650.

Beelitz, A., & Merkl-Davies, D. M. (2012). Using discourse to restore organisational legitimacy: 'CEO-speak'after an incident in a German nuclear power plant. *Journal of Business Ethics,* Vol. 108, pp. 101–120.

Bitzer, L. F. (1968). The rhetorical situation. *Philosophy & Rhetoric,* Vol. 1, pp. 1–14.

Brennan, N. M., & Conroy, J. P. (2013). Executive hubris: The case of a bank CEO. *Accounting, Auditing & Accountability Journal,* Vol. 26 (2), pp. 172–195.

Brennan, N. M., & Merkl-Davies, D. M. (2013). Accounting narratives and impression management. In L. Jack, J. Davisson and R. Craig (eds) *The Routledge companion to accounting communication* (pp. 123–146). London: Routledge.

Brennan, N. M., & Merkl-Davies, D. M. (2014). Rhetoric and argument in social and environmental reporting: The Dirty Laundry case. *Accounting, Auditing & Accountability Journal,* Vol. 27 (4), pp. 602–633.

Brennan, N. M., Merkl-Davies, D. M., & Beelitz, A. (2013). Dialogism in corporate social responsibility communications: Conceptualising verbal interaction between organisations and their audiences. *Journal of Business Ethics*, Vol. 115, pp. 665–679.

Brown, N., & Deegan, C. (1998). The public disclosure of environmental performance information—A dual test of media agenda setting theory and legitimacy theory. *Accounting and Business Research*, Vol. 29, pp. 21–41.

Cho, C. H., Laine, M., Roberts, R. W., & Rodrigue, M. (2015). Organized hypocrisy, organizational façades, and sustainability reporting. *Accounting, Organizations and Society*, Vol. 40, pp. 78–94.

Cho, C. H., & Roberts, R. W. (2010). Environmental reporting on the internet by America's Toxic 100: Legitimacy and self-presentation. *International Journal of Accounting Information Systems*, Vol. 11, pp. 1–16.

Colleoni, E., Arvidsson, A., Hansen, L. K., & Marchesini, A. (2011). Measuring corporate reputation using sentiment analysis. In *Proceedings of the 15th International Conference on Corporate Reputation: Navigating the Reputation Economy, New Orleans, USA*.

Craig, R., & Amernic, J. (2004a). The deployment of accounting-related rhetoric in the prelude to a privatization. *Accounting, Auditing & Accountability Journal*, Vol. 17, pp. 41–58.

Craig, R. J., & Amernic, J. H. (2004b). Enron discourse: The rhetoric of a resilient capitalism. *Critical Perspectives on Accounting*, Vol. 15, pp. 813–852.

Craig, R. T. (2006). Communication as a practice. In G.J. Shepherd, J.St.John, T.Striphas (eds) *Communication as… : Perspectives on theory*. Sage Publications, London, pp. 38.

Craig, R. T. (2007). Pragmatism in the field of communication theory. *Communication Theory*, Vol. 17, pp. 125–145.

Crowther, D., Carter, C., & Cooper, S. (2006). The poetics of corporate reporting: Evidence from the UK water industry. *Critical Perspectives on Accounting*, Vol. 17, pp. 175–201.

Davison, J. (2004). Sacred vestiges in financial reporting. *Accounting, Auditing & Accountability Journal*, Vol. 17, pp. 476–497.

Dellarocas, C. (2003). The digitization of word of mouth: Promise and challenges of online feedback mechanisms. *Management science*, Vol. 49 (10), pp. 1407–1424.

Entman, R. M. (2007). Framing bias: Media in the distribution of power. *Journal of communication*, Vol. 57, pp. 163–173.

Ferguson, J., de Aguiar, T. R. S., & Fearfull, A. (2016). Corporate response to climate change: Language, power and symbolic construction. *Accounting, Auditing & Accountability Journal*, Vol. 29, pp. 278–304.

Fish, S. E. (1980). *Is there a text in this class?: The authority of interpretive communities*. Cambridge, MA: Harvard University Press.

Fiske, J. (2010). *The John Fiske collection: Introduction to communication studies*. New York: Routledge.

Goffman, E. (1978). *The presentation of self in everyday life*. Harmondsworth, London: Allen Lane.

Green, S. E. (2001). *Rhetoric and the institutionalization of takeover defenses in the S & P 1500 from 1975–1998*. Cambridge, MA: Harvard University .

Hartt, C., Mills, A. J., Mills, J. H., & Durepos, G. (2012). Markets, organizations, institutions and national identity. *Critical perspectives on international business*, Vol. 8, pp. 14–36.

Higgins, C., & Walker, R. (2010). Strategies of persuasion in social/environmental reporting. In *APIRA 2010: Proceedings of the 6th Asia Pacific Interdisciplinary Research in Accounting Conference* (pp. 1–24): University of Sydney, Australia.

Hogarth, R. M., & Einhorn, H. J. (1992). Order effects in belief updating: The belief-adjustment model. *Cognitive Psychology,* Vol. 24, pp. 1–55.

Hooghiemstra, R. (2010). Letters to the shareholders: A content analysis comparison of letters written by CEOs in the United States and Japan. *The International Journal of Accounting,* Vol. 45, pp. 275–300.

Insch, A. (2008). Online communication of Corporate Environmental Citizenship: A study of New Zealand's electricity and gas retailers. *Journal of Marketing Communications,* Vol. 14 (2), pp. 139–153.

Kamla, R. (2007). Critically appreciating social accounting and reporting in the Arab MiddleEast: A postcolonial perspective. *Advances in International Accounting,* Vol. 20, pp. 105–177.

Kent, P., & Zunker, T. (2013). Attaining legitimacy by employee information in annual reports. *Accounting, Auditing & Accountability Journal,* Vol. 26, pp. 1072–1106.

La Torre, M., Sabelfeld, S., Blomkvist, M., Tarquinio, L., & Dumay, J. (2018). Harmonising non-financial reporting regulation in Europe. *Meditari Accountancy Research,* Vol. 26, pp. 598–621.

Merkl-Davies, D. M., & Brennan, N. M. (2017). A theoretical framework of external accounting communication. *Accounting, Auditing & Accountability Journal,* Vol. 30, pp. 433–469.

Merkl-Davies, D. M., Brennan, N. M., & McLeay, S. J. (2011). Impression management and retrospective sense-making in corporate narratives. *Accounting, Auditing & Accountability Journal,* Vol. 24, pp. 315–344.

Merkl-Davies, D. M., & Koller, V. (2012). 'Metaphoring' people out of this world: A Critical Discourse Analysis of a chairman's statement of a UK defence firm, *Accounting Forum,* Vol. 36 (3), pp. 178–193.

Milne, M. J., Tregidga, H., & Walton, S. (2009). Words not actions! The ideological role of sustainable development reporting. *Accounting, Auditing & Accountability Journal,* Vol. 22, pp. 1211–1257.

Moerman, L., & van der Laan, S. (2007). Pursuing shareholder value: The rhetoric of James Hardie, *Accounting Forum,* Vol. 31 (4), pp. 354–369.

Morsing, M., & Schultz, M. (2006). Corporate social responsibility communication: Stakeholder information, response and involvement strategies. *Business Ethics: A European Review,* Vol. 15, pp. 323–338.

Ng, W., & Cock, C. D. (2002). Battle in the boardroom: A discursive perspective. *Journal of Management Studies,* Vol. 39, pp. 23–49.

Palmer, I., King, A. W., & Kelleher, D. (2004). Listening to Jack: GE's change conversations with shareholders. *Journal of organizational change management,* Vol. 17, pp. 593–614.

Prasad, A., & Mir, R. (2002). Digging deep for meaning: A critical hermeneutic analysis of CEO letters to shareholders in the oil industry. *The Journal of Business Communication (1973),* Vol. 39, pp. 92–116.

Preston, A. M., Wright, C., & Young, J. J. (1996). Imag [in] ing annual reports. *Accounting, Organizations and Society,* Vol. 21, pp. 113–137.

Ricoeur, P. (1976). *Interpretation theory: Discourse and the surplus of meaning.* Fort Worth, Texas: TCU Press.

Ricoeur, P. (1978). The Narrative Function. *Semeia,* Vol. 13, pp. 177–202.

Sabelfeld, S. (2013). *Investor relations on the Web–interpretations across borders.* Förlag, Gothenburg, Sweden: BAS.

Sabelfeld, S. (2016). Redovisningskommunikation. In G. Rimmel and K. Jonäll (eds), Redovisningsteorier – viktiga begrepp och teoretiska perspektiv inom redovisning. Stockholm: Sanoma utbildning.

Shannon, C. E., & Weaver, W. (1949). The mathematical theory of information. *Urbana: University of Illinois Press*, p. 97.

Saussure, F. D. (1916). Cours de linguistique générale, publié par Charles Bally et Albert Sechehaye, avec la collaboration de Albert Riedlinger. *Lausanne/Paris.*

Stocken, P. C. (2000). Credibility of voluntary disclosure. *The RAND Journal of Economics*, Vol. 31 (2), pp. 359–374.

Thompson, J. (1990). Ideology and modern culture. Stanford, CA: Stanford University Press.

Tinker, T. (1991). The accountant as partisan. *Accounting, Organizations and Society*, Vol. 16, pp. 297–310.

Tregidga, H., Milne, M., & Kearins, K. (2014). (Re) presenting 'sustainable organizations'. *Accounting, Organizations and Society*, Vol. 39, pp. 477–494.

Vatz, R. E. (1973). The myth of the rhetorical situation. *Philosophy & Rhetoric*, Vol. 6, pp. 154–161.

Weick, K. E. (1979). *The social psychology of organizing.* Reading, MA: McGraw-Hill.

Williams, S. J., & Adams, C. A. (2013). Moral accounting? Employee disclosures from a stakeholder accountability perspective. *Accounting, Auditing & Accountability Journal*, Vol. 26, pp. 449–495.

Yuthas, K., Rogers, R., & Dillard, J. F. (2002). Communicative action and corporate annual reports. *Journal of Business Ethics*, Vol. 41, pp. 141–157.

Part IV

Capital market and audit (external perspective)

11 Sustainability reporting from a capital market perspective

Susanne Arvidsson

Abstract

This chapter provides an overview of sustainability reporting from a capital market perspective. The chapter illustrates how the capital market's view on sustainability reporting has gone from skeptical to more positive. We will highlight the ongoing process of developing the new landscape of sustainable finance where the capital market is undergoing a fierce development to be able to assist in the transformation towards more sustainable businesses. In this process it is vital for companies to enhance the value relevance, credibility and comparability of sustainability reporting in order to be considered relevant in a capital market perspective. The chapter begins with a presentation of the actors in the capital market as well as their different roles and their relationships with sustainability reporting. Section 11.2 introduces the basic differences between a shareholder focus and a stakeholder focus. Then, in Section 11.3, we discuss how companies and the capital market gradually have adopted an increased focus on corporate social responsibility and sustainable business. Section 11.4 presents how this increased focus has resulted in sustainability rankings and sustainability indices. Section 11.5 highlights studies exploring if there is any relationship between being a sustainable business and financial strength. In Section 11.6, we take a closer look at the ongoing development of a new sustainable finance landscape and how various regulations and initiatives aim at enhancing corporate disclosure. Finally, research is presented on how the relationship between sustainable business and various financial performance measures looks.

Learning outcomes

After reading this chapter, the reader is expected to be able to:

1 Describe the role of the various actors in the capital market and their relationship to sustainability reporting.
2 Explain the differences between shareholder focus and stakeholder focus.

3   Exemplify how an increased focus on corporate social responsibility and sustainable business is reflected in the capital market.
4   Describe what previous research has found on the relationship between sustainable business and financial performance.
5   Discuss how a new sustainable finance landscape is developing and how it relates to corporate sustainability reporting.

11.1 Capital market actors

The capital market is often used as a collective name for a number of different financial sub-markets, e.g., the capital market and the foreign exchange market. The foreign exchange market is the largest market, and here the trading of currencies takes place. The capital market can be seen as the channel through which companies, households, organizations and states can access capital for various investments. Conversely, this market helps investors to find interesting investment opportunities. The capital market is divided into the stock market and the credit market. In the stock market, the focus is on equity trade while the credit market is where debt trading takes place. Furthermore, the credit market is divided into the money market (maturity up till one year) and the bond market (maturity longer than one year). There are a number of different actors in the capital market such as banks, fund companies, financial analysts, brokers and investors. Below we discuss the roles of fund companies, financial analysts and investors in the capital market and how the transformation towards more sustainable business has come to influence their work.

The fund companies are examples of financial intermediaries that help households manage their savings effectively. By taking advantage of economies of scale, the fund companies can create portfolios of securities, the so-called security funds. By creating these security funds, the risks in each individual security can be spread (Riksbank, 2014). Each fund company usually offers a large number of funds with different investment directions. Fund savings in Sweden alone at the end of 2019 (2016) reached a new maximum level of SEK 4,786 (3,568) billion. Over the past decade, it has become increasingly common, both nationally and internationally, for mutual funds to focus on sustainability. This means that there is an increased interest in identifying companies that are successful in the area of sustainability and, thus, suitable to be included in a securities fund aimed at sustainability (see Section 11.4).

Financial analysts (usually divided into buy-side and sell-side analysts depending on who their client is) usually work at an investment bank and also act as intermediaries. Their task consists of gathering all available information about a company from various sources (e.g., quarterly reports, annual reports, one-on-ones with management teams, industry statistics). Thereafter, they interpret all this information in order to provide a valuation of the company. The valuation is usually communicated via an analyst report where investors are recommended to buy, sell or hold shares in the company. The corporate valuation is the basis for this recommendation. A review of 101 analyst re-ports from international investment banks for the year 1999 showed that none of these reports highlighted information related to sustainability (Arvidsson, 2003). Today, the situation looks completely different and sustainability per-spectives are often integrated in their corporate analyses and their analyst reports (see Section 11.6).

Investors are usually divided into institutional and private. Unlike pri-vate investors, an institutional investor is a legal entity. Often a narrower definition is used where an institutional investor refers to an organization that manages capital on behalf of others and brings together capital from different individuals and/or organizations to make this possible. A private investor manages his own capital. In the category of institutional investors, we find fund companies, but also pension funds and insurance companies. Institutional ownership has increased steadily and is considerably larger than private. As institutional ownership has increased, it has often been criticized for being a passive ownership that leaves the management of the owned com-panies with too much room for maneuver when the important control func-tion is neglected. This development is considered to be due to the fact that institutional ownership is not exercised by those who own the shares but by officials of, e.g., the fund company that manages the capital. A clear trend over the past decade is that investors are increasingly focusing their capital on the so-called Socially Responsible Investments (SRI), which is discussed in more detail in Chapter 12.

11.2 Shareholder focus vs stakeholder focus (Shareholder focus vs stakeholder focus)

In 1970, Milton Friedman wrote an article in *The New York Times Magazine* that came to receive much attention and is still widely referred to today when discussing social responsibility and sustainable businesses (Friedman, 1970). In the article, Milton Friedman firmly stated that a company's social respon-sibility is to increase its profits and nothing else. At that time, his thinking was not very controversial. A number of similar ideas were published in both popular science and more scientific journals. As early as 1958, Levitt warned in the *Harvard Business Review* that corporate social responsibility (CSR) had become a "... deadly serious employment"... (Levitt, 1958, p. 41). Andrews (1973) was a bit more nuanced and suggested that the underlying ideas about CSR need not necessarily conflict with increased shareholder value if these ideas were integrated into the business and its business model. Even in the 1980s and 1990s, the prevailing mantra in business society was that all cor-porate decision-making should aim at maximizing shareholder value. The owner was considered to be the company's main stakeholder. Satisfying this stakeholder was thought of as main foci.

However, in the late 1990s, the increasingly lively debate around CSR be-gan to challenge the ideas on which maximized shareholder value (shareholder value maximization) is based. The concept of stakeholder was challenged, and it became broadened from a strict ownership focus to include several of the company's stakeholders. The proposed broadening of the shareholder value concept became known as the enlightened value maximization (enlightened stakeholder theory) (see Jensen, 2001). It is interesting to note that Michael Jensen, who is considered to be some kind of founder of these ideas, himself previously advocated the strict shareholder value concept. Prior et al. (2008) argue that this means that a stakeholder/agent perspective is adopted where the company is no longer perceived as a bilateral relationship between shareholders and corporate management but a multilateral set of relationships between corporate management and several different stakeholders.

A company's stakeholders include individuals, groups and organizations that have different interests in the company. Most companies list a number of different stakeholders in their annual reports (e.g., owners, employees, customers, suppliers, NGOs, authorities), which in different ways and to varying degrees are important for and affect and/or are affected by the company's operations. In order to illustrate these mutual relationships between a company and its stakeholders, we usually use the stakeholder model. See Chapter 2 for a more detailed presentation of the stakeholder model.

Often a company's stakeholders contribute with something to the company's operations (e.g., work, capital, products). For this contribution they expect some form of remuneration (salary for their work, interest on loaned capital, payment for delivered products). The importance of different stakeholders to a company's business varies from company to company. To structure the process of identifying relevant stakeholders and assessing their importance to a company, Mitchell et al. (1997) introduced a model called the stakeholder salience. This model proposes that each stakeholder should be assessed based on three attributes: power, legitimacy and urgency. With an increased focus on social responsibility and sustainable businesses among stakeholders, companies need to act in accordance with the norms and values in society in order to be considered to fulfill its social responsibility and thereby be granted legitimacy to continue their operations (see Deegan, 2002; Dowling and Pfeffer, 1975). The process of transforming and managing sustainable businesses involves several challenges related to, e.g., reporting, governance, risk management and measurement (Arvidsson, 2019a).

11.3 Increased focus on sustainable business in the corporate world and the capital market

Over 30 years ago, the so-called the Brundtland Report "Our Common Future" (UNWCED, 1987) was published with the aim of stressing the urgent need to promote a global sustainable development. Initially, this call was not extensively acknowledged. Not until the period around the turn of the century, did the need for promoting a global sustainable development gradually gain momentum in the corporate world but to a certain extent also in the capital market. The actors in these arenas had previously been more or less uninterested in these ideas. At this time, however, we witnessed several corporate scandals related to the social, ethical and environmental arena (e.g., Enron, WorldCom, gigantic bonuses, child labor, environmental scandals, increased environmental degradation, rising CO_2 emissions), which came to undermine confidence in the way the companies were run. Ghoshal (2005) and Gray et al. (2005) criticized the theory behind an overly strict focus on maximizing shareholder value since it contributed to a short-term view, lack of morals and neglect of CSR.

Thus, this period became a perfect hotbed for the ideas behind CSR. Acting socially responsible was argued to be an efficient means for reducing the mistrust towards corporate management and, at the same time, restoring confidence in how they run our businesses. The number of CSR articles published in European financial press increased from 4 to 273 between 1996 and 2005 (Windell, 2006). In the same vein, investors in the capital market started to acknowledge that companies with a sustainability profile could be interesting investments. This interest was manifested in a steady increase in the so-called Socially Responsible Investments (SRI) (see also Chapter 14). Again, Milton Friedman entered the debate when, in Friedman and Miles (2001, p. 523), he argues that a possible reason for the increase in SRI is that investors see it as:

"… a business case, as well as, or as opposed to a moral case, for acting in a more responsible manner."

In 2006, the UN introduced its "Principles for Responsible Investments" (PRI) with the aim of offering investors guidelines on how to include a so-called ESG (Environmental, Social and Governance) perspective in their investment decision processes. These guidelines are just one example of all the commendable initiatives that have contributed to the transition towards more sustainable organizations promoting a global sustainable development. Although some countries have legislation and regulation in the area of sustainability, much of the development has been driven by voluntary initiatives (see Chapter 13). Some examples are the different standards that have been developed in the area of sustainability, e.g., UN Global Compact (principle-based standard); AA1000, SA8000, ISO26000 (certification-based standards); and integrated reporting, Global Reporting Initiative (GRI; reporting-based standards). The objective with this standard development has primarily been to increase the reliability and comparability of how companies and organizations communicate their performance in the area of sustainability. This communication has primarily been through sustainability reporting in the so-called sustainability reports, which are published as a supplement to companies' annual reports (Arvidsson, 2010). Over the past decade, the number of companies providing their stakeholders with sustainability reports has steadily increased. According to a comprehensive global survey, 93 percent of G250 companies today have a sustainability report (KPMG, 2019).

11.4 Sustainability ranking and sustainability index

Today, it has become increasingly common that a company's sustainability work is mapped and ranked by various capital market actors (Arvidsson, 2020). This is usually done on the basis of the information that the companies communicate through their sustainability reports. Waring and Edwards (2008) argue that this means that companies are under increasing pressure to provide capital market actors with good track records regarding their sustainability performance. Thus, the need for value-relevant, credible and comparable information on sustainability performance is increasing (see Arvidsson, 2019b; Arvidsson and Jonäll, 2019). Already in 2006, one in eight dollars was invested after evaluation of the investment's sustainability ranking. The KPMG Survey of Corporate Responsibility Reporting is the world's largest survey of sustainability reporting and maps the 100 largest companies in 49 countries (KPMG, 2015, 2019). In total, close to 4,000 listed and unlisted companies are included in the study. The survey is carried out every two or three years. Its focus is on the included companies' sustainability reports, the quality of these reports, the progress towards integrated reporting and the extent to which the GRI is used. Ever since KPMG's first survey, Swedish companies have been ranked very high in terms of the quality of their sustainability reporting. Another ranking is made annually by Newsweek where the 500 greenest companies are selected (Newsweek Green Ranking). Again, Swedish companies stand out as some of the best in sustainability. In the 2016 ranking, 5 Swedish companies ranked among the 100 that were considered greenest, namely SEB, Atlas Copco, Nordea, H&M and Swedbank. A total of nine Swedish companies were included in the ranking.

With an increased focus on social responsibility and sustainable businesses, both stock exchanges and various organizations have introduced sustainability indices. The most well-known sustainability indices include the Dow Jones Sustainability Index (DJSI), FTSE4GOOD Index and Ethical Sustainability Index. As early as 1999, the DJSI was introduced. This index is considered the most important sustainability index. Its importance is further increased since several ethical or green funds have decided that their funds may only consist of companies that are included in the DJSI. Companies are included in DJSI after having been ranked according to economic, environmental and social criteria. In addition to the overall DJSI World index, which consists of the 15 percent best-performing sustainability companies included in the S&P Global Broad Market Index (S&P Global BMI), there are seven additional DJSIs, each focusing on a specific region (North America, Europe, Asia Pacific, Emerging Markets) or country (Korea, Australia, Chile). DSJI Europe ranks the 20 percent best-performing European companies included in S&P Global BMI.

As more stock exchanges develop sustainability indices, it has become common for studies to examine whether it affects a company's market value if it is included or excluded in a sustainability index (see, e.g., Becchetti et al., 2012, Joshi et al., 2017, Oberndorfer et al., 2013, Van Stekelenburg et al., 2015). The results of these studies do not point in any clear direction but indicate positive impact, as well as negative and unclear impact.

11.5 Is there any relationship between being a sustainable business and financial strength?

For several decades, there has been a lively debate about whether sustainable business has a positive effect on a company's value creation and its various financial performance measures. The debate highlights both normative and ideological foundations. Various attempts have been made to measure the relationship between social performance (corporate social) and financial performance (corporate financial). The first studies that examined this relationship are considered to be Bragdon and Marlin (1972) and Moskowitz (1972). Since their initial studies, interest in this relationship has steadily increased. Margolis and Walsh (2003) contributed to this research when they reviewed 109 empirical studies that in various ways attempted to capture the relationship between social and financial performance. This review showed that of the 109 studies, 54 showed a positive while 7 showed a negative relationship. The other studies, i.e., 48, showed unclear relationships. Similar to this study, but with a refined comparison method, van Beurden and Gössling (2008) conducted a review of 34 empirical studies from the period 1991 to 2007. Of these studies, 23 showed a clear positive relationship, 2 showed a negative relationship and the other (9) showed unclear and non-significant relationships. Recent studies continue to show unclear results (see Zhao and Murrell, 2016). In recent years, researchers have analyzed the relationship between sustainable businesses, on the one hand, and the accuracy of analysts' forecasts and/ or cost of capital, on the other. While the first relationship has been found to be positive (higher social responsibility gives better forecasting accuracy) (Dhaliwal et al., 2012), the second has been found to be negative (higher social responsibility gives lower capital cost) (see Dhaliwal et al., 2014).

From the ongoing debate about the challenges with capturing this relationship, explanations with three different origins can be identified: the methodological, the skepticism driven and the ethical ideological. Van Beurden and Gössling (2008) argue that the majority of studies that have shown unclear or negative relationships over the years has primarily been older studies where the method has not been sufficiently developed. In line with this, several studies have focused on how social performance and financial performance actually are operationalized and how this relationship is measured (see Orlitzky et al., 2003; Wu, 2006; Zhao and Murrell, 2016). Carroll (2000, p. 473) goes one step further and argues that it is almost impossible to develop valid and reliable sustainability measures. This research direction can be said to propose explanations with a *methodological origin*. Another research direction including critics like Milton Friedman argues that unclear and negative relationships are strong evidence that there is no relationship between being a sustainable company with good social performance and high financial performance. This direction can be said to have a *skepticism-driven origin*. The third research direction does not focus so much on the findings of unclear relationships, but rather accepts the relatively positive relationship between social and financial performance. However, they question what is the chicken and what is the egg (see Waddock and Graves, 1997). This direction can be said to have an *ethical ideological origin*. The question they raise is whether good social performance leads to a good financial performance or whether it is instead companies that already show good financial performance that can afford to invest in achieving good social performance. As long as we do not reach clear evidence of significant relationship between social and financial performance – whether positive, negative or no – the debate will probably continue.

11.6 A new sustainable finance landscape calls for enhancing sustainability reporting

Today, there is an increased awareness and interest from external stakeholders, not the least from the financial market actors, for understanding and assessing how a company actually *performs* on the different sustainability arenas (Arvidsson, 2019c). This means that there is a need for informative and credible sustainability information. To assist in this process, several national, EU and international regulations and initiatives have been launched. Recently, there has been a shift from primarily voluntary initiatives towards legislative and normative initiatives aimed at enhancing the quality of corporate disclosure on sustainability (see, e.g., EU Commission, 2013, 2014, 2018). As a response to the argued need for legislative initiatives opt for enhancing credibility and comparability of sustainability information, came the EU directive (2014/95/EU) on non-financial reporting (EU Commission, 2014). Through national laws, this directive mandates the largest EU companies to disclose social and environmental information in their corporate reports. While the Paris Agreement from 2015 has a clear environmental focus where fighting climate change is main foci, the adoption of Agenda 2030 and the launch of the Sustainable Development Goals (SDGs) integrate *all* three dimensions of sustainability, i.e. environmental, social and economic.

A new landscape of sustainable finance is emerging where the financial market is undergoing a fierce development to be able to assist in the transformation towards more sustainable businesses (Arvidsson and Blomkvist, 2019). The recent formation of the EU High Level Expert Group (HLEG) on Sustainable Finance is a noticeable milestone. The financial markets actors, who for long time have been skeptical towards sustainability (Arvidsson, 2014; Cho et al., 2015; Friedman, 1970; Yeldar, 2012), now join forces to explore how to integrate sustainability consideration into their frameworks in order to mobilize finance for sustainable growth (EU Commission, 2018). In this process it is vital for companies to enhance the value relevance, credibility and comparability of sustainability reporting in order to be considered relevant from the perspective of financial market actors (see EVRACSI Initiative). The financial market perspective is also accentuated by the Task Force on Climate-Related Financial Disclosures (TCFD). They have developed a framework that promotes an enhancement of climate-related financial disclosure by including financial-risk and scenarios-analysis perspectives (TCFD, 2017). The establishment of the Technical Expert Group (TEG) on Sustainable Finance with the objective to develop an EU classification system of sustainable activities, i.e. the EU taxonomy is yet another example of the movement in the sustainable finance area where improved sustainability reporting is vital (TEG, 2018).

11.7 Summary

Claims such as "Good Ethics is Good Business" (van Beurden and Gössling, 2008, p. 407) have long been and still are, to some extent, controversial and challenging. Especially for the actors on the financial market where some skepticism still prevails over whether there are benefits with CSR and sustainable businesses. In recent decades there has been a trend where more and more people believe that the strict shareholder focus needs to be facilitated and supplemented with a broader stakeholder focus. This has increased the number of companies that provide sustainability reports to their stakeholders. This trend is further enhanced by an increased focus – from politicians, governments and business society – on promoting a global sustainable development and an efficient transformation towards sustainable business. Reaching Agenda 2030 and UN's SDG is high up on the agendas both in the corporate board rooms and when the world's leaders meet. We also witness a fierce development of a new sustainable finance landscape where the financial market actors are at the center of promoting an efficient transformation towards more sustainable organizations. In line with the SDGs' focus on all three dimensions of sustainability, i.e. environmental, social and economic, many corporate rankings today include environmental, social *and* economic criteria. Most stock exchanges now have a sustainability index (e.g., DJSI and FTSE4GOOD) where companies which meet different sustainability-related criteria are included. Although there is a swift and positive development towards acknowledging the need for companies to become more sustainable, the debate around whether there is a relationship between social and financial performance will probably continue.

Questions that you should be able to answer after reading this chapter:

1 Describe the various capital market actors.
2 What roles do they play and how has the increased focus on corporate social responsibility and sustainable businesses come to influence their work?

3   What are the differences between a shareholder focus and an enlightened stakeholder focus?
4   How have the thoughts developed about who the company should focus on in its decision-making process?
5   What is a sustainability index? Give a few examples.
6   Describe what research has found regarding the relationship between social and financial performance.
7   When discussing the challenges of capturing the relationship between social and financial performance, three different explanations are put forward. These can be said to have a methodological, a skepticism-driven or an ethical ideological origin. Briefly describe these three explanations.
8   Briefly explain some regulations and initiatives that underly the ongoing development of a new sustainable finance landscape.
9   In what ways are this development related to corporate sustainability reporting?

References

Andrews, K. R. (1973). Can best corporations be made moral. *Harvard Business Review*, Vol. 51 (3), pp. 57–64.

Arvidsson, S. (2020). *Rapport om hållbarhetsrankning av börsbolag 2018: Om rankningsmodell och resultat med analyser och kommentarer* (Report on the Swedish Corporate Sustainability Ranking 2019: Ranking model and results with analyses and comments), Dagens Industri, Stockholm. ISBN 978–91–519–4656-6

Arvidsson, S. (Ed.) (2019a). *Challenges in managing sustainable business: Reporting, taxation, ethics and governance*, pp. 3–24. Palgrave Macmillan.

Arvidsson, S. (2019b). An expose of the challenging practice development of sustainability reporting: From the first wave to the EU Directive (2014/95/EU). In Arvidsson, S. (Ed.), (2019), *Challenges in managing sustainable business: Reporting, taxation, ethics and governance*, Palgrave Macmillan. doi: 10.1007/978-3-319–93266-8_1.

Arvidsson, S. (Ed.) (2019c). *1st SUBREA Conference Report – A focus on challenges and future knowledge-needs, Lund University*, Media Tryck. ISBN 978–91–7267–408-0

Arvidsson, S. (2014). Corporate social responsibility and stock market actors: A comprehensive study. *Social Responsibility Journal*, Vol. 10 (2), pp. 210–225.

Arvidsson, S. (2010). Communication of corporate social responsibility: A study of the views of management teams in large companies, *Journal of Business Ethics*, Vol. 96, pp. 339–354.

Arvidsson, S. (2003). *Demand and supply of information on intangibles: The case of knowledge-intense companies*. PhD dissertation, Department of Business Administration, Lund University, Sweden.

Arvidsson, S., & Blomkvist, M. (2019). Valuation of investments from a sustainability perspective. In Arvidsson, S. (Ed.) (2019). *1st SUBREA Conference Report – A focus on challenges and future knowledge-needs* (pp. 47–59). Lund University, Media Tryck.

Arvidsson, S., & Jonäll, K. (2019). Sustainability reporting. In Arvidsson, S. (Ed.) (2019). *1st SUBREA Conference Report – A focus on challenges and future knowledge-needs* (pp. 11–30). Lund University, Media Tryck.

Becchetti, L., Ciciretti, R., Hasan, I., & Kobeissi, N. (2012). Corporate social responsibility and shareholder's value. *Journal of Business Research*, Vol. 65 (11), pp. 1628–1635.

Bragdon, J. H., & Marlin, J. A. (1972). ls pollution profitable. *Risk Management*, Vol. 19 (4), pp. 9–18.

Carroll, A. B. (2000). A commentary and an overview of key questions on corporate social performance measurements. *Business and Society*, Vol. 39, pp. 466–478.

Cho, C. H., Michelon, G., Patten, D. M., & Robets, R. W. (2015), "CSR disclosure: The more things change…?", *Accounting, Auditing and Accountability Journal*, Vol. 28 (1), pp. 14–35.

Deegan, C. (2002). Introduction – The legitimising effect of social and environmental disclosures – A theoretical foundation. *Accounting, Auditing & Accountability Journal*, Vol. 15 (3), pp. 282–311.

Dhaliwal, D., Li, O. Z., Tsang, A., & Yang, Y. G. (2014). Corporate social responsibility disclosure and the cost of equity capital: The roles of stakeholder orientation and financial transparency. *Journal of Accounting and Public Policy*, Vol. 33 (4), pp. 328–355.

Dhaliwal, D. S., Radhakrishnan, S., Tsang, A. H., & Yang, Y. G. (2012). Nonfinancial disclosure and analyst forecast accuracy: International evidence on corporate social responsibility disclosure. *The Accounting Review*, Vol. 87 (3), Vol. 723–759.

Dowling, J., & Pfeffer, J. (1975). Organizational legitimacy: Social values and organizational behavior. *The Pacific Sociological Review*, Vol. 18 (1), pp. 122–136.

European Commission (2018). *Financing a sustainable European economy*, The final report from High-level expert group on sustainable finance, Brussels.

European Commission (2014). Directive on disclosure of non-financial and diversity information by certain large companies. (2014/95/EU) Brussels.

European Commission (2013). Report on Corporate Social Responsibility: Promoting society's interests and a route to sustainable and inclusive recovery. (2012/2097(INI)). Brussels.

EVRACSI Initiative (2020). www.ehl.lu.se/om-ekonomihogskolan/hallbarhet/EVRACSI.

Friedman, A. L., & Miles, S. (2001). Socially responsible investment and corporate social and environmental reporting in the U.K.: An exploratory study. *British Accounting Review*, Vol. 33, pp. 523–548.

Friedman, M. (1970). The social responsibility of business is to increase its profits. *New York Times Magazine*, Vol. 33, pp. 122–126.

Ghoshal, S. (2005). Bad management theories are destroying good management practices. *Academy of Management Learning & Education*, Vol. 4 (1), pp. 75–91.

Gray, K. R., Frieder, L. A., & Clark, G. W. (2005). *Corporate scandals – The many faces of greed*. St. Paul, MN: Paragon House.

Jensen, M. C. (2001). Value maximization, stakeholder theory, and the corporate objective function. *Journal of Applied Corporate Finance*, Vol. 14 (3), pp. 8–21.

Joshi, S., Pandey, V., & Ross, R. B. (2017). Asymmetry in stock market reactions to changes in membership of the Dow Jones sustainability index. *The Journal of Business Inquiry*, Vol. 16 (1), pp. 12–35.

KPMG (2019). *KPMG survey of corporate responsibility reporting 2017: The road ahead*. Amsterdam: KPMG.

KPMG (2015). *KPMG international survey of corporate responsibility reporting*. Amsterdam: KPMG International.

Levitt, T. (1958). The dangers of social-responsibility. *Harvard Business Review*, Vol. 36 (5), pp. 41–50.

Margolis, J. D., & Walsh, J. P. (2003). Misery loves companies: Rethinking social initiatives by business. *Administrative Science Quarterly*, Vol. 48 (2), pp. 268–305.

Mitchell, R. K., Agle. B. R., & Wood, D. J. (1997). Toward a theory of stakeholder identification and salience: Defining the principle of who and what really counts. *Academy of Management Review*, Vol. 22 (4), pp. 853–886.

Moskowitz, M. (1972). Choosing socially responsible stocks. *Business and Society Review*, Vol. 1 (1), Vol. 71–75.

Oberndorfer, U., Schmidt, P., Wagner, M., & Ziegler, A. (2013). Does the stock market value the inclusion in a sustainability stock index? An event study analysis for German firms. *Journal of Environmental Economics and Management*, Vol. 66 (3), pp. 497–509.

Orlitzky, M., Schmidt, F. L., & Rynes, S. L. (2003). Corporate social and financial performance: A meta-analysis. *Organization Studies*, Vol. 24 (3), pp. 403–441.

Prior, D., Surroca, J., & Tribó, J. A. (2008). Are socially responsible managers really ethical? Exploring the relationship between earnings management and corporate social responsibility. *Corporate Governance: An International Review*, Vol.16 (3), pp. 160–177.

Riksbank, S. (2014). *Den svenska finansmarknaden*. Stockholm, Sweden: Printfabriken.

TCFD (2017) Recommendations of the task force on climate-related financial disclosures. The final report from TCFD.

UNWCED (United Nation World Commission on Environment and Development) (1987). *Report of the United Nation World Commission on Environment and Development 'Our Common Future' (The Brundtland Report)*. (Item 83, 42nd Session of the United Nations General Assembly).

van Beurden, P., & Gössling, T. (2008). The worth of values–A literature review on the relation between corporate social and financial performance. *Journal of Business Ethics*, Vol. 82 (2), pp. 407–424.

van Stekelenburg, A., Georgakopoulos, G., Sotiropoulou, V., Vasileiou, K. Z., & Vlachos, I. (2015). The relation between sustainability performance and stock market returns: An empirical analysis of the Dow Jones Sustainability Index Europe. *International Journal of Economics and Finance*, Vol. 7 (7), p. 74.

Waddock, S. A., & Graves, S. B. (1997). The corporate social performance–financial performance link. *Strategic Management Journal*, Vol. 18 (4), pp. 303–319.

Waring, P., & Edwards, T. (2008). Socially responsible investment: Explaining its uneven development and human resource management consequences. *Corporate Governance: An International Review*, Vol. 16 (3), pp. 135–145.

Windell, K. (2006). *Corporate social responsibility under construction: Ideas, translations, and institutional change*. Doctoral Thesis No. 123, Department of Business Studies, Uppsala University, Uppsala.

Wu, M. L. (2006). Corporate social performance, corporate financial performance, and firm size: A meta-analysis. *Journal of American Academy of Business*, Vol. 8 (1), pp. 163–171.

Yeldar, R. (2012). *The value of extra financial disclosure: What investors and analysts said*. Report commissioned by Accounting for Sustainability and The Global Reporting Initiative. www.globalreporting.org/resourcelibrary/The -value-of-extra-financial-disclosure.pdf

Zhao, X., & Murrell, A. J. (2016). Revisiting the corporate social performance-financial performance link: A replication of Waddock and Graves. *Strategic Management Journal*, Vol. 37 (11), pp. 2378–2388.

12 Socially responsible investment

Gunnar Rimmel

Abstract

This chapter presents the emergence of the Socially Responsible Invest-ment (SRI) discipline, which is a growing market in the financial in-dustry. The goal of SRI is to combine financial investments with social responsibility to create long-term competitive returns that simultane-ously have a positive socio-economic impact. Specific Environmental, Social and Governance (ESG) criteria for environmental, social and cor-porate governance reflect SRI's investment focus. This chapter provides an overview of the historical development of SRI. This chapter outlines basic sustainable investment strategies and tools within SRI and how important organizations within SRI have developed acceptance of SRI. Finally, criticism and challenges are discussed with SRI.

Learning outcomes

After reading this chapter, you are expected to be able to:

*   Explain the origin and significance of Socially Responsible Investment.
*   Understand the development of the Socially Responsible Investment field.
*   Explain basic concepts and investment strategies for sustainable SRI investments.

12.1 Introduction

During the past decades, modern capitalist society has faced a legitimacy crisis, which has led to a decline in support and trust for both economy and governments (Arjaliès, 2010). The recent economic crises with bankruptcy of some of the largest global financial institutions and financial problems for states (e.g. Ireland, Spain and Greece) have intensified the legitimacy crisis. This crisis of legitimacy has mobilized society in various ways, e.g. in the form of environmental and human rights activists and shareholder activism to change economic and political institutions.

The increased scepticism towards and scrutiny of company behaviour has pushed companies in way that they can no longer ignore their responsibility to protect society and the environment in which they operate. The two recent financial crises and the subsequent lack of trust and confidence in the private sector gave further stimulus for the pursuit of changing corporate behaviour. Increased social demands on companies have led to developments that companies had to deal with Corporate Social Responsibility (CSR) initiatives, to reduce carbon dioxide emissions, to fight child labour or to create a clear governance structure to legitimize their business operations.

The financial sector developed financial products, e.g. funds that comply with specific criteria for Environmental, Social and Governance (ESG). A new investment discipline emerged called Socially Responsible Investment (SRI), which reflects its investment focus on social responsibility to create long-term competitive returns that simultaneously have a positive socio-economic impact. ESG thinking within SRI has led to a number of sets of ESG standards in the US, Europe and Scandinavia. Regardless of the ESG standard, these generally have in common that they concentrate on the three ESG criteria. The *Environmental* criteria examine the company's impact on nature. The *Social* criteria examine how a company manages relationships with its employees, suppliers, customers and the communities in which they operate. *Governance* is about company management, director salaries, audits, internal controls and shareholders' rights.

SRIs and practices for reviewing company performance using ESG criteria are often summarized under the concept of *CSR*. Just as there is no uniform global SRI standard, neither is there a uniform definition that describes the meaning of SRI. SRI's varying practice development is dependent on different perceptions about the concept's content and meaning. Depending on their emphasis, SRI investors use alternating labels such as *Community Investments, Ethical Investments, Green Investments, Responsible Investments, Value-Based Investments* or *Sustainable Investments).*

Stakeholders play an important role within SRI in identifying, operating and monitoring the CSR of large companies. Especially financial stakeholders such as investors and shareholders are interested in connection with SRI. SRI has reversed the conceptualisation of the role of financial stakeholders. Instead of seeing financial stakeholders' main desire for companies to maximize shareholder value, in the form of the short-term return, the value is added to the long-term value potential of a company. Maximizing shareholder value is often viewed as the opposite of what is good for society. An example of this divide is the recent crises in the financial market in the form of banks' credit crises. However, this division between shareholders and society can be traced back to the protracted debate between traditional economists Milton Friedman and Edward Freeman. Friedman argued that the only social responsibility for a company is to use its resources to increase profits (Friedman, 1962). However, Freeman (1984) considered that the modern company has an obligation to all stakeholders that goes beyond value maximization for shareholders.

Institutional investors have increasingly challenged large companies to improve their information and control systems on issues such as working conditions, human rights, supplier choice, climate impact, environmentally friendly products and corruption. The reasons for these requirements are that integration of CSR-related issues can play an important role in securing long-term returns for shareholders while providing broader social welfare. Institutional investors can choose shares based on the company's CSR activities and thus follow an SRI investment strategy (see Section 12.3). For example, institutional investors may intentionally use *negative screening* and exclude companies that harm society or the environment from their funds and investment portfolios, or they include companies that are *good corporate citizens* who take account of society or the environment. Large pension funds usually have a long-term investment horizon of 20–30 years. They have begun to worry about companies' exposure to social and environmental risks, as their long-term investments are threatened with lower value development. Through their investments, these institutional investors have direct access to management decision-making. Thus, institutional investors integrate social problems into their daily decision-making.

In recent years, the market for SRI investments has increased significantly in both Europe and the United States. In Europe, the SRI market increased from EUR 1 trillion in 2005 to EUR 158 trillion at the end of 2016, covering 48 per cent of the total European professionally managed assets (Eurosif, 2016). In the United States, the volume of SRI funds increased by 573 per cent over a 5-year period, from USD 1.41 trillion in 2012 to USD 8.72 trillion in 2016 (USSIF, 2016). These figures clearly show that financial institutions and investors have begun to take more account of CSR factors in their investment decisions to invest capital.

12.2 Historical development of SRI

Responsible investment is not a new phenomenon. The older term used for responsible investment is ethical investment. In the beginning, the most prominent ethical investors were the Methodist Church and Quakers in England and the United States who did not invest in weapons or in products obtained through slavery. For originally religious reasons, these investors refused to invest capital in companies that participated in the "industries of sin". In the 1920s, the United Methodist Church began systematically through negative screening to avoid investing in "sinful" companies, such as companies involved in the production of alcohol, tobacco, weapons, gambling or pornography. In 1928, the first modern ethical foundation, the Pioneer Fund, was founded, which used negative screening based on religious traditions.

In contrast to early ethical investments based on religious traditions, modern SRI is more based on the different personal and social beliefs of individual investors. Since the 1960s, a number of social campaigns, such as the anti-war movement or the anti-racist movements, made investors aware of the social consequences of their investments. In the 1960s, therefore, demand for SRI products increased substantially. The Vietnam War laid the foundation for committed anti-war movements, and anti-racial movements made citizens, and especially investors, extremely sensitive to injustice in society and harmful corporate activities. 1971 was an important milestone for SRI development when the first SRI fund, Pax World, was founded in the United States (Renneboog et al., 2008). Originally, it was aimed at investors who opposed the Vietnam War and militarism. Gathering their resources into an SRI fund enabled investors to join a collective that expressed their dissatisfaction with companies that work with harmful products, in Pax World's case, it involved all weapons production.

The next major driver contributing to the growth of SRI funds was South Africa's apartheid system in the 1980s. In Europe the first SRI funds were founded in the 1980s in response to apartheid in South Africa. SRI investors from around the world pushed companies and the South African government to abolish apartheid. SRI funds put pressure on companies not to do business with South African companies by divesting their investments in Western companies with South African subsidiaries. The campaign was one of the most successful moments in SRI history and also resulted in several state regulations. For example, a change in the law of California, where pension funds were forced to divest more than USD 6 billion from companies operating in South Africa (Sparkes, 2001).

In the late 1980s and early 1990s, several developments in the SRI industry were noticed. In 1987, the United Nations World Commission on Environment and Development published the *Report of the World Commission on Environment and Development: Our Common Future*. The report, better known as the *Brundtland Report*, named after the President of the Commission at that time, Norway's Prime Minister Gro Harlem Brundtland. The report outlined the link between economic development and environmental degradation, and received a great deal of media attention. In the wake of the Brundtland Report, the SRI industry developed specially niche environmental funds.

Environmental disasters in the late 1980s made investors more aware of the negative environmental effects of industrial development. In 1986, the Chernobyl nuclear power plant exploded. In 1989, the oil tanker Exxon Valdez went to waste, resulting in oil spills of 11 million litres of crude oil in Alaska. It was by far the worst environmental disaster in the United States until the Deepwater Horizon oil platform sank in the Gulf of Mexico in 2010.

In 1988, the first Scandinavian environmental fund was founded, Carlson World Nature Fund, which used negative screening in its investment process and donated 2 per cent of the annual return to the World Wildlife Foundation.

In the 1990s, corporate governance became a focus area in the CSR debate. Issues such as environmental protection, human rights and labour relations had become commonplace in SRI. Corporate scandals such as Enron, Arthur Andersen, Parmalat and Skandia drew attention to deficiencies in corporate governance structures. Legislative changes in different countries increased the requirements for governance information and led to the introduction of voluntary codes of conduct in large companies. The major financial consequences of corporate scandals and the resulting increased demands for governance became an extra dimension in the Triple Bottom Line strategy for SRI. This led to the development of the concept of ESG and its criteria for investment decisions (Solomon & Solomon, 2006).

The early 2000s also saw the emergence of SRI among Swedish state and private pension funds. A change in Swedish legislation forced the five largest state pension funds to include environment and ethics in their investment policy from 1 January 2001. Swedish pension funds were among the first state pension funds that led to the trend among pension funds in Europe to include SRI in their investment strategies.

The expansion of ethical investments and SRI led to a whole new investment industry. Since the 2000s, the SRI industry has evolved from managing specialized funds for niche investors to becoming more mature and mainstream in the global investment market.

12.3 Sustainable investment strategies and tools

As described in the previous sections, SRI is about sustainable investment strategies that take ESG factors into account when choosing a portfolio and investment decisions. Because there is no globally accepted SRI standard that the SRI industry adheres to, there are a variety of different SRI strategies that SRI fund managers use for their SRI funds around the world. Usually, SRI funds apply a combination of different types of screening technology or focus in their investment strategies. Below are briefly presented seven different types of screening technology or focus that are commonly found in conjunction with sustainable SRI strategies.

Sustainable SRI investments include the following activities and strategies:

1   *Negative Screening:* Exclusion from a fund or investment portfolio for certain sectors, companies or practices based on specific ESG criteria.
2   *Positive/best-in-class screening:* Investment sectors, companies or projects selected for positive ESG performance in relation to industry partners.
3   *Norm-based screening:* Screening of investments against minimum norms for business practice based on international norms.
4   *ESG integration:* Systematic and clear introduction of SRI investment managers with ESG factors in their economic analysis.
5   *Sustainability investment:* Investments in various themes or assets that are specifically related to sustainability (e.g. environmentally friendly energy, green technology or sustainable agriculture).
6   *Impact/community investment:* Targeted investments, which are usually made in private markets. These investments are aimed at solving social or environmental problems. Social investments include investments

specifically targeted at traditionally disadvantaged communities. Investments are made in companies with a clear social or environmental purpose.

7   *Corporate Engagement and Shareholder Action*: Use of positioning as a major shareholder to influence corporate behaviour on their own, including by taking a seat on corporate boards or directly communicating with company management, or gathering other major shareholders to make demands on the company to comply with the ESG guidelines.

The goal of SRI investments is to combine financial returns with social responsibility. As described above, various SRI investment strategies are used in practice to achieve this goal. An important technique for achieving the SRI investment objective is screening. Screening is the collection and processing of information to identify potential investment opportunities. In connection with SRI investments, screening often results in the exclusion or inclusion of companies or industries. ESG criteria are often used as a filter to determine investment opportunities. Ethical funds are typical examples of investments that use screening techniques. In connection with SRI investments, three different screening methods can be distinguished: negative, positive and "best in class". Negative screening is probably the best-known screening technique, which categorically excludes companies or industries from investments based on ESG criteria. Positive screening means that companies that excel in ESG criteria are included in the investment portfolio of SRI funds. Best-in-class screening aims to create comparative criteria for leading companies in terms of ESG criteria. There is also norm-based screening where investments are made against minimum standards for business practice. This has also led to ESG integration, where fund managers systematically and clearly introduce SRI investment managers who have environmental, social and governing factors in their financial analyses.

Shareholder engagement and activism have received a lot of attention in SRI investments. They represent institutional investors' attitudes to participate in management decision-making to try to actively run companies with responsible behaviour in ESG issues (Vandekerckhove et al., 2008). Shareholder activism is often referred to as the use of formal rights attached to common stock. For example, shareholders can influence decisions at the Annual General Meeting by voting against management decisions. Shareholder activism can also include media campaigns to exert pressure on corporate management to create conditions for change (Sparkes & Cowton, 2004).

Institutional investors often use a combination of different SRI strategies to improve the ESG development of companies or industries to promote sustainable, financially profitable investments.

12.4 Important organizations within SRI

There are many organizations and networks that are trying to develop acceptance of SRI. Organizations that are often mentioned in connection with

SRI are UN Principles for Responsible Investment (UN PRI), US Social Investment Forum (USSIF) and European Social Investment Forum (Eurosif).

The *PRI* was founded in 2006 on a joint initiative of the UN Global Compact and the UN Environment Program for the Financial Program (UNEP FI). PRI's mission is to develop principles to integrate ESG issues into the general investment decision and promote the use of SRI among institutional investors. Six general principles are aimed at improving the investment process by offering investors guidance to become more responsible. In 2017, 1,248 organizations followed the PRI principles (UNPRI, 2017).

The *USSIF* is an American organization that since 2010 has the task to shift investment practice towards sustainability, focusing on long-term investment and generating positive social and environmental consequences. USSIF's members include investment managers, fund companies, financial advisors, brokers, pension funds and foundations. USSIF produces training materials and development reports to monitor the SRI industry in the United States. Development reports such as *The 2016 Report on US Sustainable, Responsible and Impact Investing Trends* play an important role in seeing how media depicts the SRI industry and in promoting society's understanding of the field (USSIF, 2016).

The *Eurosif* is a European organization whose mission is to promote SRI in European capital markets. Eurosif works in partnership with European National Sustainable Investment Forums (SIF) and has a network of 400 European-based organizations with an interest in SRI. These organizations include institutional investors, asset managers, SRI services, ESG index providers, ESG surveys and analyses totalling over EUR 8 trillion in total assets. Eurosif is also a founder of the Global Sustainable Investment Alliance, the alliance of the largest SIF members around the world. Eurosif's main tasks are public policy, research and the creation of platforms to promote sustainable investment in practice. Eurosif also provides studies such as European SRI Study 2016 to document the development of the SRI market in Europe (Eurosif, 2016).

12.5 Criticisms and challenges with SRI

Despite the dramatic increase in SRI funds as the studies of USSIF (2016) and Eurosif (2016) show, the overall increase in SRI assets is significantly less impressive compared to the increases that occurred in the total investment assets in the global fund market. As Slager (2015) points out, it is possible to argue against these successes. Although the share of the SRI market is in the total assets of about 10 per cent, 90 per cent is still in funds that do not take SRI into account.

Critics of SRI point out that the pursuit of competitive returns inevitably leads to diluted screening, which means that about 90 per cent of all companies can be considered qualified for an SRI portfolio. A fast-food company, an oil company or a mining company can sometimes be considered "best in class" for a certain part of its corporate governance practice, and this is a fundamental problem (Joly, 2010).

One challenge for the SRI industry is to pursue the same goals as the traditional financial industry, which means that SRI funds and individual SRI investments need to deliver at least the same competitive returns. Institutional investors are measured by their financial performance, and it is no different for those who follow SRI with ESG criteria. At present, it is not as easy to access SRI data on data for financial markets. This affects the quality of analyses and makes it more difficult to conduct independent analyses on the SRI market.

12.6 Summary

In this chapter, an introduction was made regarding the shift in the financial industry towards sustainable investments that take into account CSR and its impact on society. It was stated that SRI funds follow specific ESG criteria that take into account the ESG issues of the companies. An overview of the historical development of the SRI showed that the origins go far back in time to the Methodist Church and Quakers who on religious grounds refused to invest in companies involved in the production of alcohol, tobacco, weapons, games or pornography. The first ethical foundations were founded in the 1920s. In the 1960s and 1970s, SRI funds developed as a reaction to the anti-war and anti-racist movements. Environmental disasters made investors more aware of the negative environmental effects of industrial development that are included in the ESG criteria for SRI. The growth of ethical investments and SRI led the SRI industry to evolve from niche products to mainstream in the global investment market. A review of activities and strategies in sustainable SRI investments showed that there are seven different types of screening technology. Some important organizations such as PRI, USSIF and Eurosif were presented to illustrate their efforts to develop acceptance of SRI. Finally, criticism and challenges are discussed with SRI.

Study questions

1   In what way has modern society been exposed to a crisis of legitimacy?
2   What are the ESG criteria?
3   Why is maximization of shareholder value often seen as the opposite of what is good for society?
4   What does ethical investment entails?
5   How did the first Ethical Fund come into being?
6   How was SRI developed in the 1960s?
7   What role did the SRI funds play in the 1980s in response to apartheid in South Africa?
8   How was SRI developed in the 1990s?
9   What is negative screening?

10   What role does best-in-class screening play in SRI?
11   What does ESG integration mean?
12   How is the goal of SRI explained?
13   What does shareholder activism mean?
14   What criticism is being made against SRI?

References

Arjaliès, D. L. (2010). A social movement perspective on finance: How socially responsible investment mattered, *Journal of Business Ethics*, Vol. 92, pp. 57–78.

European Sustainable Investment Forum (Eurosif), hemsida: www.eurosif.org.

Eurosif (2016). European SRI Study 2016, European Sustainable Investment Forum.

Freeman, R. E. 1984. Strategic management: A stakeholder approach. Boston: Pitman.

Friedman, M. (1962). *Capitalism and freedom*, Chicago: University of Chicago Press.

Joly, C. (2010). Why responsible investment falls short of its purpose and what to do about it?, *Corporate Governance: The International Journal of Business in Society*, Vol. 10 (1), pp. 18–32.

Principles for Responsible Investment, hemsida: www.unpri.org

Renneboog, L., Ter Horst, J. & Zhang, C. (2008). Socially responsible investments: Institutional aspects, performance, and investor behavior, *Journal of Banking & Finance*, Vol. 32, pp. 1723–1742.

Slager, R. (2015). SRI Indices and responsible corporate behavior: A study of the FTSE4Good Index, *Business & Society*, Vol. 54 (3), pp. 386–405.

Solomon, J. F. & Solomon, A. (2006). Private social, ethical and environmental disclosure, *Accounting, Auditing & Accountability Journal*, Vol. 19 (4), pp. 564–591.

Sparkes, R. (2001). Ethical investment: Whose ethics, which investment?, *Business Ethics: A European Review*, Vol. 10 (3), pp. 194–205.

Sparkes, R. & Cowton, C. J. (2004). The maturing of socially responsible investment: A review of the developing link with corporate social responsibility, *Journal of Business Ethics*, Vol. 52 (1), pp. 45–57.

UNPRI. (2017). Principles for Responsible Investment–Annual Report 2017. UNPRI.

USSIF. (2016). 2016 Trends report executive summary: 2016 Report on sustainable and responsible investing trends. US SIF Foundation.

Vandekerckhove, W., Leys, J. & Braeckel, D. (2008). A speech-act model for talking to management. Building a framework for evaluating communication within the SRI engagement process, *Journal of Business Ethics*, Vol. 82 (1), pp. 77–91.

13 Sustainability audit and assurance

Gunnar Rimmel

Abstract

Sustainability audit and assurance is a relatively new phenomenon. The chapter begins with a description of the growing trend among companies to publish sustainability reports, which has increased attention towards the credibility and accuracy of sustainability information. External audits and assurance of sustainability reports have started to develop. The chapter describes that sustainability audit and assurance is an independent review of the company's internal sustainability processes and is used to increase the robustness, accuracy and reliability of information in sustainability reports for users in their decision-making. An approach with generic strategies for the sustainability audit process is described. The chapter contains a brief presentation of regulations and standards in sustainability assurance. It describes the three most well-known assurance standards: ISAE 3000, AA1000 and SA8000. Finally, criticism and challenges are discussed with sustainability audits.

Learning outcomes

After reading this chapter, you are expected to be able to:

- Explain the importance of sustainability audits and assurance.
- Describe the approaches in the process of sustainability auditing.
- Explain the differences between the most well-known standards for sustainability assurance.

13.1 Introduction

Sustainability reporting is a process that helps organizations to understand the links between sustainability-related issues and the organization's plans and strategy, goals, measurements and results. The global economy is changing towards more sustainability thinking. Sustainability is the foundation of today's global framework for international cooperation. The UN created Agenda 2030 that calls for the sustainable development of all nations around the world, and they have set specific Sustainable Development Goals (SDGs). In each of the 17 SDGs, specific goals have been set that needs to be achieved before 2030. This applies to all countries around the world. Achieving these goals requires action by all governments, companies and communities. This means that accounting for sustainability is an important factor in the development towards the UN's various goals and, as a result, the need to measure, to evaluate and to report growth increasingly.

The increasing trend in comprehensive sustainability accounting and companies' publication of sustainability reports has increased attention towards the credibility and accuracy of sustainability information. Sustainability information is considered a powerful tool for assessing the organization's current status quo and future prospects. A sustainability report is the end product where the organization reports on the important material aspects of the organization's economic, social and environmental development.

A key component of developing and implementing sustainability work within an organization involves a periodic follow-up and review of the sustainability work that focuses on issues such as "how do we do" and "where do we need to make improvements?" (Coyne, 2006). These issues reflect the basic auditing principles of management systems and sustainability processes (see Chapter 6). The application of audits helps an organization to assure and review how they are doing on the journey to sustainability. Auditing and reviewing information increases the credibility of users of sustainability reports: especially, if this is being done by independent external parties such as audit firms or other assurance companies that specialize in sustainability auditing and assurance services.

External auditing and assurance of sustainability reports can give users of sustainability reports increased security. Users of sustainability reports can be important for both external stakeholders (e.g. shareholders) and internal stakeholders such as managers (see Chapter 2). An external independent audit provides greater assurance on the quality of sustainability information by verifying its accuracy, making it more likely that the information in the sustainability reports will be relied upon and used for decision-making (Fernandez-Feijoo, Romero & Ruiz, 2016).

Although the external audit of sustainability reports contains similarities to the external audit of the companies' financial reports, there are important differences. For listed companies, auditing is a statutory requirement while auditing of sustainability reports is voluntary and unregulated. The statutory audit requirement clearly stipulates what financial reporting is intended for, and there are clear requirements for how to carry out an assurance engagement for financial reporting.

Assurance engagement is defined by the International Auditing and Assurance Standards Board (IAASB) as:

> ...an engagement in which a practitioner aims to obtain sufficient appropriate evidence in order to express a conclusion designed to enhance

the degree of confidence of the intended users other than the responsible party about the subject matter information.

(IAASB, 2016, p. 14)

Although accounting standards for financial reporting are well established, financial reports that have been assured by external auditors are considered more valuable and useful than unaudited financial reports without assurance. In the same way, it applies to an independent audit of the process behind the preparation of sustainability reports. The sustainability reports that have been audited externally through auditing or assurance services are considered more robust and more reliable in comparison with unannounced sustainability reports (Hodge, Subramaniam & Stewart, 2009).

Sustainability audits must address the issues that are most critical to managing, measuring and informing about sustainability. These issues may vary depending on the industry and company. Sustainability reporting covers various areas with criteria for environmental, social and corporate governance of the company. Sustainability information often contains a mixture of quantitative and qualitative information. Quantitative sustainability information is usually not measured in monetary units and internal control systems, and data collection processes are often not as standardized and developed as control systems, and these processes are for the company's financial information. These factors combined with the increased interest in reliable, comparable information and the accuracy of the sustainability reports create a need for external sustainability audits and assurance.

Globally applied audit and assurance standards for sustainability information have started to become developed in recent years. These standards for sustainability audit and assurance vary in focus and approach. It should also be noted that only a few countries, such as South Africa due to the King reports, focus on integrated reporting (IR; see Chapter 9) and have clearly formulated the need for sustainability reports to receive an external audit and independent assurance.

13.2 Sustainability audit and assurance approaches

Sustainability auditing and assurance is still a relatively new phenomenon. Auditing of sustainability reports is relatively new, and assurance services are offered by various suppliers, such as accounting firms and consultants. Although sustainability reporting has increased strongly with the growing acceptance of Triple Bottom Line thinking (see Chapter 7) among companies and the use of sustainability frameworks and standards such as the Global Reporting Initiative (GRI) and IR (see Chapter 9), sustainability audits have not played a strong role. The recent decades of sustainability reporting have not resulted in an equally clear need for sustainability audit and assurance. Although GRI has had requests for external audits and assurances and described their thoughts on sustainability auditing (GRI, 2013) through the different application levels in its G3 standard, GRI removed the different application levels (see Chapter 8). This indicates that sustainability reporting has had problems with the credibility and accuracy of the information due to lack of comparability and compliance in sustainability reports (Cuadrado-Ballesteros, Martínez-Ferrero & García-Sánchez, 2017).

Therefore, the use of external independent audits and assurance of companies' internal sustainability processes and external disclosures issued in sustainability reports aims to increase the rigour, accuracy and reliability of sustainability information for the users of sustainability reports for their decision-making. The terms used in the process of sustainability auditing and assurance may vary with the various standards, but usually include audit, verification, certification and external assurance (Martínez-Ferrero & García-Sánchez, 2017). There are different approaches to sustainability audit and assurance that depend on the different focus found in the standards for sustainability audit and assurance.

Sustainability audit and assurances follow a generic approach that includes the following steps:

1 Define the sustainability audit and assurance's goals, scope and agenda.
2 Select the organization for sustainability audit and assurance and minimum qualifications for audit staff or practitioners.
3 Select the organizational units to review in the process of sustainability assurance engagement.
4 Determine the criteria and frameworks to apply for sustainability reporting.
5 Determine the frequency of audits, audit method and assurance.
6 Determine the responsibility of the company in the audit and assurance process, such as data collection or the establishment of internal controls.
7 Determine the responsibility of the sustainability auditor regarding ethical and legal requirements.
8 Select audit records, checklists or guidelines to use during the audit and assurance.
9 Define procedures for reporting sustainability audit and assurance and document management.
10 Define procedures for corrective action after checking and reviewing results.

As the generic approach to sustainability audit and assurance illustrates above, the audit and assurance process will focus on data quality, specific routines about what data to collect and how it should be audited and assured. The underlying intention is to improve the quality of the information in the sustainability reports. High-quality information is seen as more credible and ultimately more useful both for the company and for the information users (Simnett, Vanstraelen, & Chua, 2009).

An independent audit and assurance of sustainability reports and the benefit of sustainability audits is challenged by two key factors. First, there are currently no widely accepted reporting criteria for sustainability reporting (although GRI has become dominant), resulting in considerable variation in scope and responsibility for sustainability audits and assurances. Accordingly, the audit reports may vary considerably depending on the regulations and standards applied while carrying out the sustainability audit and assurance work (Braama, Uit de Weerd, Hauck & Hujibregts, 2016).

13.3 Sustainability audit and assurance regulations and standards

At present, there is no globally universally accepted standard for sustainability audit and assurance. However, there are instead a number of different audit and assurance standards and initiatives. The most well-known standards for sustainability audit and assurance that have gained global distribution and use around the world are ISAE 3000, AA1000 and SA8000 (Junior, Best & Cotter, 2014). All these three standards in sustainability audit and assurance (see Table 13.1) have been developed on private initiatives. As a result, these standards have not been developed on the same grounds as auditing of financial accounting information, as these are usually derived from government initiatives. SA8000 and AA1000 AS are relatively similar in their attributes in connection with sustainability audit and assurance. Both standards have a strong focus on social responsibility. ISAE 3000 has been added later than the other two and has a greater resemblance to the audit of financial reporting.

The lack of an international common normative standard for sustainability audit and assurance has caused confusion, as the standards that exist partly have overlapping terminology, principles and guidelines. This has led to, for example, AA1000 and ISAE 3000, being used in combination to gain greater credibility for companies' sustainability reports (Junior, Best & Cotter, 2014).

13.4 ISAE 3000

The IAASB has created the ISAE 3000. It is an international standard for auditing non-financial information reporting. The IAASB is part of the International Federation of Accountants (IFAC). IFAC was founded in 1977 at the 11th World Congress of Accountants in Munich to strengthen the global accounting profession and contribute to the development of accounting and auditing. IFAC's international audit framework is developed by the IAASB in the form of International Standards on Auditing (ISA). IAASB's international audit framework defines the most important elements of an audit assignment to manage information on financial or non-financial information.

The international standard ISAE 3000 covers the control of the services provided by organizations. The purpose of ISAE 3000 is to handle various needs and reporting requirements of service organizations and to provide

Table 13.1 International standards in sustainability audit and assurance

Fundamental concepts	Standard setter	
ISAE 3000	International Auditing and Assurance Standard Board (IAASB)	• Non–stakeholder focused • Specially designed for sustainability auditing • Limited auditing is permitted for sustainability reports • Emphasizes the auditor's competence and explicit appearance of the use of experts • Procedures include audit planning, risk assessment, collection and evaluation procedures • Approved by the Federation of European Accountants (FEE)
AA1000	AccountAbility	• Core principles: materiality, inclusiveness and responsiveness • Auditing of performance information and also unexamined performance information are both permitted • Observations and recommendations are included in the audit report
SA8000	Social Accountability International (SAI)	• Non–stakeholder focused • Based on the various UN conventions and ILO recommendations • Applies to all sizes of organization in all industries • Requirements for auditing to obtain an accredited certification • Compatible with ISO 9001 and ISO 14001 standards • Approved by the Federation of European Accountants (FEE)

valuable information to meet users' needs, including risk assessment in connection with outsourcing.

Generally, ISAE 3000 is used for auditing of internal control, sustainability and compliance with laws and regulations. ISAE 3000 provides strict requirements and supplementary guidance on the performance of audit assignments, including guidance on planning of engagement and gathering of information. The standard consists of guidelines for ethical behaviour, quality management and implementation of ISAE 3000 (IAASB, 2016).

ISAE 3000 describes the basic parts of the report as follows:

- Intended users of the assurance report, e.g. management, shareholders.
- An identification and description of the subject matter information.
- Identification of the criteria – whether or not the criteria are embodied in laws or regulations, or issued by authorized or recognized bodies of experts that follow a transparent due.
- The responsibility of the practitioner and the company in the assurance engagement.
- Reference to the relevant ISAE 3000 standard.
- A summary of the work performed.
- The practitioner's conclusion in form of an assurance report.

A practitioner, not necessarily a charted accountant or auditor, must submit an audit in a separate written assurance report that is linked to the sustainability information reported on. The assurance report should be concise and contain information on the criteria used and a summary of the work performed.

In accordance with ISAE 3000, there are two levels of assurance: reasonable assurance and limited assurance. The definition of limited assurance is explained by obtaining reasonable assurance. A limited assurance is applied where a practitioner reduces the risk in the assurance engagement to a level that is acceptable under the circumstances of the assignment, but where the risk is greater than for a reasonable audit work.

The IAASB had discussed the possibilities of developing subject-specific assurance standards for sustainability, for example, the mining industry. However, with the emergence and rapid dissemination of IR and related audit and assurance issues, it is possible that the IAASB will not develop subject-specific standards for sustainability assurance (Simnett, 2012). Currently, the IAASB does not have such specified standards, but instead updates the assurance of sustainability reports in ISAE 3000.

13.5 AA1000

The AccountAbility (AA) organization launched the AA1000 standard in England in 1999 with the goal of helping companies, shareholders, auditors, consultants and certification bodies. It can be used alone or in conjunction with other standards of accountability, such as the GRI standards, ISO standards and SA8000. The AA1000 standard is a voluntary standard for social and ethical accounting, auditing and reporting. The idea for the standard came up to deal with scepticism of corporate reports on human rights, socio-economic and economic issues. Therefore, AA1000 focuses on improving the social and ethical performance of organizations through the principles of accounting, reporting and auditing of sustainability. AccountAbility developed its AA1000 Series of Standards, which are principles-based standards and frameworks used by a wide range of organizations (AccountAbility, 2008).

The AA1000 series consists of three books:

1   *AA1000 AccountAbility Principles Standard (AA1000AS, 2008) with 2018 Addendum* contains the basic principles of a policy-based framework that can be applied by organizations of all sizes.
2   *AA1000 AccountAbility Assurance Standard (AA1000AS)* (2008) content description of the methodology for sustainability-related assurance engagements to examine how an organization complies with the AA1000 principles.
3   *AA1000 AccountAbility Stakeholder Engagement Standard (AA100ES)* (2015) is the standard that supports organizations to communicate an integrated approach to stakeholder engagement.

According to the AA1000 sustainability assurance standard, there are two types of AA1000 sustainability assurance engagements. These are classified as Type 1 or Type 2.

In *Type 1 sustainability assurance engagement*, the assurance provider will review the nature and extent of the organization's compliance with AA1000. The assurance of AA1000 is intended to provide stakeholders with an audit of how an organization manages sustainability performance and how it communicates this in its sustainability reporting without verifying the reliability of the reported information. In Type 1 sustainability assurance engagement, the assurance provider concludes on the reliability of sustainability information.

In *Type 2 sustainability assurance engagements*, the assurance provider shall review the nature and extent of the organization's compliance with AA1000 AccountAbility Principles, just as for Type 1. In addition, in Type 2 sustainability assurance engagements the assurance provider shall evaluate the reliability of specified sustainability performance information. Specified information on sustainability performance is the information that the assurance provider and the reporting organization approve to include within the framework of the assurance engagement. Specified information is selected based on materiality and must be meaningful to the intended users of the assurance report.

An AA1000 assurance engagement can be performed on two different levels: a high assurance level or a moderate assurance level. A high level of assurance gives users a high degree of confidence in the organization's sustainability information. The auditor achieves a high assurance level if sufficient evidence has been obtained to support that the risk of an incorrect conclusion in the assurance report is very low. Moderate assurance level increases user trust in an organization. The auditor achieves moderate assurance if sufficient evidence has been obtained to support that the risk of an incorrect conclusion in the audit report is reduced.

Currently, AccountAbility is updating AA1000 and plans to release an update in 2020, as current topics such as IR need to be addressed in AA1000 auditing.

13.6 SA8000

In 1997, the first SA8000 standard was issued in the USA. This standard had been developed by the Council on Economic Priorities Accreditation Agency (CEPAA) to improve working conditions at a global level. Since 1998, the organization Social Accountability International (SAI) has been responsible for the standard. The standard was updated in 2001, 2008 and 2014. CEPAA focused on developing a standard that, with the help of a third-party verification system, can ensure ethical purchasing of products, goods and working conditions worldwide.

SA8000 is the first standard in corporate social responsibility that allows assurance and is compliant with the ISO 9001 and ISO 14001 standards (see Chapter 6). The SA8000 standard is based mainly on the various conventions and recommendations of the International Labor Organization (ILO), the UN Declaration on Human Rights and the UN Convention on the Rights of the Child.

This is reflected in the SA8000's nine basic requirements:

1   Child labour – *employers shall not employ children under 15 years.*
2   Forced labour – *the employer must ensure that their workers are free and do not work against their will.*
3   Health and safety – *employers must provide safeguard measures to ensure the health and safety of workers.*
4   Freedom of association and the right to collective bargaining – *workers must have the freedom to negotiate with employers, to create and become members of the trade union of their choice.*
5   Discrimination – *racial, gender and other discrimination is prohibited.*
6   Disciplinary methods – *employers may not use or support the use of disciplinary methods.*
7   Working hours – working hours must be limited to 48 hours per week and overtime 12 hours per week.
8   Compensation – *the employer must pay at least the minimum wage.*
9   Management system – *a quality management system that ensures compliance with the standard.*

The SA8000 standard applies to all sizes of organization or business in all industries. In principle, the standard is not limited to specific industrial sectors. Although SA8000 excludes agricultural and extractive industries, the SA8000 is mainly designed to manage and control the value chain. It is a voluntary standard that can be implemented by all types of organizations, regardless of size, industrial sector, geographical location or whether it is a for-profit company or a non-profit organization.

When applying the SA8000, an organization must implement a so-called Social Management System (SMS) to ensure compliance with the standard. The SA8000 SMS is designed as a quality management system and includes process phases such as planning, implementation, control and corrective measures as well as management review.

SAI has released the *Guidance Document for Social Accountability 8000* that assists with both interpretation and application of the nine requirements to obtain accredited certification (SAI, 2016). The accredited certification is considered a valuable tool for evaluating performance and driving improvements in the company's supply chain to ensure ethical purchasing of products, goods and working conditions.

13.7 Criticism and challenges with sustainability audit and assurance

Auditing and assurance of sustainability reports is an important aspect to increase the reliability of non-financial aspects of the environment, social conditions or governance. If companies cannot integrate the non-financial aspects of sustainability with financial reporting, the principle of materiality will be undermined. Sustainability reports have frequently been abused as marketing products in corporate communications. This is also due to the fact that sustainability reports have been voluntary and without independent audit. The importance of auditing in connection with sustainability reporting has increased. Criticism has been made that stakeholders do not demand sufficient sustainability reports that have been independently audited (Cuadrado-Ballesteros, Martínez-Ferrero & García-Sánchez, 2017). However, there is evidence that stakeholders value a higher level of sustainability auditing for their investment decisions. If sustainability reports do not follow known sustainability audit and assurance standards that audit corporate sustainability information on management, governance, performance and reporting, companies may fail to retain their stakeholders' trust (Fernandez-Feijoo, Romero & Ruiz, 2016).

The credibility of sustainability audit and assurance standards is very important, as corporate stakeholders must have confidence in sustainability audit and assurance process to assess sustainability report information (Simnett, Vanstraelen & Chua, 2009). So far, there are no statutory requirements for sustainability audits. The fact that the three presented audit and assurance standards partly overlap in their characteristics can be seen as a problem for companies to decide which standard they want to use. This has led some companies to follow several standards at the same time in order to gain more credibility in their sustainability reports (Junior, Best & Cotter, 2014). This entails higher costs for companies as they double-check their sustainability reports in the audit and assurance process.

Given the benefits of sustainability audits and assurances, the challenges lie in taking the initiative to legislate the requirement for sustainability audit and assurance to ensure that non-financial corporate information is as accurate in its audit and assurance as for financial accounting information. However, this requires that governments, authorities and private organizations cooperate more strongly on these issues than before. An example in the opposite direction is GRI, which removed application levels A, B, C. This showed clearly the level of independent review of sustainability reports by designating »+« to their application levels. While GRI argued that they did not want to put a quality stamp on sustainability reports (see Chapter 8), it only shows that stakeholders put confidence in independent audits and assurances of sustainability reports. Stakeholders see audits and assurances as quality enhancements of sustainability reports.

13.8 Summary

In this chapter, a review of sustainability audit and assurance was made. Audit and assurance of sustainability information increases the credibility of users of sustainability reports, if these are done by independent external parties such as audit firms or other companies that specialized in sustainability audit and assurance. Sustainability audit and assurances go through issues that are most critical for managing, measuring and reporting on sustainability. In recent years, international audit and assurance standards for sustainability information have begun to develop. These audit and assurance standards vary in focus and approach. Although there are different approaches to sustainability audit and assurance, they depend on the different focus in the standards for sustainability audit and assurance. There is a generic process in sustainability audit and assurance. The most well-known standards for sustainability audit and assurance that have been widely recognized and found application around the world are ISAE 3000, AA1000 and SA8000. The IAASB has created ISAE 3000, which is an international standard for assurance of non-financial information reporting. According to ISAE 3000, professional accountants are required to submit an assurance report linked to the sustainability information reported on. The AA1000 standard is a voluntary standard for social and ethical accounting, auditing, assurance and reporting. The SA8000 is the first standard in corporate social responsibility that allows assurance and is compliant with the ISO 9001 and ISO 14001 standards. Assurance sustainability report is an important aspect of increasing reliability in non-financial aspects of the environment, social conditions or governance. The benefits of sustainability audit and assurance can promote future initiatives to legislate the requirement for sustainability audit and assurance.

Study questions

1   How does the trend of increased sustainability reports relate to the development of sustainability audit and assurance?
2   How does the International Auditing and Assurance Standards Board define the term assurance engagement?
3   Why is sustainability audit and assurance considered a relatively new phenomenon?

4 Describe the generic steps in the sustainability audit and assurance process.
5 Describe the three most well-known characteristics of the sustainability audit and assurance standards.
6 How was the ISAE 3000 developed?
7 What are the essential elements of the ISAE 3000 in the report?
8 How was AA1000 developed?
9 How was the SA8000 developed?
10 What role does the SA8000's nine basic requirements play?
11 What is the significance of the so-called Social Management System?
12 What criticism was made against sustainability audit and assurance?

References

AccountAbility (2008). *AA1000 Assurance Standard 2008*, AccountAbility Publications.

Braama, G. J. M., Uit de Weerd, L., Hauck, M. & Huijbregts, M. A. J. (2016). Determinants of corporate environmental reporting: The importance of environmental performance and assurance, *Journal of Cleaner Production*, Vol. 129, pp. 724–734.

Coyne, K. L. (2006). Sustainability auditing–Evaluating organizations' progress toward sustainable development, *Environmental Quality Management*, Vol. 16, pp. 25–41.

Cuadrado-Ballesteros, B., Martínez-Ferrero, J. & García-Sánchez, I. M. (2017). Mitigating information asymmetry through sustainability assurance: The role of accountants and levels of assurance, *International Business Review*, Vol. 26, pp. 1141–1156.

Fernandez-Feijoo, B., Romero, S. & Ruiz, S. (2016) The assurance market of sustainability reports: What do accounting firms do?, *Journal of Cleaner Production*, Vol. 139, pp. 1128–1137.

GRI (2013). *The external assurance of sustainability reporting*, Global Reporting Initiative Research & Development Series.

Hodge, K., Subramaniam, N. & Stewart, J. (2009). Assurance of sustainability reports: Impact on report users' confidence and perceptions of information credibility, *Australian Accounting Review*, Vol. 19 (3), pp. 178–194.

International Auditing and Assurance Standards Board (IAASB) (2016). *Handbook of international quality control, auditing, review, other assurance, and related services pronouncements–2016–2017 Edition Volume I*. IFAC Handbook, International Federation of Accountants.

Junior, R. M., Best P. J. & Cotter, J. (2014). Sustainability reporting and assurance: A historical analysis on a world-wide phenomenon, *Journal of Business Ethics*, Vol. 120 (1), pp. 1–11.

Martínez-Ferrero, J. & García-Sánchez, I. M. (2017). Coercive, normative and mimetic isomorphism as determinants of the voluntary assurance of sustainability reports, *International Business Review*, Vol. 26, pp. 102–118.

Simnett, R. (2012). Assurance of sustainability reports: Revision of ISAE 3000 and associated research opportunities, *Sustainability Accounting, Management and Policy Journal*, Vol. 3 (1), pp. 89–98.

Simnett, R., Vanstraelen, A. & Chua, W. F. (2009). Assurance on sustainability reports: An international comparison, *The Accounting Review*, Vol. 84 (3), pp. 937–967.
Social Accountability International (SAI) (2016). Guidance document for Social Accountability 8000 (SA8000:2014).

International Federation of Accountants, website:

International Auditing Handbooks, Standards, and Pronouncements, www.ifac.org
International Standard on Assurance Engagements (ISAE) 3000

Accountability, website:

AA1000, www.accountability.org

Social Accountability International (SAI), website:

SA8000, www.sa-intl.org

14 Critical reflections and future developments

Gunnar Rimmel, Susanne Arvidsson, Peter Beusch,
Berit Hartmann, Kristina Jonäll, Svetlana Sabelfeld
and Matti Skoog

Abstract

This chapter aims to provide critical reflections on accounting for sustainability developments, the present situation and future developments. First, it is descried how accounting for sustainability has become an important element in companies' reporting landscape. Thereafter, a number of important players in the market for sustainability accounting are presented, and how the shift from voluntary disclosure to statutory sustainability reports has gradually changed. The chapter describes a possible turning point in accounting for sustainability, as increased legal requirements for sustainability information have resulted in growing demands on its quality. Then, current developments of sustainability reporting against aggregated reporting frameworks are discussed. Finally, some reflections are presented on the future developments of accounting for sustainability.

Learning outcomes

After reading this chapter, you are expected to be able to:

* Understand why accounting for sustainability is an important element of corporate reporting.
* Describe the turning point in accounting for sustainability.
* Describe sustainability accounting and the path to aggregated sustainability reporting frameworks.

14.1 Accounting for sustainability is an important element in corporate reporting

In today's business environment, it is no longer enough for companies to only disclose financial information. This can be seen very clearly by comparing old annual reports from the 1950s, 1960s, 1970s, 1980s, 1990s, or from the turn of the millennium. It is evident that a regular annual report in the 1950s had only 10–15 pages and simply included the balance sheet and income statement. The development of increased complexity in global trade, and the importance of the capital market to individual investors, is reflected in an increasing number of descriptions and disclosures of non-financial information that illustrate corporate operations. Non-financial information describes the company's products, markets and development as a complement to the traditional balance sheet and income statement. But even as the financial statement part has changed over time. For example, cashflow statements began to emerge in the 1990s. Currently, the annual reports grew in volume to large documents with 100–200 or even more pages containing financial and non-financial information.

As the previous chapters of this book have shown, voluntary disclosure of sustainability information has become a common part of company reporting. Voluntary information is company information that exceeds the minimum requirement according to legal requirements, such as accounting standards (Rimmel 2003). Sustainability reporting is not new on the companies' communication agenda (see Chapter 10). The first sustainability reports were published in the 1960s and 1970s (Gray et al. 2014, Dumay et al. 2015), but voluntary sustainability information existed as early as 1885, which Guthrie and Parker showed in their study of Australian mining companies (Guthrie & Parker 1989). The importance of sustainability issues has increased significantly since the first days of sustainability reporting. Companies are held accountable for their way of doing business (see Chapters 12 and 13). For companies, it is no longer a question of whether they should participate in sustainability reporting. The question for them is: what to report in their corporate reports (see Chapters 7–9), how to work on these issues internally (see Chapters 3–5) and what measures are needed to meet the needs of the capital market (see Chapter 11). Unlike accounting standards, there are few mandatory requirements for companies to report sustainability information (see Chapter 6).

In the absence of legislation and requirements, a growing number of voluntary sustainability frameworks have been developed by private initiatives and international organizations over the past two decades (Baboukardos & Rimmel 2016). These reporting frameworks can vary from focusing heavily on financial management, added value, social accounting, environmental reporting, human capital accounting or Triple Bottom Line reporting. There is also a combination of social, environmental and economic measures that have led to external audits and assurance of sustainability reports or capital market-oriented initiatives for sustainable investments.

There are a number of important players in the market that leads to international development. As explained in Chapter 8, the Global Reporting Initiative (GRI) was founded in the late 1990s by the non-profit organizations such as CERES, the Tellus Institute and the United Nations Environment Program (UNEP). GRI standards are the oldest reporting framework for sustainability and have found the greatest application of all sustainability frameworks among multinational companies and organizations. A little later, in 2000, the United Nations launched the UN Global Compact to encourage companies globally to demonstrate sustainability and social responsibility by following ten principles in the areas of human rights, manpower, environment and corruption. In 2006, the UN Principles for Responsible Investment (PRI) was introduced to show that environmental issues, social issues and governance (ESG), such as climate change and human rights, can affect the performance of investment portfolios. In the aftermath of the 2007 financial crisis, the International Integrated Reporting Council (IIRC) was founded to develop a new method for sustainability reporting, called integrated reporting (IR). In 2013, the IIRC introduced an IR framework focused on the integrated report and defined its purpose, basic content and principles. In addition to companies' efforts for sustainable development, leaders in countries around the world have signed several environmental agreements. In 2014, the European Council approved a new directive (2014/95/EU) on non-financial reporting.

The world's most widely used frameworks and standards for sustainability reporting (see Table 14.1) are not the only ones available in the market for sustainability reporting. There are a large number of other frameworks and standards that have been developed by various private initiatives. However, Table 14.1 illustrates which ones are the most prominent and have found wide application of companies or received a great deal of attention in business. The number of companies and organizations that comply with GRI, UN Global Compact, PRI, <IR> or European non-financial disclosure directives is steadily growing.

Although sustainability reporting in the beginning has been subject to scepticism from various stakeholders, abused by companies to green-wash their business or treated as a pure marketing tool with little evidence and hard facts, the latest developments in sustainability accounting have gained great acceptance with greater confidence to the data quality. Sustainability reporting began as voluntary information without legal consequences; if companies did not comply with standards or guidelines no punishment would be used for enforcement. However, this prevailing voluntary sustainability reporting regime is about to change towards regulations and requirements that will be enforced.

14.2 The turning point in accounting for sustainability

The current landscape of sustainability reporting has changed tremendously in comparison with the early days of the 1960s, 1970s or 1990s. At the time when sustainability reporting was still in its infancy, it was individual companies, organizations and other promoters who tried to change the dominant approach to financial reporting. Advocates and leaders in the development of accounting for sustainability were often criticized for not having their origins in the field of accounting. In the 1960s, 1970s or 1980s, climate change was already on the agenda, but only for researchers and environmental activists.

Table 14.1 Key players in accounting for sustainability

Organisation	Perspective	Focus	Outreach
GRI	The GRI applies a multi-stakeholder strategy for sustainability reporting.	A framework for sustainability reporting, GRI standards, based on previous reporting guideline G4 that extends from universal standards, economic standards, environmental standards and social standards.	12,000 companies, organizations and governments. 93 per cent of the world's largest companies apply GRI.
UN Global Compact	UN Global Compact developed a principle-based framework for companies.	Ten principles for companies in the area of human rights, labour, environment and corruption.	9,700 companies and other stakeholders in over 161 countries.
UN PRI	UN PRI focuses on sustainable investments in the capital market.	Six different PRI. The six principles for responsible investing are a voluntary and ambitious set of investment principles to integrate ESG issues into investment practice.	More than 1,750 signatories, from over 50 countries.
<IR>	The IIRC has developed an IR framework.	The IR framework focuses on the integrated report and defines its purpose, basic content and basic principles. Corporate communication should be about the organization's strategy, governance, results and future prospects that should lead to value creation in the short, medium and long term.	About 100 organizations, ranging from multinational companies and stock exchanges to universities.
European Commission	In 2014, the European Council approved one new directive (2014/95/EU) on non-financial reporting.	European directive requiring public companies to disclose their social, environmental, governance and versatile performance activities.	Approximately 6,000 large listed companies that will report according to the directives from 2017.

The phenomenon of climate change had not been widely acknowledged in society until the 1990s, but for the past decade it has been on the global agenda for both governments and society in general, not least through the media attention that arose in 2007 when Al Gore shared the Nobel Peace Prize with Intergovernmental Panel on Climate Change (IPCC) for generating opinion on global warming. At the same time, unbridled global capitalism on stock exchanges around the world experienced, in close succession, two of the most severe financial crises. As a result, the way in which corporate reporting was also changed. The shift in corporate reporting went from an exclusive financial approach to a holistic approach. Instead of relying solely on the financial development of the company, more and more information about the company's operations and its impact on society and the environment is now needed.

It seems that accounting for sustainability has reached a turning point, as it is no longer just a problem for individual companies or individual private initiatives. Sustainability reporting was moved from the periphery of financial reporting to become a common and important element in describing corporate responsibility towards society and the environment. In order to produce sustainability reports, internal accounting processes are required that make it easier to provide the right information. One of the important factors in the development of accounting for sustainability from niche product to mainstream may just be collaboration with the political agenda to combat climate change and the consequences of the global financial crises. In addition to these efforts by leading companies and private organizations for sustainable development, political leaders in countries around the world have signed several international environmental agreements that require sustainability information. As a result, these agreements make sustainability information a legal requirement.

In 2014, the European Council approved a new directive (2014/95/EU) on non-financial reporting. The directive aims to improve disclosure of non-financial information, such as social and environmental issues. One reason for this directive is to make it easier for the European Union (EU) to develop and take measurements to allow comparison between member states. After the directives on non-financial reporting in the EU were approved, European member states issued new legislation that made it mandatory for large companies to publish sustainability reports. These sustainability reports should provide information on how the company works on issues related to the environment, social conditions, employees, anti-corruption and human rights.

In December 2019, the new European Commission President Ursula von der Leyen announced 'The European Green Deal'. The European Green Deal aims for the EU to become the world's first climate-neutral continent by 2050. In order to achieve this, the European Commission presented in its road map that the EU will impose further statutory requirements for national EU member states, companies and stock exchanges. With increased regulation and mandatory requirements, the emphasis on which information is to be reported in sustainability reports changed. Therefore, companies and organizations must reflect on what sustainability information is crucial to achieving set sustainability goals in their operations. This needs a transformation of the financial markets towards sustainable finance. The recent formation of the EU High Level Expert (HLEG) Group on Sustainable Finance is a noticeable milestone. Further, the Task Force on Climate-Related Financial Disclosures (TCFD) have developed a framework that promotes an enhancement of climate-related financial disclosure by including financial-risk and scenarios-analysis perspectives (TCFD 2017). The establishment of the Technical Expert Group (TEG) on Sustainable Finance with the objective to develop an EU classification system of sustainable activities, i.e. the EU taxonomy is yet another example of the movement in the sustainable finance area where improved sustainability reporting is vital (TEG 2019). In beginning of February 2020, The Project Task Force of Climate-Related Reporting of the EFRAG European Lab launched its report: 'How to improve climate-related reporting – A summary of good practices from Europe and beyond'. This EFRAG European Lab report is identifying good reporting practices and assessing the level of maturity in the implementation of the TCFD recommendations, while also taking into consideration the climate-related reporting elements of the EU Non-financial Reporting Directive.

All these recent developments point out that non-compliance with reporting sustainability information would have a negative impact on the company's performance, reputation and even the ability to raise capital. Accounting for sustainability has spread to the boardroom, to the investment decision processes and to the company's stakeholders. This leaves a mark on corporate reporting to work for the integration of financial and non-financial reporting. Financial reporting has its basis in reliable data. By making sustainability reporting a legal statutory reporting requirement the pressure for non-financial information reporting increases that this type of information must be equally measurable as financial information in order to ensure maximum transparency and easy comparison.

The current challenge is to ensure that sustainability reporting accomplishes the same quality as financial reporting to enable investment decisions for the right reasons. A study by Baboukardos and Rimmel (2016) found that capital market participants in South Africa consider that mandatory sustainability information requirements in integrated reports are value-relevant. This shows that disclosure about accounting for sustainability is a value-relevant and useful proxy for investors. Instead of relying solely on financial reporting, investors should also look at sustainability measures to gain broader understanding of the company's long-term value. Accordingly, the long-term goal of sustainability reporting should be to enable comparable performance through adequate information and transparency.

14.3 Accounting for sustainability towards aggregated reporting frameworks

Sustainability reporting has undergone a fairly rapid development lately. From niche product to a global general practice in listed companies as well as to be found in Small- and Medium-Sized Entities (SMEs). With the growing interest in corporate sustainability, a number of reporting standards, guidelines and frameworks have emerged, as shown in the previous chapters. While the international landscape for sustainability reporting has spread through a variety of different standards, guidelines and frameworks, there are tendencies for different organizations to collaborate and harmonize their guidelines and frameworks. In part, this may be due to the growing number of players in the market for accounting for sustainability also increasing competition for users, i.e. companies that must follow and use the various reporting standards, guidelines and frameworks. This can be expressed in the fact that regional frameworks try to establish themselves against international frameworks.

An example could be the establishment of the Sustainability Accounting Standard Board (SASB) in the United States as a national organization that aims to develop sustainability standards that GRI also aims to achieve. Rimmel and Jonäll (2013) showed that many companies apply several different frameworks and guidelines for sustainability reporting. One of the reasons for increased application of several frameworks and guidelines for sustainability reporting may be the growing need for companies to communicate the financial consequences of sustainability to stakeholders. The problem with the use of several frameworks and standards on sustainability reporting is that this can lead to a large variation in the quality, quantity, timeliness and relevance of the sustainability information that is to be disclosed. In turn, such a large variation can cause confusion among users of the information, since comparability of sustainability information between years and companies may not be possible.

Although sustainability reporting frameworks and standards intend to share important sustainability information and create awareness, their current emphasis and perspective may be quite different. For example, the IIRC's <IR> framework provides very little guidance on how companies should report on sustainability. Whereas GRI publishes a variety of standards that contain specific disclosure requirements, SASB in the United States developed a number of industry-specific standards for sustainability reporting, which are even more specific than GRI's. However, all three of these frameworks are voluntary for the companies, as the current mandatory requirements do not explicitly advocate a specific framework or standard for sustainability reporting.

The increase in mandatory sustainability reporting in many jurisdictions (e.g. at EU or national level) will lead to an increasing number of requirements with greater complexity for businesses. It can be a burden for a company to decide on a framework if no specific framework is recommended. Assessing a number of different standards, frameworks and guidelines as the best method of sustainability reporting for a company is a major challenge, which is costly and time-consuming. Since there are many different actors within the sustainability reporting framework, all these actors would like to become the most important framework or standard.

The harmonization and standardization process will be crucial in meeting the increased demands towards relevance and comparability of sustainability information. Admittedly, there will always be specific issues that are of significant importance to various interest groups. However, like financial reporting, sustainability reporting should be the subject of high-quality data to increase confidence and transparency in information. GRI seems to be a leader in converging different frameworks for sustainability reporting. Since their G4 guidelines were launched, which have now become GRI standards, GRI now contains clear links to the UN Global Compact. Furthermore, GRI has announced that they will extend their cooperation with PRI and IIRC (GRI 2017). The collaboration makes it difficult for other frameworks (e.g. SASB) to continue its expansion in the market for sustainability accounting. Indeed, there may be parallels with the competition between the Financial Accounting Standards Board (FASB) from the United States and the International Accounting Standards Board (IASB) before embarking on their convergence project. The IIRC convenes *The Corporate Reporting Dialogue* platform, to promote greater coherence, consistency and comparability between corporate reporting frameworks, standards and related requirements. The Corporate Reporting Platform includes many leading organizations like Climate Disclosure Standards Board, GRI, IASB, IIRC, International Organization for Standardization, SASB as well as the FASB, which is participating as an observer. Maybe this will reduces the boundaries among these different reporting frameworks.

There is much to gain from a common framework for sustainability reporting. Harmonizing frameworks may increase the usability and comparability of sustainability information and reporting. If companies only needed to provide a method for sustainability information, it would reduce companies' work and costs compared to applying multiple sustainability reporting frameworks that partially overlap.

14.4 Some reflections on the future developments of accounting for sustainability

Sustainability reporting is here to stay and has become a commonplace in corporate reporting. Transparency and sustainability information are high on the corporate agenda. However, accounting for sustainability is not just for companies, but for a wide range of interests ranging from investors, customers, suppliers and employees to society and governments. Accounting can play an important role, as information in sustainability reports needs accurate accounts of companies' sustainability activities. There is a growing demand for sustainability reports. The information contained therein must be credible, reliable and powerful, and include material issues for stakeholders.

This in turn obliges companies to be knowledgeable about how the business is adapted to sustainability performance. Sustainability performance requires reliable sustainability information at management accounting level. Integrating sustainability internally with financial management leads to a better understanding of the company's strategy and ensures companies' value development and long-term survival. With increased demand for sustainability reporting, there is an increased demand for reliability in sustainability information.

External independent assurance in the form of sustainability audits will probably increase in the future to reliably show how organizations create sustainable value. Following the introduction of the first mandatory requirements for sustainability reporting, this led to an increasing number of regulations and requirements for a higher level of detail on mandatory reporting. Greater emphasis will be placed on data quality for sustainability information.

It is always difficult to predict the future, but a development that is already underway is to integrate sustainability into corporate financial management. The business systems are currently being adapted to the new requirements and will provide simpler data collection of sustainability information as well as many analysis tools that will help companies to incorporate sustainability issues into their decisions. Another trend that we have already started to see is increased collaboration among various sustainability standards and frameworks. If this trend continues and becomes converged into a Generally Accepted Sustainability Accounting Principles (GASAP), it will probably take very long. As we already know from the convergence project between IASB and FASB, there are as many own interests as there are frameworks, standards and sustainability initiatives.

14.5 Summary

This chapter describes in the introduction how accounting for sustainability has become an important element in corporate reporting. In the absence of legislation and few mandatory requirements, a growing number of voluntary sustainability frameworks have been developed on private initiatives and by international organizations over the past two decades. There are a number of important players in the market that leads to international development. The most prominent frameworks and standards for sustainability reporting have found wide application by companies and received a great deal of attention in business. The volume of companies and organizations complying with GRI, UN Global Compact, PRI, <IR> or European directives is steadily growing. The shift in corporate reporting went from an exclusive financial approach to a holistic approach. Instead of relying solely on the financial development of the company, more and more information about the company's operations and its impact on society and the environment is now needed. It seems that accounting for sustainability has reached a turning point, as it is no longer just a matter for individual companies or for individual private initiatives. Sustainability reporting was moved from the periphery of financial reporting to become a common and important element in describing corporate responsibility towards society and the environment. The challenge is currently to ensure that sustainability reporting achieves the same quality as financial reporting to ensure investment decisions on the right grounds. Many companies apply several different frameworks and guidelines for sustainability reporting. The increase in mandatory sustainability reporting in many jurisdictions (e.g. at EU or national level) will lead to an increasing number of requirements with greater complexity for companies. Harmonization and standardization of the approach will be crucial in meeting the increased relevance and comparability of sustainability information.

Finally, some reflections were presented on the future developments of accounting for sustainability. Integrating sustainability internally with financial management leads to a better understanding of the company's strategy that ensures companies' value development and long-term survival. With increased demand for sustainability reporting, there is an increased demand for reliability in sustainability information. The business systems are currently being adapted to the new requirements and will provide simpler data collection of sustainability information as well as many analysis tools that will help companies to incorporate sustainability issues into their decisions. Accounting for sustainability is here to stay.

References

Baboukardos, D. & Rimmel, G. (2016). Relevance of accounting information under an integrated reporting approach: A research note, *Journal of Accounting and Public Policy*, Vol. 35 (4), pp. 437–452.

Council Directive 2014/95/EU of 22 October 2014 on amending Directive 2013/34 EU as regards disclosure of non-financial and diversity information by certain large undertakings and groups [2014] OJ L330/1.

Dumay, J., Frost, G. & Beck, C. (2015). Material legitimacy: Blending organisational and stakeholder concerns through non-financial information disclosures, *Journal of Accounting & Organizational Change*, Vol. 11 (1), pp. 2–23.

EFRAG Reporting Lab (2020). How to improve climate-related reporting – A summary of good practices from Europe and beyond, www.efrag.org/Assets/Download?assetUrl=/sites/webpublishing/SiteAssets/European%20Lab%20PTF-CRR%20%28Main%20Report%29%20PRINT.pdf

Gray, R., Adams, C. A. & Owen, D. (2014). *Accountability, social responsibility and sustainability: Accounting for society and the environment*. Edinburgh: Pearson Education.

GRI (2017). www.globalreporting.org/information/news-and-press-center/Pages/GRI-and-UN-Global-Compact-partner-to-shape-the-future-of-SDG-reporting.aspx

Guthrie, J. & Parker, L. D. (1989). Corporate social reporting: A rebuttal of legitimacy theory, *Accounting and Business Review*, Vol. 19 (76), pp. 343–352.

Rimmel, G. (2003). *Human resource disclosures: A comparative study of annual reporting practice about information, providers and users in two corporations*. Göteborg: BAS Publishing House.

Rimmel, G. & Jonäll, K. (2013). Biodiversity reporting in Sweden–Corporate disclosure and preparers' views, *Accounting, Auditing & Accountability Journal*, Vol. 25 (5), pp. 746–778.

TCFD (2017).Recommendations of the task force on climate-related financial disclosures, The final report from TCFD.

TEG (2019). Technical expert group – Taxonomy technical report, https://ec.europa.eu/info/sites/info/files/business_economy_euro/banking_and_finance/documents/190618-sustainable-finance-teg-report-taxonomy_en.pdf

Index

Note: Page numbers in **bold** refer to figures; Page numbers in *italic* refer to tables.

Made in the USA
Las Vegas, NV
14 January 2022

41209170R00129